HANDMADE
INTERIORS

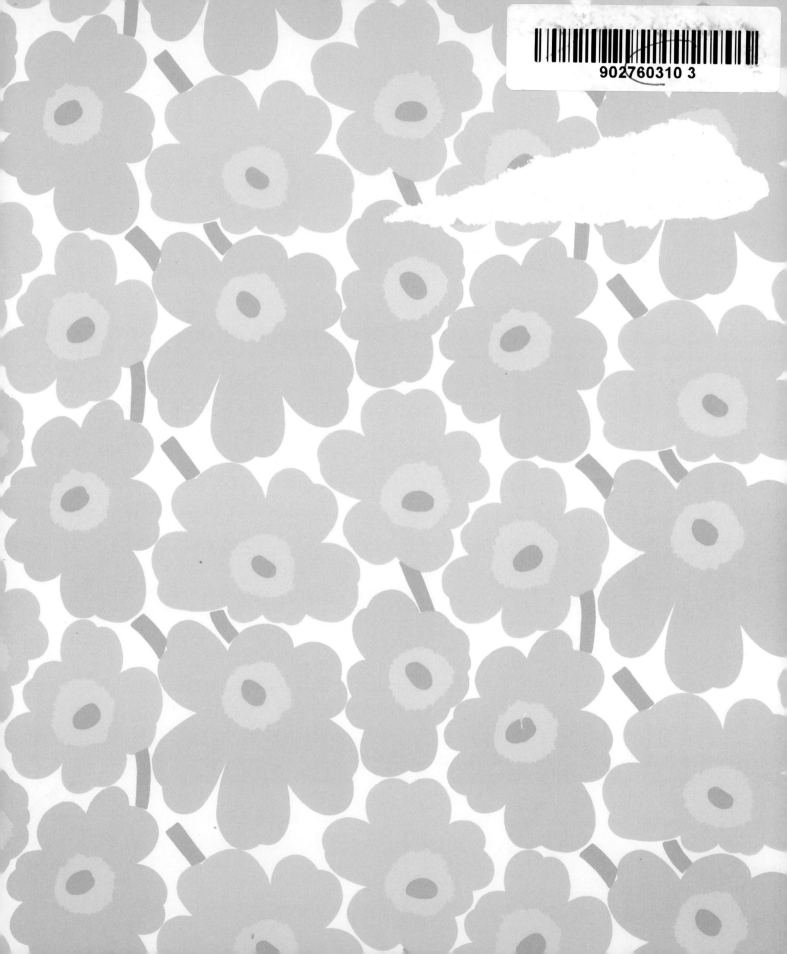

HANDMADE INTERIORS

Penguin Random House

Project editor Laura Palosuo
Senior designers Glenda Fisher, Clare Shedden,
Claire Patane, Sadie Thomas, and Samantha Richiardi
Senior editors Hilary Mandleberg and Wendy Horobin
Additional editing Kate Meeker, Toby Mann
and Anne Hildyard
Design assistant Stefan Georgiou
Project design and consultants Bevelee Regan
and Danielle Budd
Photographer Penny Wincer
Stylist Mia Pejcinovic
Art direction for photography Glenda Fisher
and Mia Pejcinovic
Managing editor Penny Smith
Managing art editor Marianne Markham
Senior jacket creative Nicola Powling
Producer, pre-production Dragana Puvacic
Senior producer Ché Creasey
Creative Technical Support Sonia Charbonnier
Creative director Jane Bull
Category publisher Mary Ling

First published in Great Britain in 2015 by
Dorling Kinderlsey Limited
80 Strand, London WC2R 0RL

Copyright © 2015 Dorling Kindersley Limited
A Penguin Random House Company

VELCRO is a trade mark of Velcro Industries B.V.

10 9 8 7 6 5 4 3 2 1
001- 256500-August/2015

A CIP catalogue record for this book is available from the British
Library
ISBN: 978-0-2411-8638-1

Printed and bound in China

All images © Dorling Kindersley Limited
For further information see: www.dkimages.com

A WORLD OF IDEAS:
SEE ALL THERE IS TO KNOW
www.dk.com

Contents

INTRODUCTION TO SOFT FURNISHINGS

Sewing MACHINE

Although some soft furnishings can be made by hand, we recommend using a sewing machine. It will save you time and effort, providing strong, even stitching and ensuring a professional finish. You only need a basic sewing machine to make the projects in this book but if you're not yet ready to buy a machine, you could always borrow one.

Useful features

A modern sewing machine comes with a multitude of features, some of which are essential for making soft furnishings. Check your machine's user's manual for instructions on how to use these features.

• The **balance wheel** is used to move the needle up and down manually. It is helpful in positioning the needle at the start of work that requires precise stitching, such as inserting a zip.

• The **needle plate** sits under the needle and has a printed or engraved grid on its surface. Aligning the edge of your work with the gridlines helps you maintain a constant seam allowance (see p.18) and sew precise seams.

• **Stitch length selectors** allow you to alter the length of the machine's stitches. This feature is useful in creating stitches such as the ease and stay stitches (see p.19) that you will use for making your soft furnishings.

Overlocker

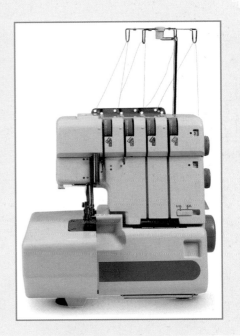

An overlocker is not necessary for making any of the soft furnishing projects in this book, but it is a useful, timesaving tool for neatening seams and other raw edges (see p.19). It provides a clean, professional finish by "locking" the edge with a 3- or 4-thread stitch that prevents the fabric from fraying. At the same time as the overlocker stitches, it cuts away the surplus fabric from the edge using its built-in knives. You will still need a sewing machine to join the fabric pieces, but an overlocker, although pricey, will give your work a smart finish.

Sewing machine feet

The machine foot "runs" over the fabric, holding it in place while you are stitching. There are several types of specialist feet that can be used for different tasks. For the projects in this book, you will need the **all-purpose foot**, as well as a **zip foot** and a **buttonhole foot**.

A **zip foot** allows you to stitch close to the zip's teeth. It attaches left or right of the needle, according to the side of the zip you are sewing.

A **buttonhole foot** enables you to stitch a perfectly sized buttonhole. You slip a button in the holder at the back of the foot, attach the foot to your machine, lower the machine's buttonhole lever, and stitch to complete.

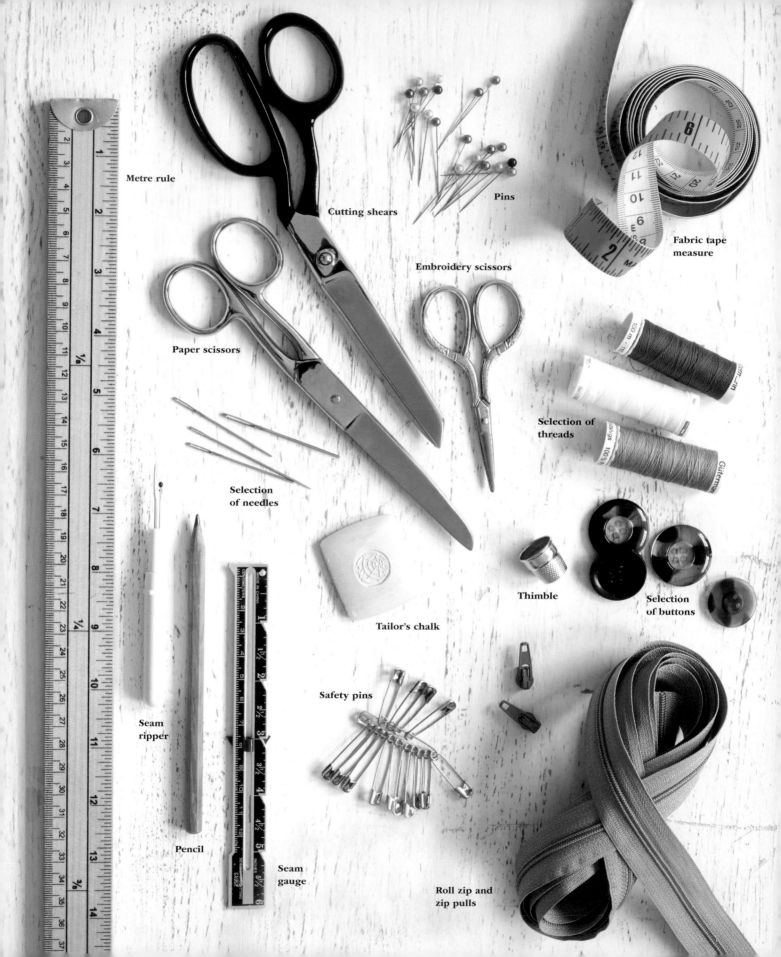

Metre rule

Cutting shears

Pins

Fabric tape measure

Paper scissors

Embroidery scissors

Selection of threads

Selection of needles

Thimble

Selection of buttons

Tailor's chalk

Seam ripper

Safety pins

Seam gauge

Pencil

Roll zip and zip pulls

Essential SEWING KIT

A sewing machine is key to making the projects in this book but you will also need other tools and accessories to cut, measure, mark, and pin fabric, as well as for the finishing touches required to create professional-quality items. Your basic sewing kit should include the items shown here, most of which are not very costly. You can add extra tools and equipment gradually as you undertake more complex projects.

Cutting tools

You will need a variety of cutting tools for different purposes, but one rule applies to all: buy good-quality equipment that can be resharpened. It is also advisable to keep a separate pair of scissors for cutting paper templates: that way you will not blunt your fabric shears by using them to cut paper. A seam ripper saves time when undoing seams and removing tacking stitches. Useful cutting tools include:

- Fabric shears
- Paper scissors
- Embroidery scissors
- Trimming scissors
- Snips (for quickly cutting off the ends of your thread)
- Seam ripper
- Pinking shears

Measuring tools

No sewing kit is complete without the correct tools for accurate measuring. Keep these tools to hand for measuring fabrics and seam allowances, as well as finished lengths as you make up each project. Useful measuring tools include:

- Fabric tape measure
- Metre rule or short ruler
- Seam gauge

Marking aids

The trick to marking fabric is to find a way of making marks that show up when you are assembling your project, but can be removed easily once the item is complete. Tailor's chalk comes in many different colours, is easy to remove, and can be used on all types of fabric. Water-soluble pens are good for accurate marking and can be removed by spraying the fabric with water. Ordinary pencil can be used in places where the marks won't show. Always test your marking tool – and whether you can remove the marks – on a scrap of fabric before you start, and be careful never to press over the marks as this may set them permanently.

Needles and pins

Using the correct pin or needle for your work is extremely important as the wrong choice can damage fabric or leave small holes, so always have a selection to hand. Keep them in good condition by storing pins in a pin cushion and needles in a needle case. Pins and needles to buy include:

- A selection of "sharps" in sizes 6–9
- Milliner's, or straw, needles
- Glass-headed pins
- Dressmaker's pins
- Safety pins

Threads

There are many types of thread to choose from. Polyester thread is the most popular as it has a slight "give" and is suitable for sewing almost all fabrics. Cotton thread is firm and strong, while silk thread can be removed without leaving a mark, making it a good choice for tacking. Always use silk thread for sewing silk fabric. Threads to buy include:

- Polyester all-purpose thread
- Cotton thread
- Silk thread

Fastenings

The projects in this book require a variety of different fastenings. Hook-and-loop tapes, such as Velcro tape, are used on projects such as blinds, to attach the blind to the batten. Roll zip is particularly versatile as it can be cut to the exact length required. Buttons can be used for closing cushion covers as well as for decoration. Useful fastenings to buy include:

- Velcro fastening tape
- Roll zip and zip pulls
- Buttons in various sizes
- Metal self-cover buttons

Useful extras

There are many other items that make sewing easier. These include:

- Thimble
- Needle threader
- Tweezers

> ### TOP **TIP**
>
> *It's best to keep all your essential sewing and cutting equipment in one good-sized sewing box. You will work much more efficiently if your tools are organized and easy to find.*

Soft furnishing TOOL KIT

Making soft furnishings often involves more than just sewing. The projects in this book require you to measure, cut, fasten, glue, staple, and more. Having the right tools to hand will help you complete these tasks safely and will produce the professional results you are after.

Scalpel and cutting mat

No tools are more useful than a scalpel (or craft knife) and a cutting mat when it comes to precisely cutting a shape from the centre of a piece of fabric, leaving the edges intact. You will use this technique when you are making the handle cutouts for the various storage baskets in this book.

Saws

Use saws to cut the battens, rods, and laths required when making blinds. Hacksaws are lighter and easier to work with when cutting small pieces of wood or cutting into tight spaces or corners. A tenon saw is more cumbersome, but is better for cutting larger pieces of wood.

Bradawl

Use a bradawl to create holes in wood, for example, when attaching screw eyes to battens when you are making blinds. Pushing the bradawl into the wood and rotating it helps to prevent the wood from splitting or splintering when the nail or screw is driven in.

Staple gun

A staple gun is similar to a regular stapler but it applies much greater force. This allows you to attach fabrics to wood quickly, easily, and securely. It is useful for fixed covers, for attaching fabric to headboards, and for covering battens when making window blinds.

Hammer

Keep a hammer handy for knocking in loose staples. The claws of the hammer can also be used for removing staples if you have inserted them in the wrong place.

Glue

Strong craft glue is essential for glueing layers of padding together, such as when making headboards.

Long pins

Use long pins to hold several layers of fabric together temporarily, as you do when making a bedspread. Long pins will hold the layers together more securely during sewing than short pins.

Pliers

Use pliers to grip small objects, for example when pulling staples out of wood or for snapping the back onto a self-cover button.

Upholstery needle

A strong, thick upholstery needle is used for stitching through several layers, for example, when attaching a deep button.

Measuring tools

Accurate measuring is key to making bespoke soft furnishings to exactly the dimensions you require – and starting with precise measurements saves time further down the line.

Fabric tape measure

The measuring tool favoured by most sewers, a fabric tape measure is essential for measuring around corners or over a curved surface. Be careful not to stretch it when measuring.

Tape measure

Use a metal tape measure for measuring straight lines. It really comes into its own, though, when you need to measure long lengths such as the length of a curtain, the drop of a blind, or the width of a fabric.

Metre rule

A metre rule is perfect for quickly measuring fabric as you unwind it off a roll. It's also great for measuring mid-range lengths while you are making your project.

Rulers

Shorter rulers are good for measuring seam allowances or the depth of a hem. A metal ruler can also double up as a straight-edge guide when you are using a scalpel.

Set square

A set square is used to keep corners at exactly 90 degrees when you are squaring off fabric. You can buy extra large set squares in specialist shops.

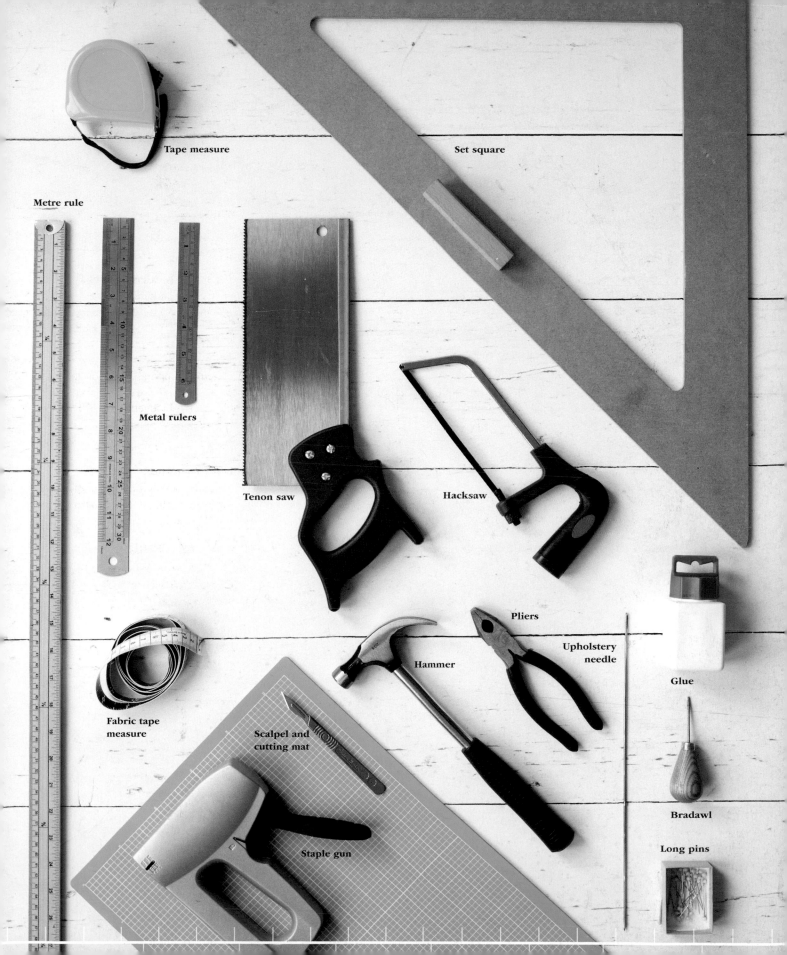

Tape measure

Set square

Metre rule

Metal rulers

Tenon saw

Hacksaw

Pliers

Upholstery
needle

Glue

Hammer

Bradawl

Fabric tape
measure

Scalpel and
cutting mat

Staple gun

Long pins

Soft furnishing FABRICS

These days there is an impressive selection of fabrics in shops and online, so it's no wonder many people are choosing to make soft furnishings that can reflect their own unique taste and style. From different widths, weights, and fibres, to almost endless pattern and texture options, read on to discover more about the wide range of soft furnishing fabrics that are available.

Common fibres

Cotton

Cotton is one of the most common furnishing fabrics thanks to its versatility, durability, and ease of care. It comes in different weights, weaves, and finishes, as well as in any number of prints. You can use it for everything from curtains and cushions to bedding and accessories.

Wool

Wool is resilient and durable and it holds its shape well. It also resists creasing and dirt, and is a good insulator. It can be used for almost any soft furnishings, whether curtains, cushions, or slipcovers.

Linen

Produced from the flax plant, linen works well for items such as curtains and cushions, but it does have a tendency to crease. You can find it in different weights, weaves, and prints, while washed linen is great for a vintage look.

Silk

This luxurious fabric is produced by silkworms. It has a natural sheen, is strong, and has good insulation properties. It looks beautiful made up into curtains but since it can be damaged by sunlight, it is best to use an interlining, which will also make the curtains look fuller and even more luxurious. Silk can also be used for cushions, lampshades, and other items not subject to much wear.

Synthetic

These fabrics are woven from man-made fibres rather than natural ones. Examples of synthetic fabrics include polyester, nylon, acrylic, and rayon. Synthetic and natural fibres are often blended together to give fabrics that have the best qualities of each fibre.

Widths

Most furnishing fabrics are made in 132cm (52in), 137cm (54in), or 140cm (56in) widths, with sheers made much wider at 3m (3¼yds). The width is measured from selvedge to selvedge, not including the width of the selvedge itself. The width is usually marked on the bolt of fabric, but if in doubt, ask the retailer.

Weight

Fabrics are normally classified as being lightweight, medium-weight, or heavyweight, but you might occasionally hear the weight described according to the number of grams per square metre or ounces per square yard.

Drape – the way a fabric hangs – and weight should not be confused. You can have a heavyweight fabric that drapes well, while a lightweight fabric can be stiff and starchy. For curtains, you would normally look for a fabric that drapes well, while drape is not usually important for furniture covers.

Generally, the heavier a fabric, the more durable it is, but durability is also influenced by factors such as the fibres the fabric is made from and how tightly they are woven together. Most soft furnishings use light- to medium-weight fabrics, with heavyweight fabrics used more often for slipcovers. Note that heavyweight fabrics are usually bulky so they can be difficult to work with.

Prints, patterns, and texture

Printed linen
Linen absorbs dye well so lends itself perfectly to a wide range of prints.

Linen blend
For greater resistance to creasing, linen can be blended with other fibres.

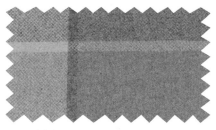

Wool-blend tartan
Wool mixed with cotton makes a durable plaid for soft furnishings.

Velvet
Whether silk or synthetic, pay attention to the nap of velvet when cutting out.

Printed silk
Silk absorbs dye well. It looks especially attractive with delicate prints.

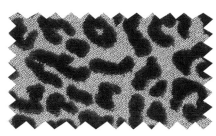

Textured synthetic
Velvet embellishments in the fabric give an interesting pattern and texture.

Cotton stripes
Stripes are classic. Pick a width that is in proportion to the item you are making.

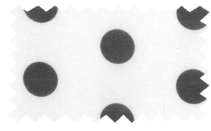

Cotton-blend polka dots
Polka dots on a polyester-cotton blend are a good choice for children's rooms.

Cotton-blend chevron
Chevrons are a bold but on-trend choice. Try them on curtains and cushions.

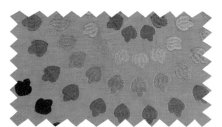

Embroidered embellishments
Embroidered embellishments add pattern, texture, and richness.

Appliqué embellishments
Appliqué motifs are another way of adding texture, colour, and pattern.

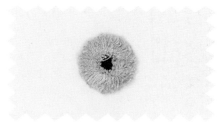

3D embellishments
These may require special care, so don't use on items subject to heavy wear.

Using FABRIC

Checking fabric before you buy and cutting it out correctly are essential. Look out for flaws, such as a pattern that's been printed awry or a faulty weave. Once you're home, check that the fabric has been cut from the roll at a right angle to the selvedge. If it hasn't, start by squaring the edge.

Fabric grain

Always cut out your fabric on the correct grain to ensure it will hang correctly without twisting. The grain is the direction in which the yarns or threads of a woven fabric lie. Mostly, you must cut parallel to the warp threads, or lengthwise grain. For some of the projects in this book, you will actually mark the straight of grain symbol (an arrow) on your pattern pieces.

Finding the grain

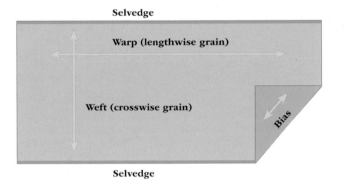

Selvedges
The woven, non-frayable edges of the fabric that run parallel to the warp grain.

Weft
The threads in the fabric that run crossways, over and under the warp threads.

Warp
The threads that run the length of the fabric. They are stronger than weft threads and are less likely to stretch.

Bias
The bias grain is diagonal, running at 45 degrees to both the warp and weft.

Marking and cutting out

Mark your pieces using a water-soluble pen or tailor's chalk. The easiest way to measure and cut your fabric is to lay it out on a smooth, flat surface. If you do not have a large enough table, you may find it easiest to work on the floor. When cutting out make sure you use a sharp pair of fabric scissors. And remember, always measure twice to cut once!

Squaring a cut edge

Using a set square
You can use a large set square to straighten the edge of a fabric. Align one perpendicular edge of the set square with the selvedge, then mark along the other perpendicular edge. Cut along the line.

Using the edge of a table
Start by aligning the selvedge with the long side of a table. Allow the cut end of the fabric to overhang the end of the table. Run chalk along the edge to mark a line, then cut along the line.

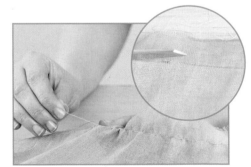

Pulling a thread
On a loose-weave fabric you can use a pulled thread to get a straight edge. Snip into the selvedge, find one single thread, and tug gently to pull it out. Carefully cut along the line left by the thread.

Laying out a pattern

As well as paying attention to fabric grain (see left) when laying out your pattern pieces, you must also consider whether you need to cut one fabric piece from a single layer of fabric, two matching pieces from a double layer, or one symmetrical piece cut on the fold from doubled fabric. If using patterned fabric, be sure to consider pattern placement, too, so that motifs can be centred on an item or so that a pattern matches across two joined pieces.

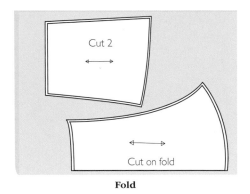

Fold

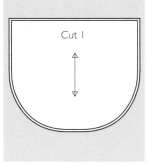

Single layer

Adding a seam allowance

A seam allowance is the area between the edge of a piece of fabric and the stitching line. For some of the projects in this book, you add the seam allowance to the pattern piece itself. In others, you add and mark it on the fabric. Here's how.

1 Lay the fabric face down with the pattern piece on top. Checking the project instructions, use a ruler to measure the length of the seam allowance from the edge of the pattern. Mark this distance at intervals along the pattern edge, then join up the marks to draw a solid line. This is your cutting line.

2 Before removing the pattern piece from the fabric, transfer any notches or other markings from the pattern piece to the fabric. Also mark any corners with a dot. Since you should not sew through a seam allowance, these dots will act as guides for where to start and stop stitching your seam.

Calculating fabric requirements

How much fabric you will need for an item will vary depending on the fabric you choose, how wide it is, and the pattern repeat. Here are some tips to get you started.

- Determine the width of the fabric. Many furnishing fabrics come in a standard 137cm (54in) width, but always double-check as fabric widths can vary.
- Take into account the pattern and nap of the fabric. If you need to match a pattern repeat, this will require more fabric, and the larger the repeat, the more fabric you will need. "Nap" can refer to the pile of a fabric – the way it "shadows" when it is smoothed in one direction – or to a one-way pattern or uneven stripes. If your fabric has a nap, you should buy extra.

- Whenever possible, make a paper pattern first, then lay it out properly on your work surface, factoring in any pattern repeat and nap. This gives you a pretty accurate guide to how much fabric you should buy.
- Always take into account shrinkage and fraying. If you plan to wash the item in the future, it is advisable to pre-wash the fabric, so that any shrinkage occurs before cutting. And if the fabric is prone to fraying, also buy a little more.
- In any event, always buy some extra fabric. If you make a mistake or a miscalculation, you may not be able to find more of the same fabric from the same bolt. Similarly, dye lots can vary from bolt to bolt, so you may not get an accurate colour match if you have to buy more fabric later.

Machine **STITCHES**

Your sewing machine will really come into its own as you make up the projects in this book. Here we show the types of stitches you will need and we introduce you to seam allowances.

Straight stitch

The straight stitch is your sewing machine's default stitch setting and you will use it in most situations and for most fabrics. You can alter your stitch length to suit the type of seam and fabric using your machine's stitch length selector. For most seams and fabrics, you need stitch length 2 but for decorative work, such as topstitching (see below), switch to stitch length 3.

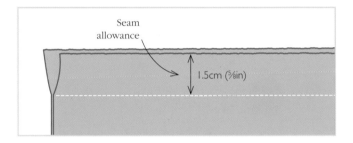

Seam allowance

1.5cm (⅝in)

Seam allowance

This is the distance between your line of stitching and the edge of the fabric. You should use the guide lines on your machine's needle plate to ensure that you keep the seam allowance constant as you work. Simply take care always to align the edge of your fabric along the same guide line. The size of the seam allowance will depend on the project you are working on, but in most cases it will be 1.5cm (⅝in).

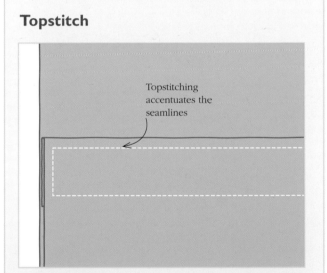

Topstitch

Topstitching accentuates the seamlines

This stitch holds layers of fabric together, which makes it a functional stitch, but since it is worked on the right side of the fabric, where it accentuates the seamline, it is also decorative. In certain situations, you topstitch using contrasting, sometimes thicker, thread and an even longer stitch, to accentuate the seamline more.

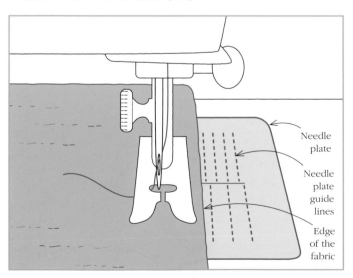

Needle plate

Needle plate guide lines

Edge of the fabric

Stay stitch

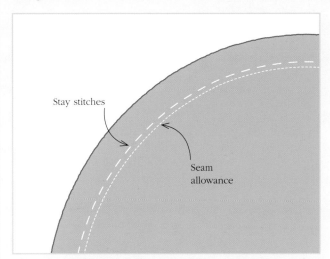

You will often use a line of stay stitches between the seam allowance and the curved raw edge of a single thickness of fabric. Stay stitches reinforce the curved edge, reducing the chances of the curve stretching or twisting before the fabric is attached to another piece. Stay stitches will not be visible on the finished item.

Ease stitch

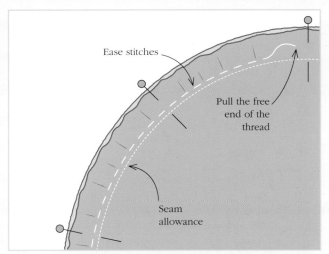

These are used when you need to fit an edge to an edge that is shorter, for example when joining two pieces along a curve. Using a long stitch, simply sew a line of stitching within the seam allowance. Backstitch at the start but leave the end free. Pull the free end to gather the fabric gently until the edges of the two pieces of fabric match.

Neatening fabric edges

Once you have cut a piece of woven fabric, the edges will start to fray – and loosely woven fabrics fray very quickly. To avoid fraying, neaten the edges before you begin to construct the item, using one of the techniques shown below. To save time, neaten all the edges in one go when you have cut out all the pieces.

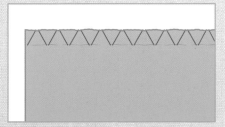

Zig zag

All sewing machines have a zig zag stitch. It is suitable for use on any fabric but you should adjust the width and length according to the fabric.

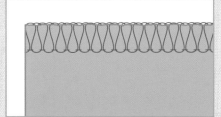

Overlocking

This stitch requires an overlocker (see p.9) and is the most secure way to neaten a fabric edge. There are both 3- and 4-thread overlocking stitches, although the former is more common.

Pinking

Pinking is the quickest and easiest means of neatening an edge, although loosely woven fabrics still fray somewhat after pinking. Simply cut along the fabric edge using pinking shears.

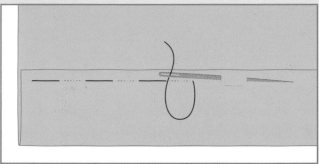

Hand STITCHES

Although most of your sewing for the projects in this book will be done by machine, there are times when stitching by hand will achieve the best results. Examples are when you are finishing curtain hems or attaching interlinings. Here are the hand stitches you will need for success every time.

Tacking stitch

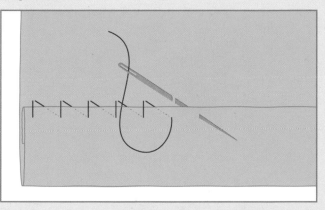

Use tacking stitches to securely hold two or more pieces of fabric in place before machine stitching them together. It is best to tack in a contrasting colour; this makes it easier to see and remove the tacking stitches once the seam is complete.

Slipstitch

Slipstitch is a useful hem stitch since the stitches do not show on the right side. It is also commonly used to close the opening on an item that has been machine stitched on the wrong side, then turned to the right side through the opening, for instance when making a fixed cushion cover (see the Round cushion, pp.42–47). When finished, the stitches will be hidden inside the seam.

Professional results

Using the correct hand-stitching techniques for each project ensures you achieve a professional finish. Practise stitching on spare pieces of fabric until you are confident that you have mastered the techniques.

Ladder stitch

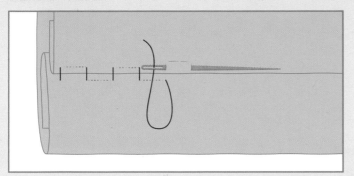

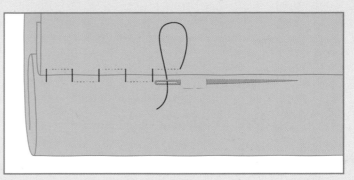

1 A ladder stitch is an almost invisible stitch used to join two folded edges, as when joining the lining to an interlined curtain. Start by inserting the needle into one thickness of fabric, close to the fold. Pass it horizontally inside the fold, then bring it out again.

2 Now take the needle vertically across the fold. Insert the needle into the other fold, in the same way as before. Pass it inside the fold and out again. Repeat to complete the seam. Only the tiny vertical stitches will show, forming a "ladder" across the seamline.

Locking stitch

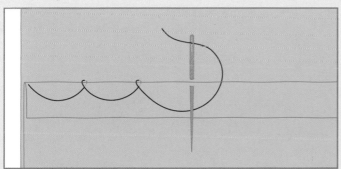

A locking stitch is used to anchor or "lock" the interlining fabric to the main fabric when making an interlined curtain. Take care only to stitch through a few threads of the main fabric so the stitches don't show on the right side. Start by taking the needle through the folded edge of the interlining, then catch just a few threads of the main fabric with the needle, allowing the thread to form a loop across the interlining. Take the needle inside the loop, then through the folded edge of the interlining again. Repeat to complete the seam.

Herringbone stitch

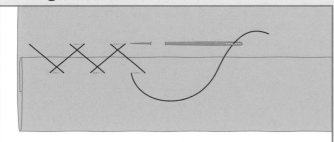

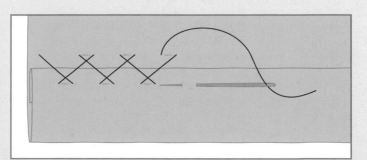

1 A herringbone stitch is a very secure stitch for a hem and for attaching interlinings. Working from the left, start by taking a short horizontal stitch from right to left, on one side of the fold.

2 Pull the thread through, then take the needle diagonally across the fold and take another short stitch from right to left. Repeat to complete the hem.

CUSHIONS

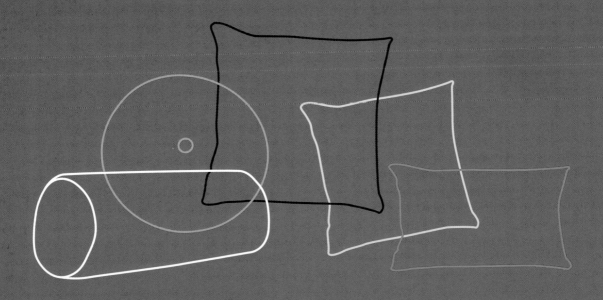

Making **CUSHIONS**

When we talk about making cushions, we really mean cushion covers. Start by buying a synthetic or feather-filled cushion pad, then use the magic of sewing to create the perfect cover. The projects in this book will teach you how and will inspire you to design your own.

Choice of shapes

Cushions are generally square, rectangular, round, or bolster-shape. Round and square cushions work well as seat cushions, while bolsters are traditionally used on a bed or at either end of a sofa or daybed.

 **Square**　　 **Rectangular**　　 **Round**　　**Bolster**

Calculating fabric

The starting point for calculating how much fabric you need for a cushion cover is always the dimensions of your cushion pad. If you like a plump cushion –and who doesn't? – make the cover to the same measurements as the pad. You do not need to add seam allowances; that way the pad will fit snugly inside the cover. If you're not sure of the dimensions of a pad you already have, measure it from seam to seam.

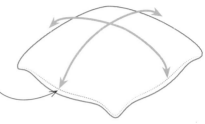

Measure from seam to seam with a fabric tape measure

Closures for your cushions

Some cushion pads are simply inserted through an opening in an envelope cover. The opening can be left open, in which case it is purely utilitarian and will be at the back of the cover, or it can be closed with decorative buttons at the front. Most of the cushion cover projects in this book, though, are closed with a zip.

Using roll zip

If the zip for your cushion cover is not a standard length, roll zip will come to your rescue. Cut the zip a little longer than you need. The zip pull comes separately and must be added before you stitch the zip in place.

1 With one side of the zip tape in one hand, insert the teeth into the corresponding side of the zip pull with the other.

2 Draw the zip pull about 5mm (³⁄₁₆in) along the teeth, then insert the other side of the tape into the other side of the zip pull.

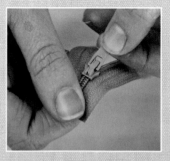

3 Draw the zip pull along until it catches the teeth on both sides of the tape.

Types of cushions

Mixing and matching cushion shapes, sizes, closures, fabrics, and embellishments will add the wow factor to any room scheme.

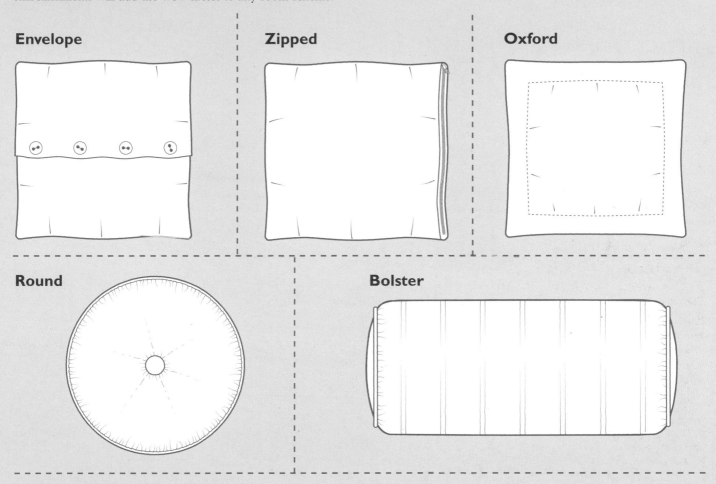

Envelope

Zipped

Oxford

Round

Bolster

Decorative cushion fronts

Inject personality into your cushions by joining striped fabric panels to create a mitred front, by using panels of varying widths and fabrics, or by adding tucks. You can also use buttons, piping, and other trims (see pp. 38–39).

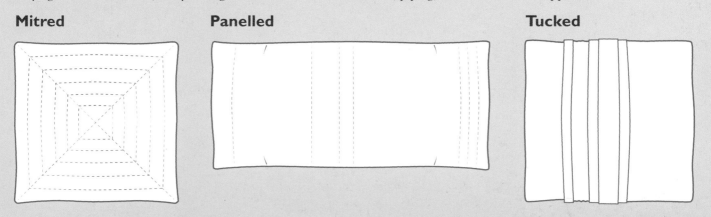

Mitred

Panelled

Tucked

Envelope **CUSHION**

One of the simplest cushion covers to sew, an envelope cover can be made with or without buttons.
The traditional version often has the closure at the back, but these zany contrasting buttons on a smartly
tailored band make the closure the star attraction on the front of the cushion.

YOU **WILL NEED**

Materials

- *45 x 45cm (18 x 18in) cushion pad*
- *50cm (20in) light- or medium-weight furnishing fabric*
- *Matching thread*
- *4 x 3cm (1¼in) buttons*

Tools

- *Scissors* • *Ruler* • *Tailor's chalk*
- *Pins* • *Iron* • *Sewing machine*
- *Buttonhole foot* • *Seam ripper*

Working out the measurements

These instructions are for a cushion pad that is 45cm (18in)
square. You can use the diagram below to work out the
measurements for a cushion pad of your choosing.

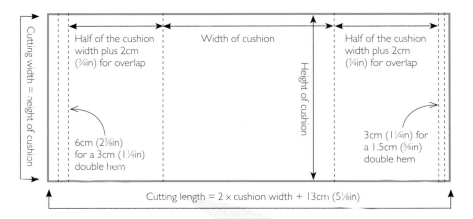

Cutting width = height of cushion

Half of the cushion width plus 2cm (¾in) for overlap

Width of cushion

Half of the cushion width plus 2cm (¾in) for overlap

Height of cushion

6cm (2⅜in) for a 3cm (1¼in) double hem

3cm (1¼in) for a 1.5cm (⅝in) double hem

Cutting length = 2 x cushion width + 13cm (5⅛in)

Cutting out and marking

Centre point

Join the points on both sides of the centre with a chalk line

To make an envelope cover
for a 45 x 45cm (18 x 18in)
cushion pad, cut a fabric
rectangle 106cm (42⅜in) by
45cm (18in). On the wrong
side, lightly mark the centre
point of one long edge with
tailor's chalk, then mark
22.5cm (9in) to the right
and 22.5cm (9in) to the left.
Repeat along the other edge,
then join these points with
chalk lines. This gives the
outline of the cushion back.

Making the hems

1 With the wrong side face up, turn over 3cm (1¼in) along one of the short edges and press. Turn over another 3cm (1¼in) and pin. Using stitch length 3, sew in place. Add a line of topstitching (see p.18) as close to the outer folded edge as possible.

2 Turn over and press 1.5cm (⅝in) along the other short edge, then turn over another 1.5cm (⅝in) to create a double hem. Pin and machine stitch as before. Press to set the stitches.

Adding buttons and buttonholes

1 Fold the fabric along the marked lines, wrong sides together, so the 3cm (1¼in) hem is on top. Place the buttons on this hem, spacing them out by eye. Make sure that the outer buttons aren't too close to the edges.

2 Measure between the buttons to ensure they are evenly spaced and adjust if necessary. Place pins either side of the buttons. These mark the position of the buttonholes.

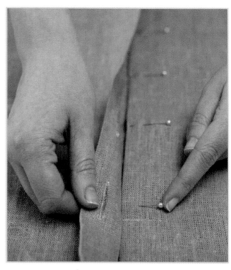

3 Unfold the fabric. Using a buttonhole foot and following the manufacturer's instructions, machine stitch each buttonhole, starting at the pin that is closest to you. Remove the pins as you go.

4 Reposition a pin at each end of a buttonhole. Insert a seam ripper at one pin and push it forward to the next pin to open the buttonhole. Repeat for the other buttonholes.

5 Refold the fabric along the marked lines so that the buttonholes overlap the 1.5cm (⅝in) hem. Fold back the buttonhole hem and mark the centre of each buttonhole with a pin on the narrower hem. Attach the buttons at the marked points.

Assembling the cushion

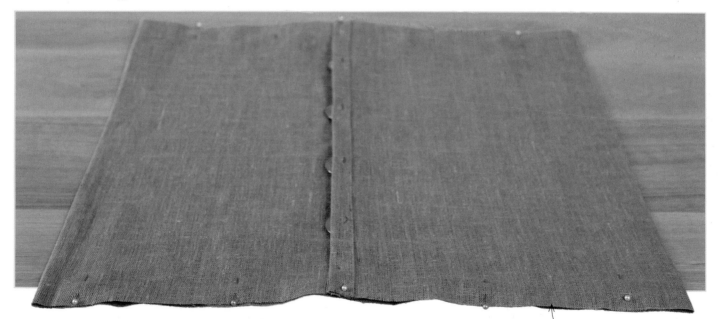

Pin the raw edges together and then stitch to finish the cushion cover

Unfold the fabric then refold it, right sides together at the chalk lines and so that the edge with the buttons lies on top of the edge with the buttonholes. Pin the raw edges together then stitch with a 1.5cm (⅝in) seam allowance. Turn the cushion cover to the right side and push the corners out. Press, then insert a cushion pad and fasten the buttons.

Zipped **CUSHION**

Either side of this smart cushion can be used as the front, thanks to an invisible zip fitted into the bottom seam. Make it using two fabrics in different colours or textures to create a clever 2-in-1 cushion or to showcase an extra special fabric by pairing it with a plain backing.

 YOU **WILL NEED**

Materials

- *1m (40in) medium-weight furnishing fabric for the cushion front*
- *1m (40in) medium-weight furnishing fabric for the cushion back*
- *50cm (20in) invisible zip*
- *Matching thread*
- *60 x 60cm (24 x 24in) cushion pad*

Tools

- *Tailor's chalk • Ruler • Scissors*
- *Iron • Sewing machine • Zip foot*

Cutting the pieces

Decide which part of the pattern you would like to show on the front of the cushion. Then, using tailor's chalk and a ruler, measure and mark the exact dimensions of the square cushion pad on the wrong side of the fabric. Cut out the cushion front. Repeat to cut out the cushion back. Neaten all four sides of each square (see p 19).

Inserting the zip

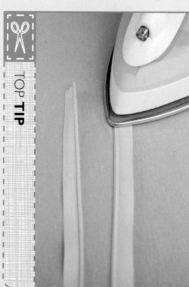

TOP **TIP**

To make a neater job of attaching the concealed zip, lay the open zip face down on the ironing board. Using the tip of the iron and a synthetic setting, press the zip tape flat. Avoid leaving the iron on the teeth too long.

2 Along the bottom edge of the cushion front, turn back then press a 1.5cm (⅝in) seam allowance towards the wrong side of the fabric. Repeat on the cushion back. Turn the front face up and unfold the seam allowance. With the zip face down and open, centre one side of the zip along the bottom edge, as shown, aligning the teeth with the fold.

3 Pin the zip in place along the fold. When you reach the end of the zip, fold back and pin the excess zip tape as shown.

4 Using a zip foot and adjusting the needle so it is as close to the teeth of the zip as possible, stitch the zip in place. Stitch as close to the closed end of the zip as you can and backstitch at the start and end of the zip to secure it. Do not sew over the pins but remove them as you go. If you prefer, you can tack the zip in position, then machine it in place.

5 With the cushion back right side up, unfold the seam allowance. Place the cushion front on top, right side down. Align the teeth of the unattached side of the zip with the fold in the cushion back. Check that the front and back of the cushion are aligned, then pin and machine the zip to the cushion back as before.

Joining front and back

I With the zip open and the right sides of the front and back of the cushion cover facing, pin the corners together. Then pin around the edges, placing a pin as close to the beginning and end of the zip as possible.

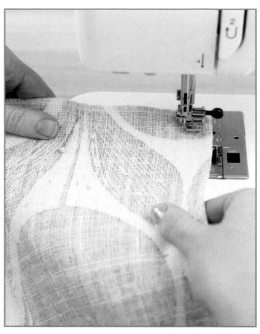

2 Using the balance wheel on your sewing machine, lower the needle into the cushion cover at the pin marking the start of the zip and 1.5cm (⅝in) from the fabric edge. You will be sewing away from the zip, so make sure the zip lies behind the presser foot. Check that the needle is as close as possible to the zip but not on top of the teeth. Backstitch to secure.

3 Sew to the corner, with a 1.5cm (⅝in) seam allowance. At the corner, with the needle down, lift the presser foot to pivot the fabric. Sew all four sides in the same way until you reach the other end of the zip.

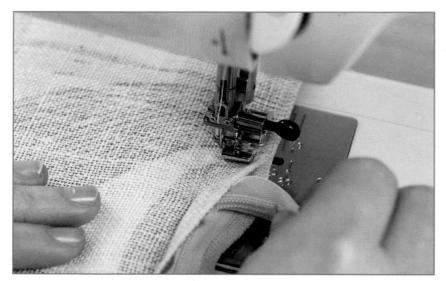

4 As you approach the end of the zip, remove the pin and pull the end of the zip towards the seam allowance. Sew as close as possible to the end of the zip, again using the balance wheel for accuracy. Backstitch to finish.

5 Trim off the corners of the cushion cover to reduce bulk but make sure you do not cut through your stitches. Turn the cover to the right side and push the corners out. Press to finish and insert a cushion pad.

Oxford CUSHION

The laid-back luxe of an Oxford pillowcase, its border showcasing a plump pillow, lends relaxed charm to any room in the house and is simplicity itself to sew. The two-part back incorporates a zip, while the very last step is to stitch the band around the edge.

YOU **WILL NEED**

Materials

- *45 x 45cm (18 x 18in) cushion pad*
- *1m (40in) medium-weight furnishing fabric*
- *Matching thread*
- *35cm (14in) invisible zip*

Tools

- *Tailor's chalk* • *Ruler* • *Scissors*
- *Iron* • *Pins* • *Sewing machine*
- *Zip foot* • *Masking tape (optional)*

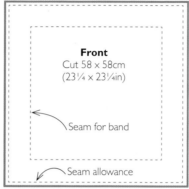

Front
Cut 58 x 58cm
(23¼ x 23¼in)

Seam for band

Seam allowance

Cutting the front

For the front of a cover to fit a 45cm (18in) cushion pad, cut out a square of fabric 58 x 58cm (23¼ x 23¼in). This allows for the 5cm (2in) wide band all around, plus two 1.5cm (⅝in) seam allowances.

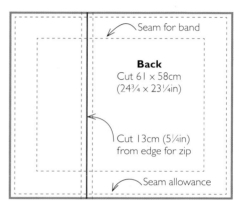

Seam for band

Back
Cut 61 x 58cm
(24¾ x 23¼in)

Cut 13cm (5¼in)
from edge for zip

Seam allowance

Cutting the back

For the back, cut out a piece of fabric 61 x 58cm (24⅜ x 23¼in). This allows for the 5cm (2in) wide band all around, plus 1.5cm (⅝in) seam allowances as shown. Cut this piece in two, 13cm (5¼in) from one short edge, to form the opening for the zip.

Preparing the pieces

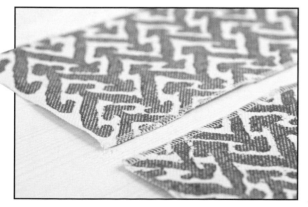

1 Using tailor's chalk and a ruler, measure and mark the dimensions of the front and back of the cushion on the wrong side of the fabric. Cut the cushion back in two, according to the measurements above. Neaten both edges of this cutting line (see p.19).

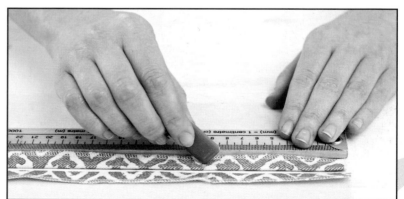

2 With the cushion back pieces face down, fold back then press a 1.5cm (⅝in) seam allowance along the two neatened edges. Mark points 9cm (3⅝in) from each end to indicate where the beginning and end of the zip will go.

Inserting the zip

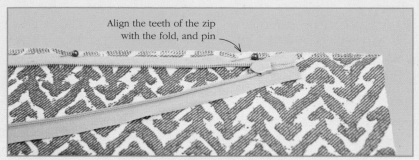

Align the teeth of the zip with the fold, and pin

1 Unfold the seam allowances. With one of the cushion back pieces right side up and the zip face down and open, place one side along the neatened edge, aligning the teeth with the fold, 1.5cm (⅝in) from the edge. Pin between the two marks.

2 At the open end of the zip, fold back and pin the excess tape. Using a zip foot and with the needle close to the teeth, stitch the zip in place. Stitch close to the closed end of the zip and backstitch at the start and end of the zip.

5 With right sides facing, pin the rest of the seam together above and below the zip. Switch the zip foot and needle to the left side to allow you to stitch as close as possible to the zip. Stitch along the pressed fold at both ends of the zip, stitching as close as possible to the beginning and end of the zip.

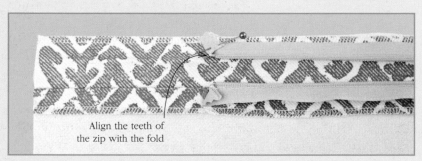

Align the teeth of the zip with the fold

3 Lay the other back piece right side up and place the first piece on top, right side down. Align the teeth of the unattached side of the zip with the other fold. Pin and machine the zip to the other back piece as before.

4 Close the zip and check that the folded edges of the back pieces are still aligned. If they are not, unpick the zip, realign it between the marks, and pin it in place, placing a pin every 3cm (1¼in). Stitch in place.

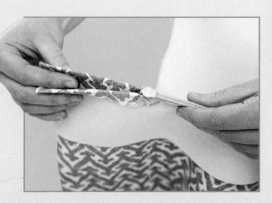

6 Press the seams open from the right side, ensuring that the seam allowance lies flat either side of the seams.

Joining front and back

1 With the zip open, place the front and back pieces right sides together. Pin the corners, then pin around the sides. Stitch with a 1.5cm (⅝in) seam allowance around all four sides, pivoting at the corners.

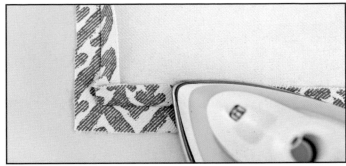

2 Lay the cushion cover flat with the zipped back piece on top. Press back the seam allowance of the zipped piece all the way around.

3 Trim the seam allowance of the front piece all the way around. Snip the corners of the back piece. This helps the seam to lie flat when the cushion is turned to the right side.

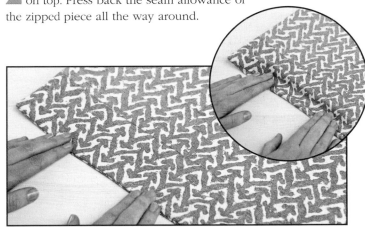

4 Turn the cushion cover to the right side and push the corners out. Finger-press the edges, rolling the seam towards the edge so it lies flat. Press.

Creating the band

1 Pin around all four sides of the cushion cover to hold the layers in place, placing the pins perpendicular to the edge.

Masking tape

2 Machine 5cm (2in) from the edge, over the pins. Backstitch at the beginning and end. Pivot at the corners. If your needle plate does not have a 5cm (2in) marker, measure this distance to the right of the needle and use a length of masking tape to mark a line. Remove the pins and insert the cushion pad.

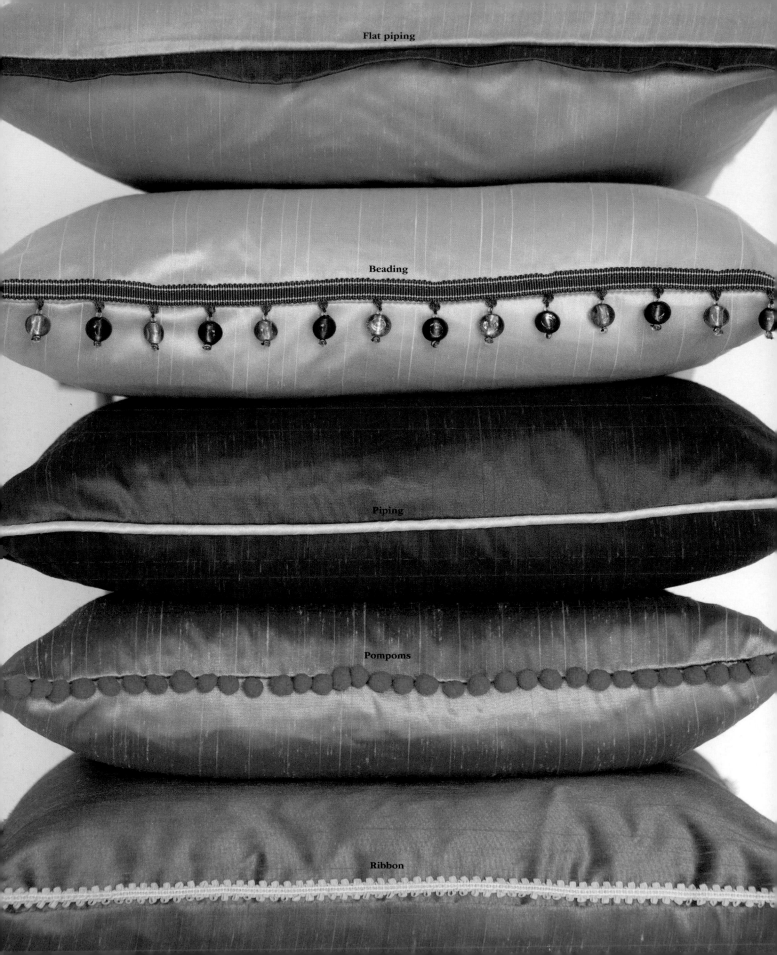

Flat piping

Beading

Piping

Pompoms

Ribbon

Cushion **TRIMS**

Whether the cushion covers you make are bright or muted, patterned or plain, a great way to give them some extra pizzazz, personality, and a professional finish, is to add a decorative trim. You can easily make a piping trim from matching or contrasting fabric, or you can buy beaded trims, pompom trims, and other novelty trims ready-made.

Flat piping

Flat piping is made in a similar way to regular piping, but is less tricky as it doesn't need to be cut on the bias (see pp.40–41). Nor does it involve sewing piping cord inside. As with regular piping, the raw edges are hidden in the seam as the piping is sewn in place. The finished piping adds a really smart, classy look to your cushion.

Beading

There's no need to worry about sewing individual beads on a ribbon with this trim, since you buy it ready-made online or from good haberdashery stores. As with piping, you can sew the beaded trim into the seam of your cushion as you join the cushion pieces together: that way the beads appear to be bursting through the seam. Alternatively, as here, you can slipstitch the trim around the edge of your cushion.

Piping

Piping is created by stitching piping cord into a length of either matching or contrasting fabric that has been cut on the bias (see pp.40–41). Once you've completed that step, you join the cushion pieces together, enclosing the raw edges of the piping in the seam. This popular trim will give your cushion a neat, tailored look.

Pompoms

Pompom trim consists of pompoms attached to a ribbon – much like beading trim – and as with piping, you usually sew the ribbon part into the seam as you join your cushion pieces together. Pompoms come in all colours and sizes, and will give your cushion a fun, quirky finish. When you turn the cushion to the right side to press the seam, make sure that you don't squash the pompoms with your iron.

Ribbon

The sky's the limit when it comes to the myriad colours, widths, weaves, and finishes of the ribbons that are on the market. You can really go to town with ribbon, using it to add a truly personal touch to your cushions. Either machine stitch it to the cushion cover before you join the cushion pieces together, or hand stitch it in place afterwards.

Making *PIPING*

Piping, whether in matching or contrasting fabric, gives a smart and tailored finish to cushions and slipcovers and is easy to make. Strips are cut on the bias and joined. Piping cord is then stitched in.

Cutting the bias strips

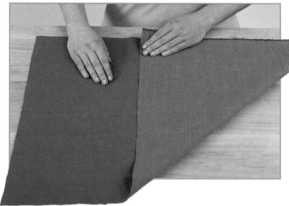

I Place the fabric on the work surface wrong side up. Find the bias (see p. 16) by folding the top edge to the bottom so the edges are aligned. Press the diagonal fold. This is the bias.

2 Open out the fabric and cut along the fold.

3 Measure and mark 4cm (1⅝in) at regular intervals along the cut edge.

4 Join the marks together with a line. Mark more lines with the same spacing between them as many times as necessary until you have the number of strips required. Cut along the lines to cut the bias strips.

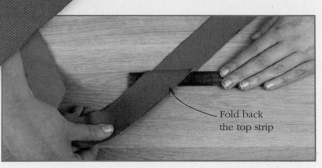

90-degree angle

Joining the strips

1 Lay two strips right side to right side at 90 degrees to each other, matching their short edges to make a horizontal line. Move the top strip so that its outer corner sits 2.5cm (1in) in from the outer corner of the bottom strip.

The short edges match to create a horizontal line

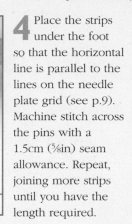

Fold back the top strip

2 Place a ruler over the aligned short edges to hold the strips together at the horizontal line, then fold back the top strip over the ruler. If the line formed by the long edges of the strips looks continuous, then the strips are in the correct position. Adjust them if they they are uneven.

3 Fold the top strip back and secure the short edges with vertical pins across the horizontal line.

4 Place the strips under the foot so that the horizontal line is parallel to the lines on the needle plate grid (see p.9). Machine stitch across the pins with a 1.5cm (⅝in) seam allowance. Repeat, joining more strips until you have the length required.

5 Press the seams open and trim off the corners at each seam.

Sewing the piping

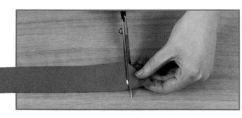

1 Square off one end of the completed bias strip. Measure and cut the strip to the required length and square off the other end. Take care not to stretch the strip when measuring.

2 Cut piping cord to the length of the strip. With the bias strip face down, lay the piping cord along the middle of the strip. Fold the strip over the cord, keeping the cord centred and matching the raw edges of the fabric. Secure with pins, leaving the first 8cm (3¼in) of the strip unpinned.

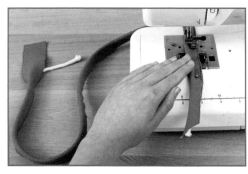

3 Using a piping or zip foot, place the strip under the foot and lower the needle at the start of the pins. Ensuring that the piping cord is under the notch in the foot, machine stitch in place, making sure that the raw edges of the strip stay aligned. Do not backstitch at the start or finish. Leave approx 8cm (3¼in) unstitched at the end.

Round **CUSHION**

Contrast piping and a button lend a touch of glamour to a round cushion that would grace any sofa, chair, or bed. The design of this fixed cover works equally well in a patterned fabric; simply pick out one of the colours for the piping.

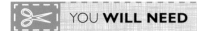

YOU **WILL NEED**

Materials

- *Calico*
- *Medium-weight fabric in main colour*
- *Matching thread*
- *Piping cord*
- *Light or medium-weight fabric in contrast colour for piping and buttons*
- *Contrast thread*
- *Round cushion pad*
- *Two metal self-cover buttons*
- *Nylon twine*

Tools

- *Ruler • Pencil • Masking tape*
- *Compass or string • Scissors*
- *Pins • Hand sewing needle*
- *Sewing machine • Zip foot*
- *Pliers (optional) • Upholstery buttoning needle*

Measuring

Measure the distance across the cushion pad to find the diameter. Divide this amount by two to find the radius.

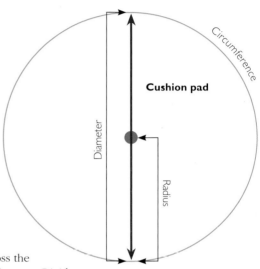

Circumference

Cushion pad

Diameter

Radius

Making the pattern and cutting out

1 Fold a square of calico in half then in half again. Work out the radius of the cushion pad, then add a 1.5cm (⅝in) seam allowance. Measure and mark this distance on two adjacent edges of the calico, starting at the folded centre point.

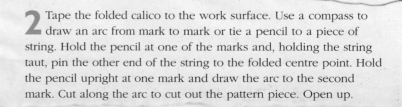

2 Tape the folded calico to the work surface. Use a compass to draw an arc from mark to mark or tie a pencil to a piece of string. Hold the pencil at one of the marks and, holding the string taut, pin the other end of the string to the folded centre point. Hold the pencil upright at one mark and draw the arc to the second mark. Cut along the arc to cut out the pattern piece. Open up.

3 Position the pattern piece on the main fabric. Secure with pins around the edge, then cut out the circle. Cut a second circle in the same way.

4 Fold each fabric circle in half then in half again. Make a single tacking stitch through the centre point of each fabric circle.

5 Open out the circle and make a few more tacking stitches. The tacking stitches mark where the button will be attached later.

Attaching the piping

1 Make piping (see pp.40–41) from the contrast fabric, 4cm (1½in) longer than the circumference of the fabric circle.

2 Cut notches into the seam allowance of the piping. Align the raw edge of the piping with the edge of one fabric circle and pin in place. Leaving 10cm (4in) of piping unstitched at each end, machine the piping to the fabric. Use a zip foot positioned next to the stitching on the piping.

3 Lay the cut ends of the piping on top of each other, then cut the piping casing to give a 4cm (1½in) overlap.

✂ TRADE **SECRET**

4 Open out each end of the piping casing, pull the piping cord out of the way, and hold the ends with the wrong side of each facing you. Leaving the left-hand end where it is, twist the right-hand end away from you so the right side of the casing is now facing you.

5 Holding the ends in this position, overlap them, left over right, so that the short end of the left-hand piece lines up with the long edge of the right-hand piece, and the corners match up. Pin from top to bottom, as shown.

6 Machine stitch the two ends together across the corner over the pins. Remove the pins and trim the raw edges of the seam to 1cm (½in).

7 With the casing opened out, overlap the ends of the piping cord and cut them level. Avoid cutting directly on top of the seam in the casing as it leads to too much bulk.

8 Tuck the ends of the cord inside the casing, then bring the raw edges of the casing together. Pin, then machine stitch them closed.

Joining the front and back

TRADE **SECRET**

1 Stay stitch (see p.19) the other fabric circle within the seam allowance. This is the cushion back. Fold in half, then in half again and mark the half and quarter points with pins. Repeat on the cushion front.

2 With right sides together and matching the half and quarter points, pin the front and back together. Ease in any excess fabric.

3 With the circle that has the piping attached on top, and using a zip foot, machine between three of the markers, leaving an opening. Having the piping on top helps you ease in the excess fabric as you sew.

4 Turn the cushion cover to the right side and insert the cushion pad. Pin the opening closed, starting from the middle of the opening and working towards either end.

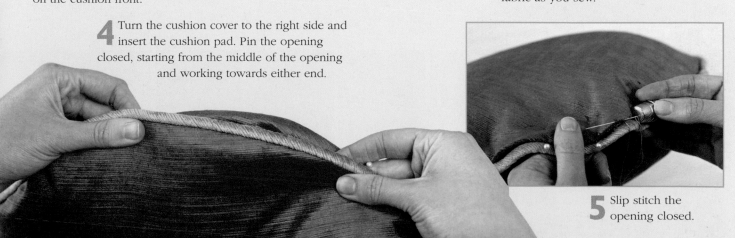

5 Slip stitch the opening closed.

Covering the buttons

1 Cut a circle from the contrast fabric approximately 2cm (¾in) bigger all round than the button to be covered. Holding the button and fabric circle together, snip notches around the edge of the fabric to ease it around the curve.

2 Hold the button and fabric together in one hand and use the other hand to push the fabric over the edge of the button until the fabric catches on the teeth.

3 Continue until the fabric is caught on the teeth all the way round. As you go, check that the fabric is taut on the front of the button and snip off any excess fabric. This is tricky and takes time and patience. Don't snip too close to the teeth as the fabric may fray.

Snip off any excess fabric as you go

4 Snap the back of the button in place, using pliers if necessary. Repeat to cover a second button.

Attaching the buttons

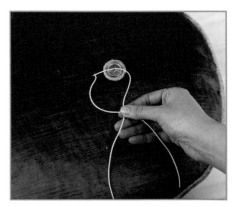

1 Feed a long piece of nylon twine through the shank of one of the buttons, then thread the free ends of the twine through the eye of the upholstery buttoning needle.

2 Push the needle straight through the cushion at one marked centre point and out through the second centre point on the other side. Keep the needle as straight as possible all the time.

3 Remove the needle then thread one free end of the twine through the shank of the second button. Pinch the two ends of twine between your thumb and index finger.

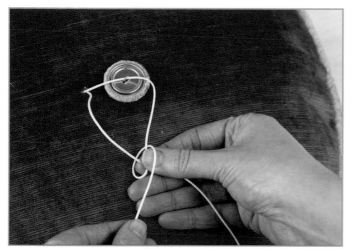

4 Loop the left-hand end of the twine under and then over the right-hand end.

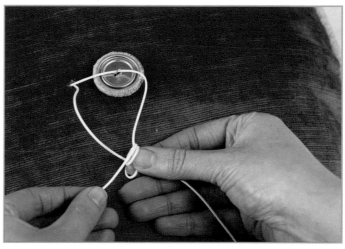

5 Loop it under and over the right-hand end a second time to form a slip knot.

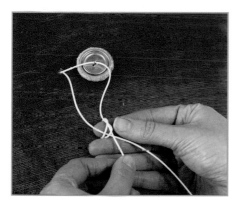

6 Pull the end through the original loop.

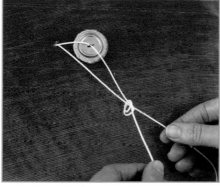

7 Pull the right-hand piece of twine until the knot tightens.

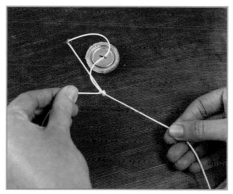

8 Pull on the right-hand piece so the knot moves towards the button.

9 Pull hard to make the knot as tight as possible.

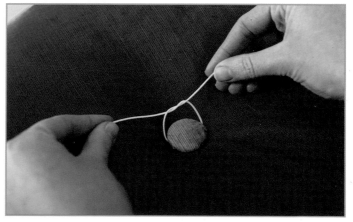

10 Once the buttons fit snugly in the cushion, wrap the remaining twine around the button once and tie a couple of knots to secure. Snip off the ends of the twine.

Bolster CUSHION

Emphasizing the cylindrical shape of the bolster, the candy-coloured stripes and contrasting end pieces of this bolster cover are sure to add a wow factor to a neutral sofa or bed. Matching piping around the ends gives a neatly tailored look, and the whole cover unzips for easy removal. If stripes aren't for you, try a patterned fabric with contrast piping and ends, or use two boldly contrasting plains.

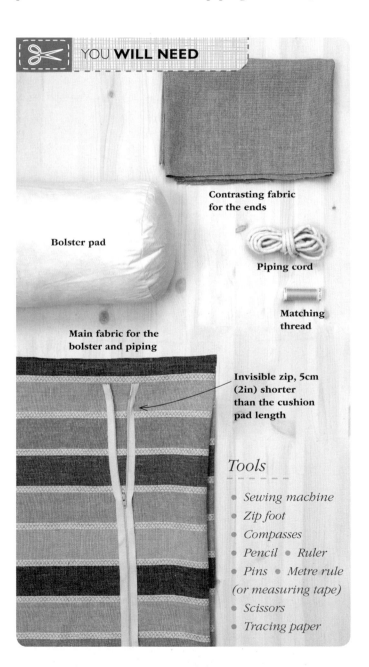

YOU WILL NEED

Contrasting fabric for the ends

Bolster pad

Piping cord

Matching thread

Main fabric for the bolster and piping

Invisible zip, 5cm (2in) shorter than the cushion pad length

Tools

- *Sewing machine*
- *Zip foot*
- *Compasses*
- *Pencil* • *Ruler*
- *Pins* • *Metre rule*
  (or measuring tape)
- *Scissors*
- *Tracing paper*

Cutting measurements

Measure the diameter and length of the bolster pad and then work out the measurements as below.

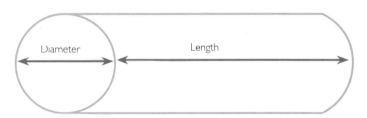

Diameter   Length

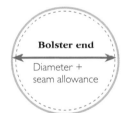

Bolster end

Diameter + seam allowance

Calculating circumference

To find the circumference of the bolster end (also the length of the end side of the bolster body) multiply the diameter of the bolster pad by π (3.14).

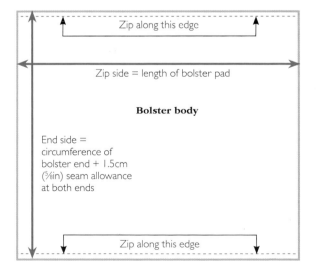

Zip along this edge

Zip side = length of bolster pad

Bolster body

End side = circumference of bolster end + 1.5cm (⅝in) seam allowance at both ends

Zip along this edge

Cutting the pattern

| For the ends of the bolster, divide the diameter of the bolster pad by two. Set your compasses to this measurement and draw a circle on paper. Now add 1.5cm (⅝in) to your compasses setting and draw a second circle outside the first. Cut out the pattern piece around the second circle.

2 For the bolster body, work out the measurements from the diagram on p.49. Draw this rectangle on paper, then add a 1.5cm (⅝in) seam allowance to the end side measurement (see diagram). The zip sides and end sides may look similar in length so label them on the pattern.

3 If using striped fabric, place the pattern for the bolster body so that the end side is parallel to the stripes. Cut out, then neaten (see p.19) the zip edges. Pin the pattern for the ends to the contrasting fabric and cut two end pieces.

Inserting the zip

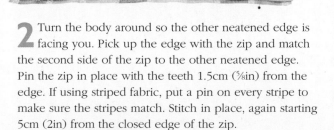

Position the open end of the zip 5cm (2in) in from the edge

Start stitching 5cm (2in) from the closed end of the zip

Start stitching 5cm (2in) from the closed end of the zip (marked here with a pin)

| With the bolster body right side up and the zip face down and open, place one side of the zip with its teeth 1.5cm (⅝in) from the neatened edge and with its open end 5cm (2in) from the raw edge. Pin in place, folding back and pinning the excess tape at the end of the zip. Starting 5cm (2in) from the closed end, stitch the zip in place, stitching as close to the teeth of the zip as possible.

2 Turn the body around so the other neatened edge is facing you. Pick up the edge with the zip and match the second side of the zip to the other neatened edge. Pin the zip in place with the teeth 1.5cm (⅝in) from the edge. If using striped fabric, put a pin on every stripe to make sure the stripes match. Stitch in place, again starting 5cm (2in) from the closed edge of the zip.

3 Pin the open ends of the zip side together. Stitch to the marker pins, pulling the end of the zip out of the way to sew as closely as possible to the zip.

4 Topstitch four or five stitches across each end of the zip and backstitch at the start and end to strengthen.

Making the ends of the bolster

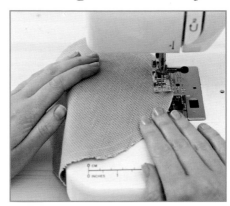

Snip the seam allowance at 1.5cm (⅝in) intervals to ease the piping around the curves

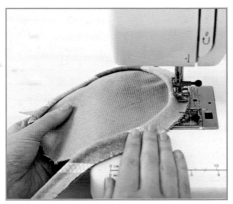

1 Stay stitch 1cm (⅜in) from the edge of the end pieces (see p.19) to help stabilize the circles.

2 Make two lengths of piping (see pp.40–41) from the main fabric, at least 4cm (1⅝in) longer than the circumference of the bolster. Leave 5cm (2in) of each end unstitched.

3 Align the raw edge of the piping with the edge of an end piece. Using a zip foot, machine the piping to the end piece, leaving 5cm (2in) unstitched at the start and finish.

4 Lay the end piece right side up, with the unstitched ends lying on top of each other. Measure and mark the casing to give an overlap of 4cm (1⅝in). Snip off the excess.

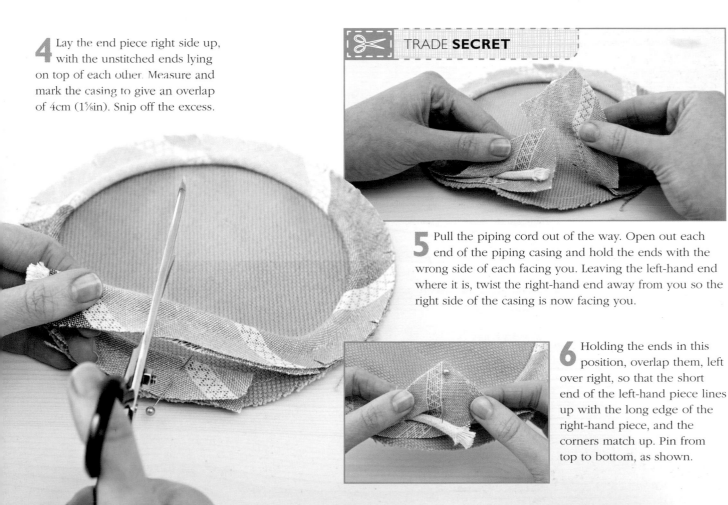

✂ TRADE **SECRET**

5 Pull the piping cord out of the way. Open out each end of the piping casing and hold the ends with the wrong side of each facing you. Leaving the left-hand end where it is, twist the right-hand end away from you so the right side of the casing is now facing you.

6 Holding the ends in this position, overlap them, left over right, so that the short end of the left-hand piece lines up with the long edge of the right-hand piece, and the corners match up. Pin from top to bottom, as shown.

7 Machine stitch the two ends together, across the pin. Remove the pin and trim the seam allowance to 1cm (⅜in).

8 With the casing opened out, overlap the ends of the piping cord and cut them level. Avoid cutting directly on top of the seam in the casing as it leads to too much bulk. Tuck the ends of the cord inside the casing.

9 Bring the raw edges of the casing together and pin. Machine stitch them closed.

10 Fold the end piece in half and mark the halfway point with pins on opposite edges. Fold in half again the other way and mark the quarter points. Avoid folding directly on the join in the casing. Repeat Steps 3–10 for the other end piece.

Joining the body and the ends

1 Fold the bolster body in half widthways, then in half again. Mark the half and quarter points with pins. Clip the seam allowances along the raw edges at 1.5cm (⅝in) intervals.

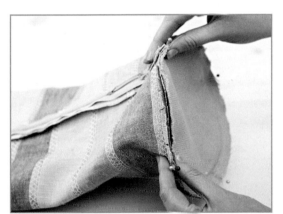

2 With right sides together, first match the half and quarter pins on the body and on one end piece, then pin all the way around, matching the raw edges.

3 Using the zip foot and with the bolster body on top, stitch the two pieces together. Stitch as close to the piping as possible and pull gently on the body so that all the raw edges are aligned. Turn to the right side to check the stitching. If the stitches are visible alongside the piping or if the piping feels too loose, stitch around again, this time a little closer to the piping. Open the zip then repeat Steps 2 and 3 to attach the other end piece to the body.

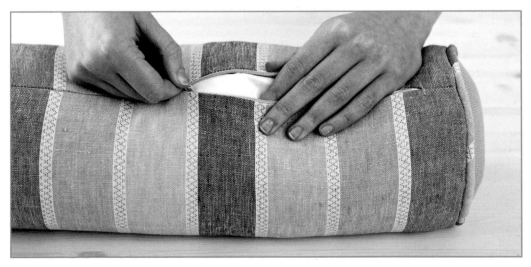

4 Place the bolster pad inside the cover. It should be a tight fit. Manipulate the cover so that the bolster pad fits inside evenly and close the zip.

Panel **CUSHION**

Contrasting panels of printed and plain fabric in differing widths lend a slightly Oriental mood to this rectangular cushion cover. We have made ours in silk but any fabrics will do, as long as they are all of similar weight. You might even be able to use oddments from your fabric box.

YOU **WILL NEED**

Materials

- *30 x 50cm (12 x 20in) cushion pad*
- *5 or 6 pieces of fabric in various colours and patterns at least 30cm (12in) tall for the cushion front*
- *1 piece of fabric large enough to cut a 30 x 50cm (12 x 20in) cushion back*
- *Matching thread*
- *40cm (16in) invisible zip*

Tools

- *Tailor's chalk* • *Scissors* • *Pins*
- *Sewing machine* • *Zip foot* • *Ruler*

Making the front

1 Cut the fabrics for the cushion front into pieces that are the height of the cushion pad and approximately one-third of its width.

Cutting out the back

Using tailor's chalk and a ruler, measure and mark the exact dimensions of the cushion pad on the wrong side of the cushion back fabric. Cut out the cushion back, then neaten the edges (see p.19).

2 Press a 1.5cm (⅝in) seam allowance towards the wrong side of the fabric along the left edge of each piece. Decide the order the panels will go in and lay them out with right sides facing. Adjust the overlaps to give some wider and some narrower panels, while checking that the overall width is the same as the cushion back.

Remove the pins and trim the excess fabric after tacking

3 Once you are happy with the layout, pin one front piece at a time to its adjacent piece, inserting a pin top and bottom into the folded seam allowance.

4 Unfold the pressed seam allowance and check that the top and bottom edges of the pieces are level. Add another pin between the top and bottom pins, then tack (see p.20) along the foldline.

5 Stitch the pieces together following the line of tacking. Continue pinning, tacking, stitching, and trimming the seam allowances until you have joined all the front pieces together. Press each seam open and neaten the edges (see p.19). Finish by pressing the cushion front.

6 Measure the cushion front. If the front is wider than the back, mark with tailor's chalk, then trim.

Inserting the zip

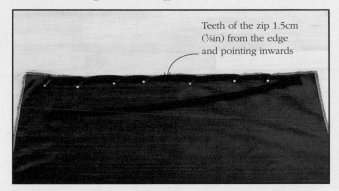

Teeth of the zip 1.5cm (⅝in) from the edge and pointing inwards

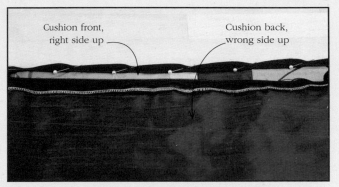

Cushion front, right side up

Cushion back, wrong side up

1 With the cushion back right side up and the zip face down and open, centre one side of the zip along one long edge. Position the teeth 1.5cm (⅝in) from the edge. Pin in place. Fold back and pin the excess tape at the end of the zip. Using a zip foot and with the needle adjusted so it is as close to the teeth as possible, stitch the zip in place.

2 With the cushion front right side up, lay the back with its zip attached on top. Position the teeth of the other side of the zip 1.5cm (⅝in) from the edge of the front. Pin and then machine the zip to the front as before, backstitching at the beginning and end. Open the zip.

Joining front and back

1 With the right sides of the front and back of the cushion cover facing, pin the corners together, then pin around the edges. Beginning as close as possible to the start of the zip, backstitch to secure your stitching, then stitch around all four sides with a 1.5cm (⅝in) seam allowance, pivoting at the corners. You can continue with the zip foot unless your fabric is slippery, in which case change to a straight-stitch foot.

2 When you reach the end of the zip, pull it towards the seam allowance and then sew as close as possible to the end of the zip. Backstitch to secure your work. Turn the cushion and insert your cushion pad.

Mitred **CUSHION**

Crisp geometry is the focal point of a cushion that is equally at home in the living room or the bedroom. Harnessing the power of stripes and mitred edges, this stylish cushion looks more complex than it is. For a kaleidoscopic effect, try the same technique using fabric with an all-over pattern.

YOU **WILL NEED**

Materials

- *50 x 50cm (20 x 20in) cushion pad*
- *1m (40in) light or medium-weight furnishing fabric*
- *Matching thread*
- *40cm (16in) invisible zip*

Tools

- *Tracing paper* • *Scissors* • *Pins*
- *Metre rule* • *Pencil* • *Sewing machine*

Making the pattern and cutting out

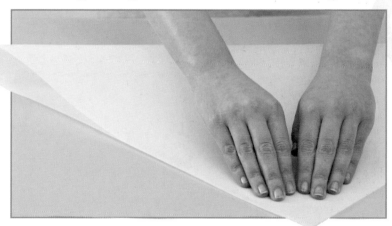

1 To make the pattern for the cushion back, draw a square the same size as the cushion pad on pattern or tracing paper. Cut it out. Check that the pattern is square by folding it in half corner to corner – the sides should line up exactly.

TOP **TIP**

2 Square off the fabric (see p.16), then place the pattern on top. Using tracing paper allows you to see the fabric through the paper. Align the straight edges of the paper pattern with the stripes on the fabric. Centre the pattern, then pin and cut out the cushion back. Neaten the edges of the cut piece (see p.19).

3 To make the pattern for the cushion front, fold the pattern for the back from corner to corner, then fold it in half again. Open it up and cut out one of the triangles.

4 Place the triangle on another piece of pattern or tracing paper and trace around it with a pencil. Add a 1.5cm (⅝in) seam allowance to the two sides that form the right angle. Cut out this larger triangle.

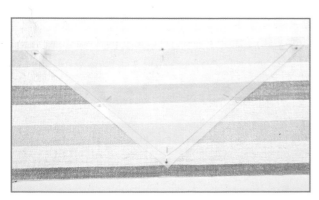

5 Lay the triangular pattern on the fabric and adjust its position to make the most of the striped fabric. Pin the pattern then cut out the fabric triangle. Cut another three triangles with the stripes in exactly the same place.

Joining the cushion front pieces

1 Stay stitch (see p.19) along the sides of the fabric triangles, 8mm (¼in) from the edge. Neaten the edges (see p.19) starting from the right-angled point.

2 Matching the stripes, pin two fabric triangles together, right sides facing, along one short side. Machine stitch with a 1.5cm (⅝in) seam allowance. Press the seam open and double check that the stripes match. Join the other two triangles in the same way.

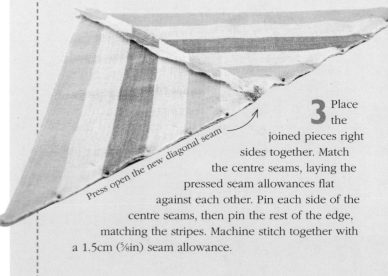

Press open the new diagonal seam

3 Place the joined pieces right sides together. Match the centre seams, laying the pressed seam allowances flat against each other. Pin each side of the centre seams, then pin the rest of the edge, matching the stripes. Machine stitch together with a 1.5cm (⅝in) seam allowance.

Fold back
and pin the
excess tape

Inserting the zip

I With the cushion front right side up and the zip face down and open, centre one side of the zip along one edge of the cushion front. Position the teeth 1.5cm (⅝in) from the edge. Pin the zip in place. Fold back and pin the excess tape at the end of the zip. Using a zip foot and adjusting the needle so it is as close to the teeth of the zip as possible, stitch the zip in place, going as close to its closed end as you can and backstitching at the beginning and end of the seam to secure your stitching.

2 With the cushion front on top of the back, right sides together, position the teeth of the other side of the zip 1.5cm (⅝in) from the edge of the back. Pin and then machine the zip to the back. Close the zip, leaving just a hand's width open.

Joining front and back

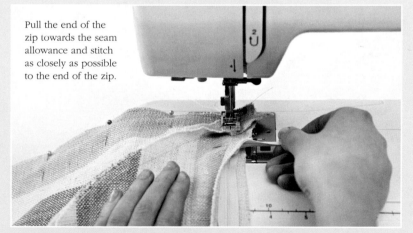

Pull the end of the zip towards the seam allowance and stitch as closely as possible to the end of the zip.

I With the cushion front and back right sides together, pin the corners, then the edges. Starting as close to the beginning of the zip as possible, sew with a 1.5cm (⅝in) seam allowance around all four sides, pivoting at the corners. When you reach the end of the zip, pull it towards the seam allowance, then sew as close as possible to the end of the zip. Backstitch to secure.

2 Clip the corners to reduce bulk, but do not cut through your stitches. Turn the cover to the right side, push out the corners, then press and insert the cushion pad.

Tuck front CUSHION

Tucks in varying widths and of varying complexity are a great way to enliven an otherwise plain cushion. Here a single tuck and a double tuck combine to bring an air of quiet elegance to a comfy plump cushion.

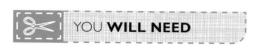
YOU **WILL NEED**

Materials

- *Medium-weight furnishing fabric*
- *Matching thread*
- *Contrast thread*
- *30cm (12in) invisible zip*
- *40 x 40cm (16 x 16in) cushion pad*

Tools

- *Scissors • Ruler • Tailor's chalk in two colours • Hand sewing needle • Pins • Sewing machine • Masking tape (optional) • Iron • Zip foot*

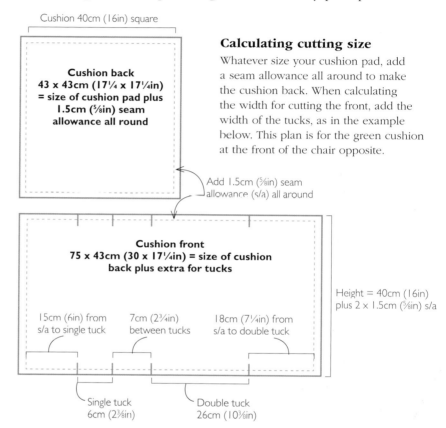

Cushion 40cm (16in) square

**Cushion back
43 x 43cm (17¼ x 17¼in)
= size of cushion pad plus
1.5cm (⅝in) seam
allowance all round**

Add 1.5cm (⅝in) seam allowance (s/a) all around

**Cushion front
75 x 43cm (30 x 17¼in) = size of cushion
back plus extra for tucks**

Height = 40cm (16in) plus 2 x 1.5cm (⅝in) s/a

15cm (6in) from s/a to single tuck

7cm (2¾in) between tucks

18cm (7¼in) from s/a to double tuck

Single tuck 6cm (2⅜in)

Double tuck 26cm (10⅜in)

Calculating cutting size

Whatever size your cushion pad, add a seam allowance all around to make the cushion back. When calculating the width for cutting the front, add the width of the tucks, as in the example below. This plan is for the green cushion at the front of the chair opposite.

Cutting out and marking

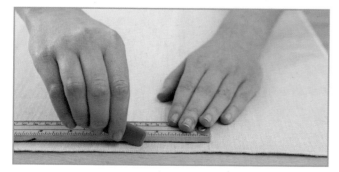

Cut out the cushion front and back. Neaten (see p.19) all the edges. Lay the front face down. Using tailor's chalk and a ruler, transfer all the tuck markings to the fabric along the top and bottom edges (see diagram).

2 Join the marks from top to bottom. The pair of lines that are 6cm (2⅜in) apart mark the single tuck. The set of lines that are 26cm (10⅜in) apart mark the double tuck.

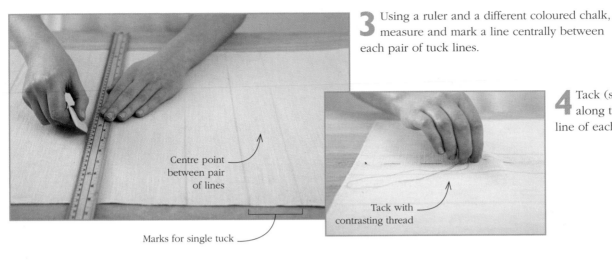

3 Using a ruler and a different coloured chalk, measure and mark a line centrally between each pair of tuck lines.

Centre point between pair of lines

Marks for single tuck

4 Tack (see p.20) along the centre line of each tuck.

Tack with contrasting thread

Creating the tucks

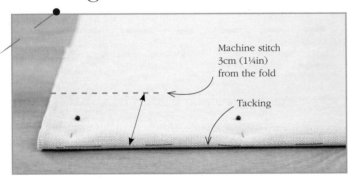

Machine stitch 3cm (1¼in) from the fold

Tacking

1 With wrong sides facing, fold the fabric along the line of tacking between the 6cm (2⅜in) lines to make a single tuck. Ensure that the top and bottom edges of the fabric are aligned. Secure with pins. Machine stitch from top to bottom, 3cm (1¼in) from the fold and over the chalk line. If your needle plate does not have a 3cm (1¼in) marker, measure this distance to the right of the needle and use a length of masking tape to mark a line.

2 Open out the fabric. With wrong sides facing, fold along the line of tacking between the 26cm (10⅜in) lines to make the double tuck, ensuring the edges are aligned. Pin in place.

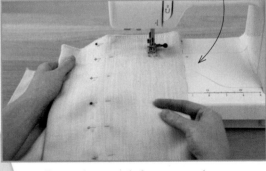

Use masking tape as a guide

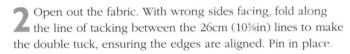

Single tuck

Sew the first seam 13cm (5¼in) from the fold

Sew the second seam 5cm (2in) from the fold

3 Machine stitch from top to bottom 13cm (5¼in) from the folded edge. To help keep your stitching straight, measure 13cm (5¼in) to the right of the needle and use a length of masking tape to mark a line. Stitch a second seam 5cm (2in) from the folded edge. Again, use a length of masking tape to help keep the stitching straight.

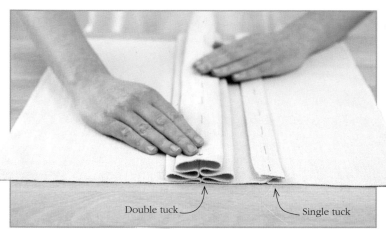

4 To complete the single tuck, centre the tacked fold line over the seam made in Step 1. Press in place. For the double tuck, centre the tacked fold line first over the 5cm (2in) seam and then over the 13cm (5¼in) seam made in Step 3. Press in place.

5 Secure the ends of the tucks with pins then tack in place. Press.

Double tuck — Single tuck

Press flat

Inserting the zip

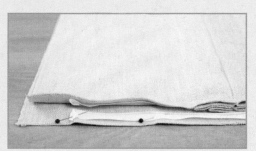

1 With the cushion front right side up and the zip face down and open, centre the zip across the folds at one edge with the teeth of the zip 1.5cm (⅝in) from the edge. Pin in place, folding back and pinning the excess tape at the open end of the zip. Sew the zip in place using a zip foot, stitching as close to the teeth of the zip as possible.

2 Lay the cushion front on top of the back, right sides together. Pin the other side of the zip along the edge of the back and stitch in place. Close the zip, leaving just a hand's width open.

Joining front and back

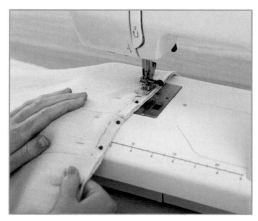

1 With the right sides of the cushion front and back facing, pin the corners together. Then pin around the edges. Starting at the end of the zip and with a 1.5cm (⅝in) seam allowance, machine around the cushion to the other end of the zip, pivoting at the corners and sewing over the tucks. Stitch as close to the ends of the zip as possible.

Push out the corners

2 Remove the tacking stitches. Clip the corners to reduce bulk, but do not cut through your stitches. Turn the cover to the right side, push out the corners, then press and insert the cushion pad.

SEAT CUSHIONS, SLIPCOVERS, AND FIXED COVERS

Making SEAT COVERS

If you're looking to refresh the appearance of a chair you love, or your budget doesn't extend to buying new, there are simple ways to update the pieces you already have, or have purchased second-hand. Adding a new seat cushion to a wooden chair or bench, making a slipcover for an upholstered chair, or attaching a fixed cover to a padded headboard are all simple-to-do transformations.

Seat cushions

A new seat cushion can work wonders for a chair or bench seat. Some shapes suit certain pieces of furniture better than others. Choose from a variety of cushions with a box edge or go for a flat pad, and leave it plain or dress it up.

Box

This is a square or rectangular cushion with edges at 90 degrees to the top and bottom. A firm filling works best.

Shaped box

This type of cushion is made to a specific shape, for example to fit a chair with a curved back or a bay window seat.

Seamless box

Using a different pattern a box cushion can be made without a seam around the top edge. Best for uneven edges.

Flat pad

A flat pad is a traditional choice for a wooden chair. It is simple to make and is usually attached to the chair with fabric ties.

A custom-made seat pad

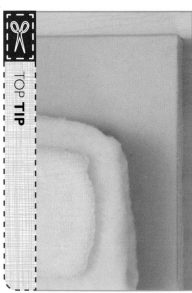

TOP **TIP**

When your seat isn't a standard size, make your own seat pad from foam cut to size, wadding, and stockinette. Wrap the foam in wadding and fold in the ends. Finally, so it's easier to insert the pad in the cushion cover, wrap it in stockinette.

Piping

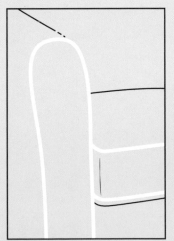 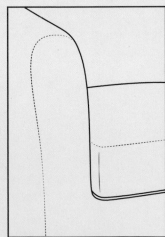

With piping

Piping gives chair covers a formal, tailored look. You can make the piping either from matching or contrasting fabric.

Without piping

Seat covers without piping look relaxed and informal and are easier to make. Try them when you want a contemporary look.

Fixed covers versus slipcovers

Reupholstering furniture with a fixed cover is a job that is usually best left to a professional (though see below for some exceptions), but making a slipcover is well within the reach of a competent sewer. Also, a slipcover can be removed and laundered or dry-cleaned whenever it needs a freshen-up. Always make a calico pattern before cutting out your fabric.

Slipcovers

Think of a slipcover as being like a dress for your furniture. It can hide a multitude of sins – out-of-date upholstery, stains, holes, a fabric that no longer matches your scheme. You can custom-make a slipcover to fit over any piece of furniture. What is more, it is an extremely cost-effective way to change the look of a room. If your fabric is washable, always pre-wash it before you make your cover; it will prevent shrinkage during future washes.

Hemmed edge
The bottom edge of the slipcover is hemmed so it hangs just below the original, fixed, upholstery.

Fixed edge
For an upholstered look, the bottom edge of the slipcover is turned under and attached to the underside of the chair with strips of Velcro tape. You can still remove the slipcover for cleaning, though.

Skirts and edges
You have a choice of lengths and finishes for the bottom edge of your slipcover. For a relaxed, modern look, simply hem the bottom edge all around at a length that suits you. A variation on this theme is to add a "skirt" that reaches to the floor. This gives a more formal look and can hide ugly chair legs. Alternatively, leave the legs on show but turn the edge of the slipcover under and fix it to the underside of the chair with Velcro tape. This makes the slipcover look more like fixed upholstery.

Fixed covers

It isn't tricky to make a professional-looking fixed cover for an item, providing it has only a few angles or curves. Recovering a drop-in seat pad (see pp.120–123) or a simple padded headboard (see pp.140–145) does not even involve any sewing skills and takes very little time. The result? A whole new look for your room or a new lease of life for a charity-shop find.

Covered seat
Recovering a drop-in seat pad is simplicity itself. All you need is a fabulous piece of fabric and a few tools. And since you don't require a lot of fabric, you might find an offcut in the sales, or could treat yourself to a really luxurious fabric that would normally be unaffordable.

Piped SEAT PAD

Contrast piping never dates and neither do zingy, classic cotton prints. Here the two combine to make a piped seat pad cover for a boldly coloured, modern, plastic chair that works indoors as well as out. The seat pad is attached to the chair with self-fabric ties and the entire cover easily unzips for washing.

YOU WILL NEED

Main fabric and contrast fabric for piping

Calico for pattern

Invisible zip

Matching thread

Foam pad of 5cm (2in) thickness

Piping cord

Tools

- Scissors • Masking tape (optional)
- Tailor's chalk • Sewing gauge
- Sewing machine • Zip foot
- Tape measure • Iron

Cutting the foam pad to shape

Use the calico pattern you make as part of this project to cut your foam pad. Just trim off the seam allowance, draw around the pattern piece, and cut out along the line.

Making the pattern

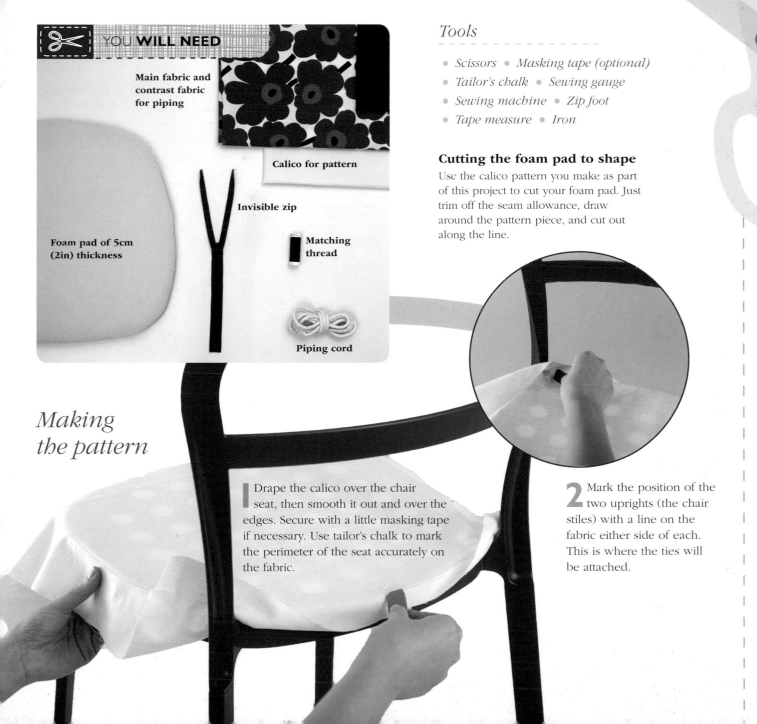

1 Drape the calico over the chair seat, then smooth it out and over the edges. Secure with a little masking tape if necessary. Use tailor's chalk to mark the perimeter of the seat accurately on the fabric.

2 Mark the position of the two uprights (the chair stiles) with a line on the fabric either side of each. This is where the ties will be attached.

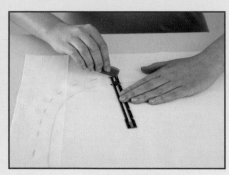

3 Remove the pattern and fold it in half to check that it is symmetrical. Adjust if necessary.

4 Lay the pattern flat on the work surface and use a sewing gauge and tailor's chalk to mark a series of points 2cm (¾in) from the seat perimeter. Join the points. This will be your cutting line. It allows for a 1.5cm (⅝in) seam allowance and 5mm (¼in) for ease, so the fabric can be wrapped around the seat pad. Cut out the pattern.

5 Fold the seat fabric in half, right sides together. Place the pattern on top and pin it in place. Cut out to produce two pieces – one for the top of the seat pad and one for the bottom. Neaten the edges of both (see p.19). Line up the pattern on top of each piece in turn and cut notches in each piece at the marks for the uprights.

Attaching the piping

1 Put a pin in the edge of one piece of seat fabric and from here, measure the perimeter. Make a length of piping (see pp.40–41) at least 4cm (1⅝in) longer than the perimeter.

Cut notches into the seam allowance

2 Starting at the back of the seat and leaving 8cm (3in) of piping unattached at the start, pin the piping to one of the seat pieces. Align the raw edge of the piping with the neatened edge of the seat fabric. To tease the piping around the curves, cut a few notches into its seam allowance. Machine the piping to the fabric, using a zip foot positioned right next to the stitching on the piping. Leave 8cm (3in) of piping unstitched at the end.

3 Lay the cut ends of the piping on top of each other, then cut the piping casing to give a 4cm (1⅝in) overlap.

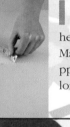

4 Open out each end of the piping casing, pull the piping cord out of the way, and hold the ends with the wrong side of each facing you. Leaving the left-hand end where it is, twist the right-hand end away from you so the right side of the casing is now facing you.

5 Holding the ends in this position, overlap them, left over right, so that the short end of the left-hand piece lines up with the long edge of the right-hand piece, and the corners match up. Pin from top to bottom, as shown.

Stitch across the pin

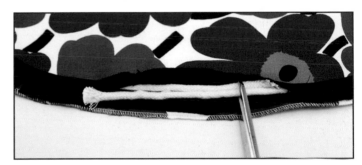

6 Machine stitch the two ends together horizontally across over the pin. Remove the pin and trim the raw edges of the seam to 1cm (⅜in).

7 With the casing opened out, overlap the ends of the piping cord and cut them level. Avoid cutting directly on top of the seam in the casing as it leads to too much bulk. Tuck the ends of the cord inside the casing, then bring the raw edges of the casing together and machine stitch them closed.

Making the ties

1 Cut a long strip the width of your fabric and 6cm (2⅜in) wide. Fold in half lengthways, wrong sides facing, then press. Open out, then fold the raw edges into the centre fold. Press again. Cut into two equal lengths.

2 To neaten the ends, fold the ties right sides together in the opposite direction, with the raw edges pointing away from you. Pinch the ends together, matching the folded edges.

3 Machine stitch across each short end with a 1cm (⅜in) seam allowance.

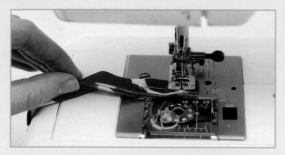

4 Turn the tie right side out and tuck in the ends.

5 Pin the long edges of each tie closed, then topstitch (see p.18), including the ends.

6 Lay the top of the seat pad right side up. Fold each tie in half and place the fold over the notches that mark the uprights, aligning the folded edge of the tie with the raw edges of the seat pad and the piping. Lay the ends of the tie on top of the seat pad, then slightly pull them apart, creating a "V". Machine stitch across the "V" within the seam allowance.

Inserting the zip

1 With the zip face down and open, centre one of its sides between the ties. Position the teeth right on top of the piping. This will allow you to stitch close enough to cover the stitching in the casing. Fold back the loose end of the zip tape and pin at 3cm (1¼in) intervals.

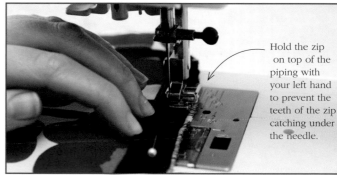

Hold the zip on top of the piping with your left hand to prevent the teeth of the zip catching under the needle.

2 Use a zip foot and adjust the needle. Stitch the zip in place, using your left hand to hold the teeth in position on top of the piping. Backstitch at the start and end of the seam to secure your stitching.

TRADE SECRET

3 Fold the bottom of the seat pad in half, then in half again, and mark the half and quarter points with pins. Repeat for the top of the seat pad.

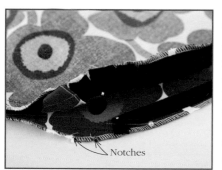
Notches

4 Lay the bottom of the seat pad right side up and lay the top, with its zip attached, right side down. Centre the other side of the zip between the notches on the bottom of the seat pad. Ensure that the notches on the bottom of the seat pad align with the ties on the top. Pin in place with the teeth of the zip 1.5cm (⅝in) from the edge and the excess tape folded back. Stitch as before.

5 Close the zip, leaving a hand's width open. Working from the top of the seat pad and with the ties tucked between the top and bottom, match the edges of both, first at the halfway points, then at the quarter-way points. Pin at these points, then pin the remainder of the edges together, easing in any excess fabric.

6 Using a zip foot, having adjusted the needle and working from the top of the seat pad so you can stitch closer to the piping, start machining at one end of the zip. Use the balance wheel to lower the needle and manoeuvre the fabric until the needle is as close to the end of the zip as possible. Ensure that the zip foot is close to the stitching line, then machine round the edges of the seat pad, backstitching at the start to secure your stitching. Check regularly while you sew that the raw edges of the top and bottom of the seat pad are aligned.

7 As you approach the end of the zip, pull the end towards the seam allowance. Sew as close as possible to the end of the zip, again using the balance wheel for accuracy. Backstitch several times to finish. Clip the curved seams, making sure you do not cut through your stitches. Turn the seat pad to the right side and insert the foam.

Bench SEAT CUSHION

What could be more inviting to sit on than this deliciously plump cushion with its smart, contrasting piping? Make one and transform any bench or chest into a statement piece of furniture. The cushion gets its plump appearance from a layer of wadding and stockinette stitched around the foam pad.

YOU **WILL NEED**

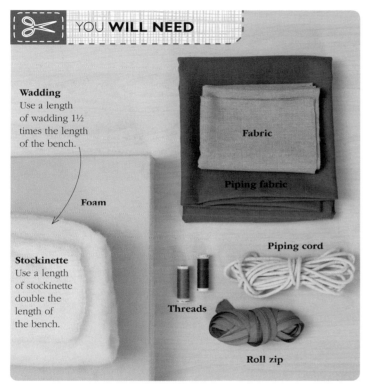

Wadding
Use a length of wadding 1½ times the length of the bench.

Foam

Fabric

Piping fabric

Stockinette
Use a length of stockinette double the length of the bench.

Piping cord

Threads

Roll zip

Tools

- Scissors • *Ruler* • *Tailor's chalk*
- *Sewing machine* • *Pins* • *Zip foot* • *Pencil*

Side band

The side band wraps around the front and sides of the cushion. Depending on the width of your fabric, you will probably have to make it in three pieces – one long and two short. To calculate the length of the short pieces, add one seat length and two seat widths to give the distance around the front and sides of the cushion (L + 2W). If the width of your fabric is less than this measurement you will need to add the difference as two pieces of equal length. Each piece will need its 2 x 1.5cm (⅝in) seam allowances all around.

W · L · H
Foam pad

Foam

Choose the right thickness of foam for your project and have a piece cut to match the length (L) and width (W) of your bench. For a bench like this one, 10cm (4in) thick foam is a good choice. The height (thickness) of the foam is measurement H.

Calculate the cutting sizes

Use the measurements of the foam pad to calculate the sizes of the fabric pieces you need to cut.

Top and bottom of seat

For these pieces, use the L and W measurements and add 3cm (1¼in) to each, giving you 2 x 1.5cm (⅝in) seam allowances along each side.

Zip bands

The zip bands sit either side of the zip along the back edge of the cushion. Their length is L + (2 x 1.5cm/⅝in) seam allowances and their width is ½H + (2 x 1.5cm/⅝in) seam allowances.

L + 3cm (1¼in)

Seat x 2

W + 3cm (1¼in)

L + 3cm (1¼in)

½H + 3cm (1¼in)

Zip bands x 2

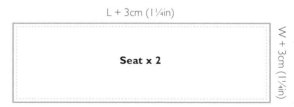

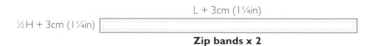

Overall length = Distance around front and sides (L + 2W) + seam allowances

H + 3cm (1¼in)   **Side band**

Cutting out

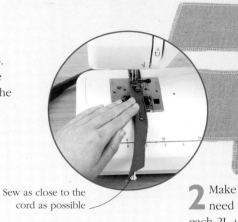

1 Lay out the fabric, wrong side up. Using your cutting sizes, measure and mark the length of the top of the seat along the width of the fabric, then mark the width. Repeat to mark the bottom of the seat, the side band pieces, and the zip bands. Cut out all the pieces and neaten the edges (see p.19).

Sew as close to the cord as possible

2 Make the piping (see pp.40–41). You will need two continuous lengths of piping, each 2L + 2W + 4cm (1⅝in) long.

Attaching the piping

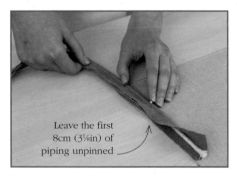

Leave the first 8cm (3⅛in) of piping unpinned

1 Lay the top of the seat on the work surface, right side up. Starting at a short edge, place the piping with its raw edge to the neatened edge of the top. Place the first pin 8cm (3⅛in) from the end of the piping.

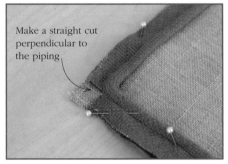

Make a straight cut perpendicular to the piping

2 Continue pinning until 1.5cm (⅝in) before the corner. Snip a straight cut into the seam allowance of the piping at this point. Guide the piping around the corner. Continue pinning the piping around the rest of the seat top, snipping each corner in the same way.

3 Leaving the first unpinned 8cm (3⅛in) of piping free, machine the piping to the seat top, using a zip foot positioned right next to the stitching on the piping. Stitch up to the first corner.

At the corners, pivot the fabric

4 Leaving the needle in the fabric, raise the presser foot and pivot the fabric, lower the foot, then carry on machining. Continue around the seat top, finishing stitching 8cm (3⅛in) before the end of the piping.

Measure an overlap
of 4cm (1½in) and
snip off the excess

5 To join the ends of the piping, place the seat top on the work surface, right side up, with the unstitched ends of the piping lying on top of each other. Pull the piping cord free of the casing at each end, then measure and mark the casing to give an overlap of 4cm (1½cm). Snip off the excess casing.

✄ TRADE **SECRET**

The wrong side of
the piping casing
is facing you

6 Still keeping the piping cord out of the way, open out each end of the piping casing and hold the ends with the wrong side of each facing you.

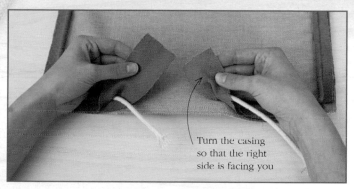

Turn the casing
so that the right
side is facing you

7 Leaving the left-hand end where it is, twist the right-hand end away from you so the right side of the casing is now facing you.

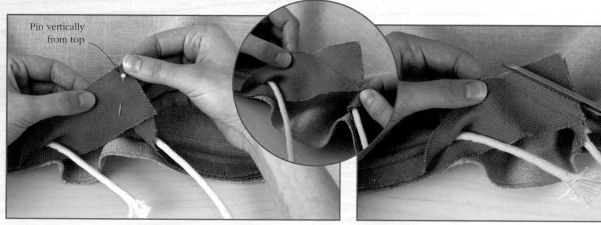

Pin vertically
from top

8 Holding the ends in this position, overlap them, left over right, so that the short end of the left-hand piece lines up with the long edge of the right-hand piece, and the corners match up. Pin from top to bottom, as shown.

9 Machine stitch the two ends together, across the pin. Remove the pin and trim the raw edges of the seam to 1cm (⅜in).

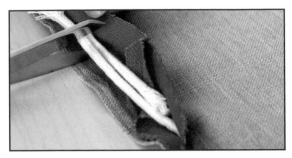

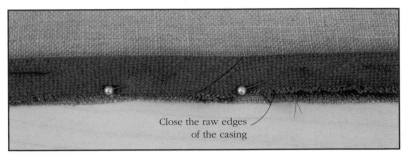

Close the raw edges
of the casing

10 With the casing opened out, overlap the ends of the piping cord and cut them level. Avoid cutting directly on top of the seam in the casing as it leads to too much bulk. Tuck the ends of the cord inside the casing,

11 Bring the raw edges of the casing together, pin, and stitch them closed. Check that the piping lies flat. Troubleshoot any wayward corners by making extra snips into the seam allowance of the piping until it lies flat. Repeat Steps 2–11 to add piping to the seat bottom.

Inserting the zip

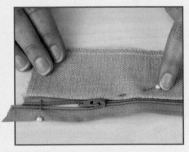

1 To assemble the side band, with wrong sides together and at a 1.5cm (⅝in) seam allowance, join the short side of one small piece to one short side of the long piece. Next join one short side of the other small piece to the other side of the long piece to make a continuous band.

2 Lay the zip bands face down and press back a 1.5cm (⅝in) seam allowance on each band. Cut a piece of zip from the roll zip so that it is slightly longer than the zip bands.

3 Insert a zip pull into the zip and secure the ends of the zip tape with a pin. Align the pressed edge of one of the zip bands with the zip teeth, as shown, and pin in place.

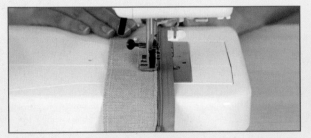

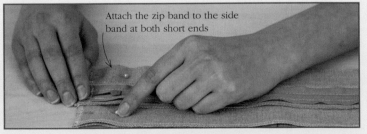

Attach the zip band to the side band at both short ends

4 Using a zip foot, stitch the zip in place as close to the zip as possible while still leaving room for the zip to open. Repeat to attach the other side of the zip to the other zip band.

5 Join the side band to the assembled zip band. Place the pieces right sides together and pin one short end of the zip band to one short end of the side band. Stitch together with a 1.5cm (⅝in) seam allowance. Repeat at the other end to create a continuous side band. Press the seam allowances open.

Joining the pieces

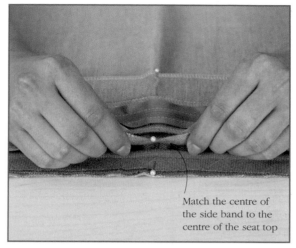

Match the centre of
the side band to the
centre of the seat top

1 Fold the seat top and bottom in half crosswise and mark the halfway points on each long edge with a pin. Fold in half again the other way and mark the quarter points. Fold the side band in half, matching the seams either side of the zip band, and mark the halfway points. Fold the band in half again and mark the quarter points.

2 With the pins as a guide, place the side band along the long side of the seat top, matching the half points. Repeat to match at the quarter points, then pin in place.

3 Using a zip foot, stitch the band to the seat top. Sew with the piped side facing up to enable you to stitch close to the piping. When you reach a corner, snip the seam allowance of the band, leave the needle in the fabric, raise the presser foot, and pivot the fabric. Open the zip, then repeat Steps 2–3 to attach the other edge of the side band to the seat bottom.

4 Turn the cover the right way out, pushing out the corners from the inside. Wrap the foam pad in a piece of wadding, fold in the ends and secure with some loose tacking stiches. To make it easier to insert it in the cover, wrap the wadding-wrapped foam in stockinette in the same way. Slip the foam into the cover and close the zip to finish.

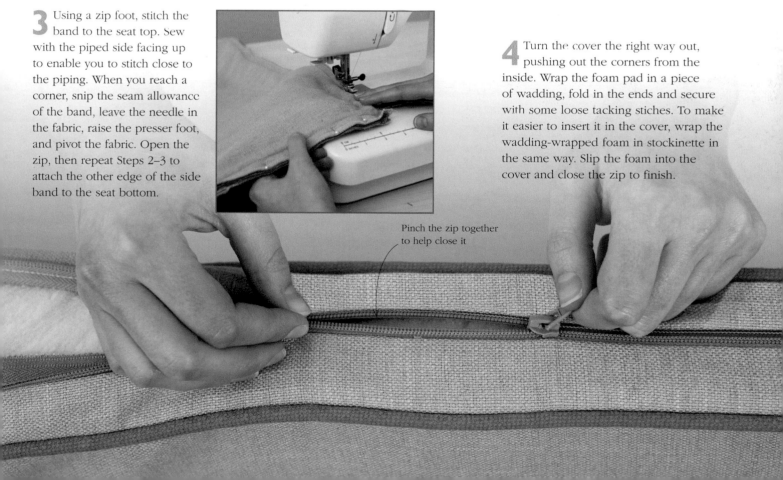

Pinch the zip together
to help close it

Footstool **SLIPCOVER**

Upcycle an old-fashioned footstool with this neat little slipcover. In fact, it's so easy to make that you won't have to worry if it gets worn and dirty. You can make another one in just an afternoon. Or better still, make a couple in different fabrics from the word go, then you can ring the changes every few months.

YOU **WILL NEED**

Materials

- *Medium-weight furnishing fabric (see cutting diagram)*
- *Matching thread*

Tools

- *Fabric tape measure* • *Dressmaker's curve or small plate* • *Marker pen (optional)* • *Pins* • *Ruler* • *Tailor's chalk* • *Scissors* • *Hand sewing needle*
- *Sewing machine*

[Diagram of footstool showing Width, Depth, and Height measurements]

Preparing the pieces

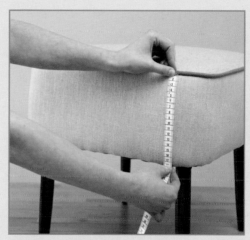

I Measure the width and depth of the footstool seat and the desired height of the cover. Calculate the cutting measurements (see left).

2 Place a dressmaker's curve at the corner of the footstool and shape it to fit the curve. Alternatively, place a small plate on the corner and slide the plate backwards until the straight sides of the footstool intersect with the edges of the plate. Make a mark on each side of the plate at these points.

Cutting measurements

Top (cut 1): Width of seat + 3cm (1¼in) seam allowance x Depth of seat + 3cm (1¼in) seam allowance

Skirt (cut 2): Height + 1.5cm (⅝in) seam allowance + 4cm (1⅝in) allowance for the hem x Width of fabric

3 Use pins to plot the measurements for the footstool top on the wrong side of the fabric. Join the pins with lines using a ruler and tailor's chalk.

4 Plot the measurements for the skirt on the fabric in the same way. Cut out the top and the two pieces for the skirt.

5 To mark the curved corners of the top, place the dressmaker's curve or the plate on one corner of the top. Position the dressmaker's curve so that the shape made by the fabric beyond the curve is symmetrical. If using a plate, slide it until the marks on the plate meet the straight sides of the top. Draw in the curve and cut along the line.

6 Fold the curved corner to meet an opposite corner. Pin together then cut around the curve.

7 Fold the fabric top in half the other way so that its curved corners meet the opposite edge. Pin and cut the remaining two corners.

8 Fold the top in half crosswise, then in half again. Mark the half and quarter points with pins. Set the top aside.

Making the skirt

1 With right sides face up, fold under the short edge of one of the two skirt pieces and lay it on the short edge of the other. If using a patterned fabric, align the pieces so the pattern matches. Press.

2 Pin in place, then slipstitch (see p.20) along the pressed edge to join the two pieces.

✂ TRADE **SECRET**

3 Unfold the top piece so that the two pieces are right sides together. Machine along the line of slipstitches. Trim the seam allowance to 1.5cm (⅝in).

4 Place the top on the work surface. "Walk" a fabric tape measure around the top to measure its perimeter. Divide this measurement by two and add a 1.5cm (⅝in) seam allowance.

5 Place the skirt on the work surface. Starting at the seam, measure along the long side of the skirt by this amount. Draw a chalk line across the skirt at this point and cut along the line. Again starting at the seam but working in the other direction, repeat and cut the other end of the skirt along the marked line.

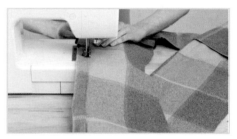

6 With right sides facing, pin the two short ends of the skirt together. Stitch a 1.5cm (⅝in) seam and press open. The skirt should now form a continuous loop.

7 With the skirt face down, fold back then press 4cm (1⅝in) along one long side. Fold under 1cm (⅜in) towards the foldline. Pin this hem in place.

8 Using a number 3 stitch, machine around the hem as close to the folded edge as possible.

Assembling the cover

1 Place the skirt right sides together, matching the seams. Pin at the seams to mark the half points. Fold in half again and mark the quarter points.

2 Lay the raw edge of the skirt on the edge of the top with right sides facing. Match the half and quarter points on the two pieces. Ease the fabric between the points and secure with pins.

3 With the skirt on top, stitch the top and the skirt together with a 1.5cm (⅝in) allowance. Turn to the right side and slip the cover over your footstool.

Chair SLIPCOVER

A beautiful printed slipcover will transform an upright chair from the ordinary to the extraordinary. The back of this slipcover has a surprise in store – fabric-covered buttons and dainty rouleau loops to fasten them. Once you've mastered the art of making these lovelies, you could use them on a dress or blouse.

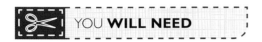 YOU **WILL NEED**

Materials

- *Fabric for chair cover*
- *3 metal self-cover buttons*
- *Matching thread*

Tools

- *Calico* • *Pins* • *Fabric tape measure*
- *Pencil* • *Scissors* • *Ruler*
- *Sewing machine* • *Blind cord*

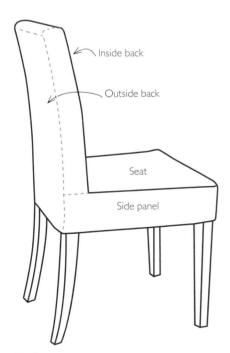

Inside back

Outside back

Seat

Side panel

Before you start
Examine your chair to make a mental note of its seamlines. Use these to plan the sections of your seat cover.

Making the calico pattern

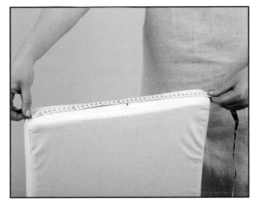

1 Find the centre point of the seat back by measuring from edge to edge. Mark this point with a pin.

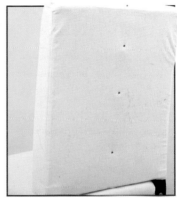

2 Starting from that pin, measure and mark a line of pins down the outside back.

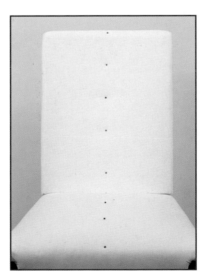

3 Measure and mark a line of pins down the inside back and along the centre line of the seat in the same way.

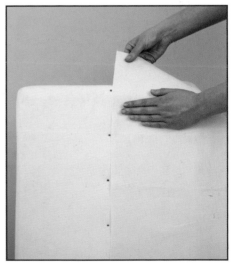

4 Align the selvedge of a piece of calico with the line of pins along the inside back, cutting the calico so it overlaps the chair's top and side seams by 20cm (8in).

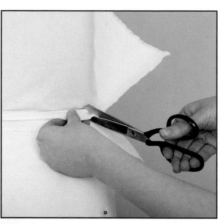

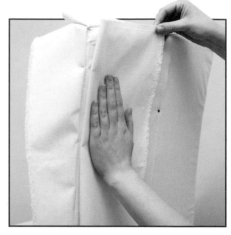

5 Pin the inside back piece of calico in place with a few pins. Align the selvedge of another piece of calico with the line of pins on the seat of the chair in the same way and pin in place.

6 Snip into the excess fabric around the inside edges to allow the calico to follow the curves of the chair.

7 Align the selvedge of another piece of calico with the line of pins on the outside back. Pin in place. Fold back the excess fabric so the fold is aligned with the side seam of the seat back. Crease along this line with your hand.

8 Open out the crease and draw in the line with a pencil.

9 Fold back the inside back piece so the fold is aligned with the side seam. Mark the crease with a pencil. Bring the inside and outside back pieces together and pin through the pencil lines.

10 Pinch the excess fabric at the top corner of the inside back piece to make a dart.

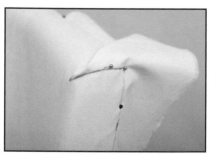

11 Ensuring the fabric is lying flat along each side, pin the dart in place. Draw in the dart on both sides with a pencil.

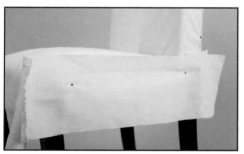

12 Moving pins as necessary, fold up the seat calico along the seat edge. Cut a strip of calico for the side panel. Pin to the chair in several places, keeping the grainline of the calico vertical.

13 Fold back the seat and side panel pieces so that they meet at the seat edge. Crease both along the seat edge. Unfold the creases one at a time and draw along them with a pencil.

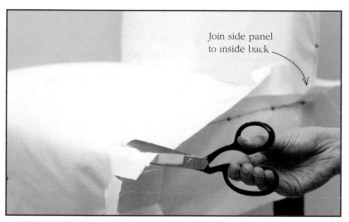

Join side panel to inside back

14 Fold the side panel and the inside back together and mark the creases with pencil lines. Pin the pieces together through the pencil lines. Clip the seam allowance of the seat piece so the fabric lies flat around the curve.

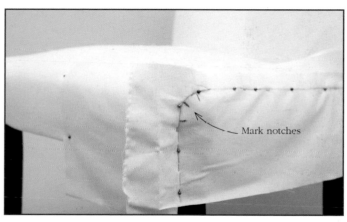

Mark notches

15 Following the seam at the front of the chair, draw in the remainder of the seamline on the side panel. Mark notches along the curve, then mark corresponding notches on the seat piece.

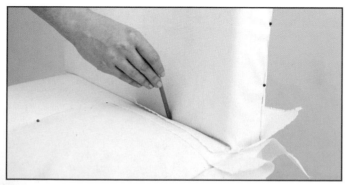

16 Tuck the inside back piece into the join between the chair seat and the inside chair back. Run a pencil along this join. Repeat, tucking in the back edge of the seat piece.

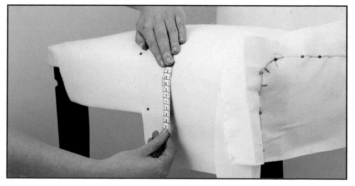

17 Measure the desired finished length along the front of the seat piece and along the side panel. Draw a line to this length to mark the bottom edge of the seat and the side panels. Continue the line along the outside back piece.

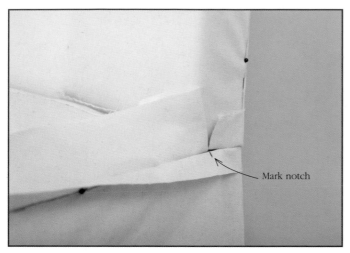

Mark notch

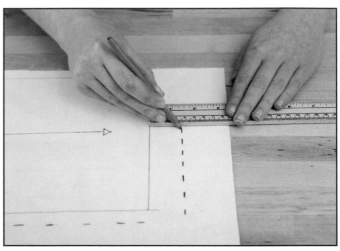

18 Mark a notch on all front pattern pieces at the point where the seat and back pieces meet the side panel seam. Mark the grainlines (see p.16) on all the pattern pieces. Remove the pattern pieces from the chair.

19 Unpin the pattern pieces. Add a "cut on fold" arrow along the selvedges of the seat and of the inside back pieces. Add a 1.5cm (⅝in) seam allowance to all seams that will be joined together. Add 3.5cm (1⅜in) to all bottom edges for a hem. Cut out the pattern pieces.

Cutting out the fabric

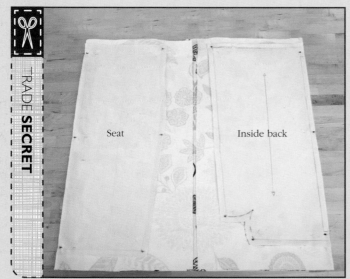

TRADE **SECRET**

Seat   Inside back

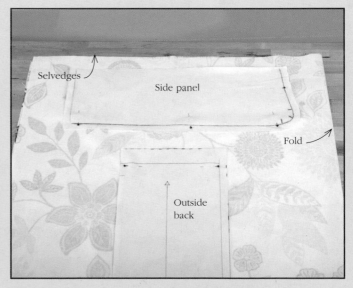

Selvedges   Side panel

Fold

Outside back

1 Fold a piece of chair cover fabric so the selvedges meet in the middle. Pin the seat and inside back pattern pieces along the folds, flipping one pattern piece so that when the fabric is cut out, the pattern will run in the same direction on both pieces. Pin and cut out. Transfer all notch and dart markings to the fabric. Neaten the edges of both pieces.

2 Fold the remaining fabric along the selvedges, right sides together. Pin the side panel and outside back pattern pieces on the fabric, following the grainline. Cut out through both layers of fabric to create two symmetrical pieces for each. Transfer all notch markings to the fabric and neaten the edges of all four pieces.

Making the rouleau loops

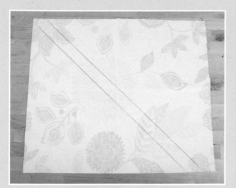

1 Cut a bias strip 5cm (2in) wide and at least 30cm (12in) long (see p.40).

Use a thick needle and strong thread

2 Lay a piece of blind cord along the right side of the strip. Fold the strip in half lengthways over the cord and machine stitch across one short end to secure the end of the cord.

3 Stitch along the long edge of the strip to enclose the cord, aligning the right-hand side of the machine foot with the raw edges of the strip.

4 Trim the seam allowance close to the seam.

5 Hold the closed end of the strip in one hand and pull the cord with the other until the strip has turned right-side out. This can be tricky, but the strip should eventually all turn through.

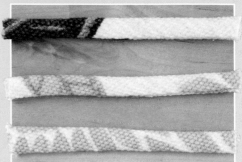

6 Cut off the closed end of the strip with its cord attached, then remove the rest of the cord. Cut the strip into three equal pieces.

7 Cut a piece of fabric 17 x 17cm (6¾ x 6¾in) and neaten the edges. Measure up 7cm (2¾in) from the bottom left-hand corner and mark with a pin. Loop one strip so that its seam is on the inside of the loop. Match the raw edge of the rouleau loop to the edge of the fabric and pin to the fabric immediately above the marker pin. Pin on the remaining rouleau loops in the same way.

8 Sew close to the edge of the fabric to attach the rouleau loops.

Joining the outside back pieces

1 Lay the two outside back pieces on the work surface, right sides up. With right sides together, place the panel with its rouleau loops along the bottom of the left-hand outside back, aligning the ends of the loops with the inside edge of the outside back. Secure with pins, then stitch in place.

2 Open out the joined pieces. With right sides together, align the free edge of the rouleau loop panel with the inside edge of the right-hand outside back. Pin and machine stitch in place.

3 Keeping the rouleau loop panel out of the way, place the free edges of the outside back pieces right sides together. Pin, then sew from the top edge of the outside back pieces to the seam allowance of the rouleau loop panel.

4 Lay the joined outside back pieces face down. Press the seam open. Centre the rouleau loop panel over the seam to form a box pleat and pin in place across the top, either side of the seam.

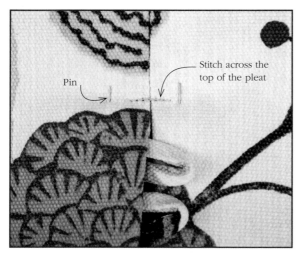

Pin

Stitch across the top of the pleat

5 Turn the piece over and stitch across the top of the pleat between the pins to hold the rouleau loop panel in place.

Covering and attaching the buttons

1 Use a pencil through the loops to mark the position of the buttons.

2 Cut a circle of fabric roughly 2cm (¾in) bigger all around than the button to be covered. Snip notches around the edge of the fabric circle to ease it around the curve.

3 Hold the fabric and button together in one hand and use the other hand to push the fabric over the edge, until the fabric catches on the teeth and is gathered inside the button front.

4 Snip off any excess fabric then snap the back of the button in place. Make two more buttons in the same way. Handstitch the buttons to the back of the seat cover at the pencil marks.

Assembling the slipcover

1 With right sides together, pin the dart on one side of the inside back piece. Stitch along the line of pins.

2 Snip into the seam allowance of the dart to allow it to open out fully. Press open. Repeat for the dart on the other side.

3 With right sides together, pin the seat piece to the inside back, between the marked notches. Start stitching 1.5cm (⅝in) in from the first notch and finish stitching 1.5cm (⅝in) before the other notch.

4 Before attaching the side panels, you will need to manoeuvre the pieces you have just joined so their outer edges line up. To do this, keep the seat piece flat and rotate or fold the inside back inwards across it. The outer edges of both pieces should now line up and be roughly horizontal.

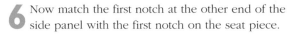

5 With right sides together, place the side panel along the edge of the inside back, matching the marked notch in the side panel with the seam that joins the seat to the inside back. Pin in place.

6 Now match the first notch at the other end of the side panel with the first notch on the seat piece.

7 Matching the other notches, pin the side panel to the seat at regular intervals, snipping the curve to ease the fabric around as you go.

8 Starting at the front, join the side panel to the seat. Ensure that the fabric does not pucker when stitching around the curve. Press the seam open. Repeat for the other side panel.

9 With right sides together, align the top edges of the inside and outside back pieces. Pin together along the top edge.

10 Ensuring the seam allowance of the darts is open and flat, continue pinning the pieces together along the sides. Stitch along the pinned lines to join the pieces.

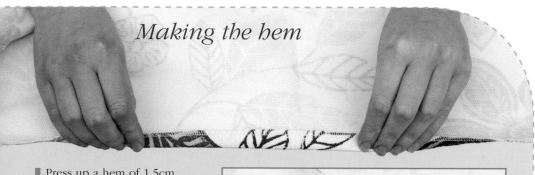

Making the hem

1 Press up a hem of 1.5cm (⅝in) around the bottom edge of the seat cover.

2 Fold up a further 2cm (¾in) and machine stitch in place with a number 3 stitch. Press as close to the edge of the first fold as possible to set the stitches.

3 Fit the cover. For a neat, professional finish, ensure that all the seam allowances face in the same direction.

Square armchair COVER

A modern square armchair gets an update with this glamorous, easy-to-fit slipcover. A linear graphic printed fabric, like the one we use here, emphasizes the armchair's geometric lines. The seat and back cushions make it super-comfy to sit on. Once your slipcover's made, sit back and relax!

YOU **WILL NEED**

Materials

- 7.5m (25ft) fabric
- Matching thread
- Roll zip
- Velcro fastening strip

Tools

- Calico • Tape measure • Extra-long pins
- Pencil • Ruler • Sewing machine

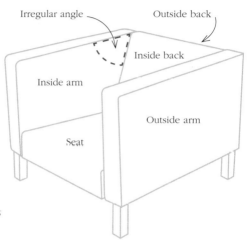

Irregular angle — Outside back — Inside back — Inside arm — Outside arm — Seat

Before you start

When making a slipcover for an armchair or sofa with rectangular arms, you don't need to make a full calico pattern. Any right-angled pieces can simply be measured and cut from fabric. You will need to make a calico pattern for any irregular angles, however. Start by identifying them on your chair. Make a calico pattern for those pieces, then measure the others. In this example you will need to make a pattern for the inside arms and back.

Making the calico pattern

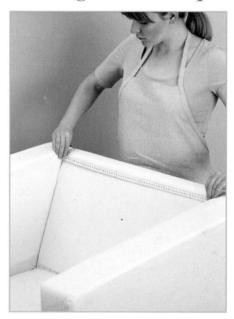

1 Measure the back of the chair to find the centre point, then mark the centre of the inside back with a line of pins.

2 Place the selvedge of a large piece of calico along the line of pins and smooth it flat.

3 Tuck the calico into the inside arm and seat back creases, cutting off the excess fabric so the calico lies flat.

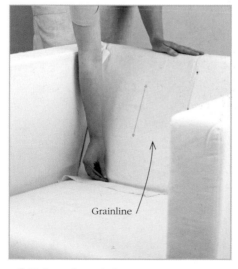

Grainline

4 Follow the existing seams to draw the inside arm and seat back seamlines. Cut off the excess fabric along the lines. Mark an arrow for the vertical grainline as a guide when cutting the main fabric.

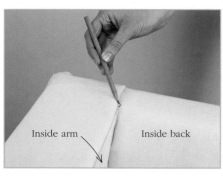

Inside arm   Inside back

5 Place a second piece of calico along the inside arm. Smooth it and tuck it into the creases. Draw in the seamlines and trim the excess.

6 Take note of where the inside arm and inside back pattern pieces meet and mark these points with notches.

7 Follow the existing seamlines to measure all the right-angled pieces – the outside arm, outside back, seat (including its front edge), and arm band (see left). Measure at least two points across the widths and lengths to allow for variations. Since the chair is symmetrical, you only need to measure each piece once. Make a note of the measurements for each piece.

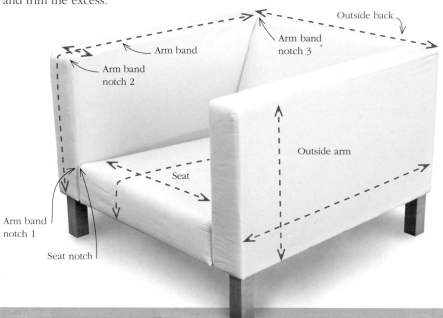

Outside back

Arm band notch 3

Arm band

Arm band notch 2

Outside arm

Seat

Arm band notch 1

Seat notch

8 Add 8cm (3¼in) to the bottom edge of the seat, the outside arm, and the outside back to allow for a double hem of 2.5cm (1in). Add a 1.5cm (⅝in) seam allowance to all the other measurements. Measure where you need to mark notches following the photograph on the left and add these measurements to your list. You will mark the notches on the fabric when you cut out the pieces.

Cutting the pieces

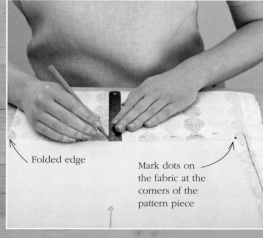

Folded edge

Mark dots on the fabric at the corners of the pattern piece

1 Look for any vertical or horizontal pattern in the fabric. Decide which part of the pattern would work best centred along the midline of the chair. This will guide the placement of the pattern for all pieces that cross the midline.

2 Cut out the inside back. Fold the fabric right sides together so the part of the pattern you have chosen to be the midline is on the fold. Lay the midline of the inside back pattern piece along the fold and draw a 1.5cm (⅝in) seam allowance along the three sides not on the fold. Transfer the notch marked in Step 6 to the fabric. Mark dots on the fabric at the corners of the pattern piece. Cut out the piece along the outer lines.

3 For the inside arms, lay a single thickness of main fabric face down with the inside arm pattern piece on top. Draw a 1.5cm (⅝in) seam allowance along all four sides and mark dots on the fabric at all the corners. Cut out. For the other inside arm piece, flip the calico pattern and repeat, checking the pattern of the fabric to ensure that the second inside arm piece is a mirror image of the first.

4 To cut two outside arms, one outside back, one seat, and two arm bands, use the measurements in your list to plot the pieces on the main fabric, paying attention to the positioning of the pattern of the fabric. For each piece, square off the fabric (see p.16). Add hem and seam allowances, and notches according to your list. Label all the pieces and neaten the edges (see p.19).

Assembling the slipcover

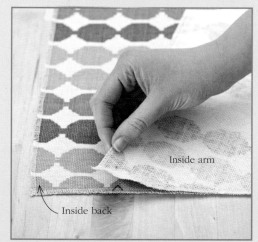

Inside arm

Inside back

1 Place one inside arm and the inside back right sides together, matching the notch on the inside back with the dot at the top corner of the inside arm. Pin. Machine stitch with a 1.5cm (⅝in) seam allowance, stopping at the dots in order not to stitch into the seam allowance.

2 Pin the other inside arm to the inside back in the same way. Pin and machine stitch together.

3 Lay the joined pieces on the chair to check that the seams line up with the existing seamlines of the chair.

4 Snip the seam allowance at the notches on both sides of the inside back, stopping just short of the stitching line. This releases the tension in the seam allowance.

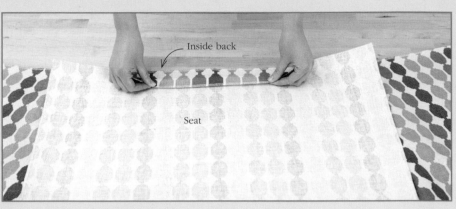

5 With right sides together, align the back of the seat with the bottom edge of the inside back, matching the pattern exactly.

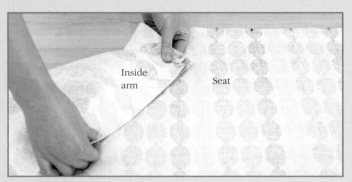

6 Pin together. With right sides together, align the bottom edge of an inside arm with the corresponding side edge of the seat, pivoting around the right-angled corner of the seat. Pin together.

7 Pin the bottom edge of the other inside arm to the seat in the same way. Stitch around all three sides of the seat with a 1.5cm (⅝in) seam allowance, stopping at the dots in order not to stitch into the seam allowance. Press the seam open.

8 Lay the joined pieces on the chair to check the fit. Put to one side.

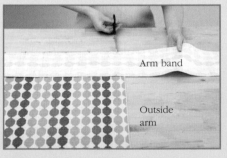

9 With right sides together, align the top edge of an outside arm with a long edge of the corresponding arm band. Match the middle notch in the arm band with the seam allowance at the front edge of the outside arm. Clip through the notch.

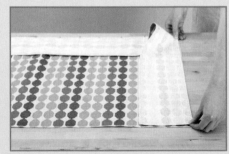

10 Pivot the band 90 degrees at the notch to match the edge of the band with the front edge of the outside arm. Pin and stitch in place with a 1.5cm (⅝in) seam allowance. Press the seam open. Repeat to join the other arm band to the other outside arm.

Attaching the outside back

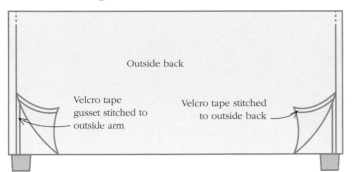

1 The outside back attaches to the inside back at the top edge. The cover is held on the chair with Velcro tape down each side and the edges above the Velcro are joined to the corresponding edges of the outside arms.

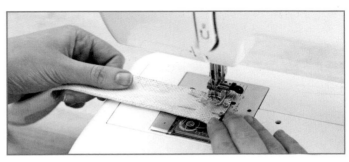

2 To make the Velcro tape gussets, cut two strips of fabric, each 7cm (2¾in) wide and 10cm (4in) less than the height of the outside arm. Fold each strip right sides together lengthwise and pin. Machine stitch along both pairs of short sides with a 1.5cm (⅝in) seam allowance.

3 Trim off the seam allowance at the short sides and turn the strip right side out. Stitch the long sides together from the right side and neaten the edges. Cut a piece of Velcro tape to the length of the strip. With the right side of the strip uppermost, lay the hooked side of the Velcro tape on top. Stitch in place.

4 Measure 5cm (2in) from the bottom of the back edge of an outside arm and mark with a pin. With its Velcro side down, align the strip with the pin, with its long edge matching the back edge of the outside arm. Pin and stitch from top to bottom within the seam allowance. Repeat Steps 12 and 13 for the other outside arm.

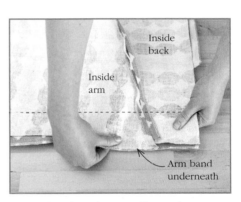

5 With right sides together and starting from the back edge, match the notch on the arm band with the seam that joins the inside arm to the inside back. Ensuring the seam is open, pin in place.

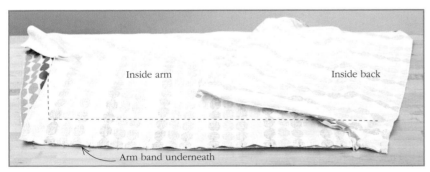

6 Continue pinning along the long edge. Match the notch on the arm band with the dot on the corner of the inside arm piece. Clip through the notch as before. Stitch with a 1.5cm (⅝in) seam allowance.

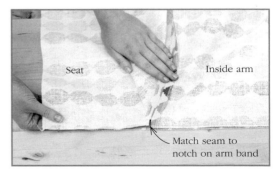

7 With right sides together, pin the front edge of the inside arm and of the seat to the front edge of the arm band. Stitch with a 1.5cm (⅝in) seam allowance.

8 With the outside back face down, fold back and press a 1.5cm (⅝in) seam allowance along one side. Measure 5cm (2in) from the top and bottom and mark with pins. Pin the looped side of the Velcro tape within the markers. Stitch in place from top to bottom. Repeat on the other side of the outside back.

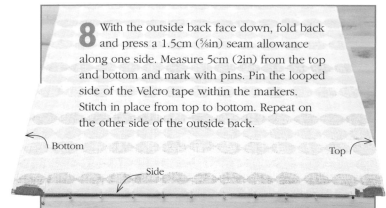

Bottom

Side

Top

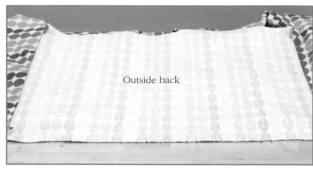

Outside back

9 With right sides together and matching the pattern exactly, align the top edge of the outside back with the top edge of the inside back, including the edge of the arm bands. Pin and stitch within the seam allowance.

Outside back

10 Snip across the seam allowance at the top of each Velcro strip on the outside back.

11 With right sides together, pin and stitch the edges above the Velcro strips to the corresponding edges of the outside arms. Backstitch at the beginning and the end.

12 Check the fit of the armchair cover.

13 With the cover face down, turn up 2.5cm (1in) all around the bottom edge and press. Turn up another 2.5cm (1in) to make a double hem. Use stitch length 3 to machine the hem in place. Press to set the stitches.

Cushion 1: Seat back cushion cover

The technique used for making this cushion cover is useful when dealing with an irregular shape, such as the trapezium shape of this seat back cushion.

The front and sides of the cushion cover are cut in one cross-shaped piece that is joined at the corners. The back has seams along all four sides to join it to the front and sides. There is a zip along one of the long seams that joins the front to the back; it cannot be seen when the cushion is in place since it is at the back of the chair

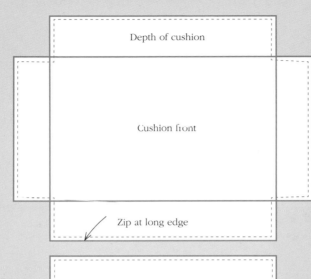

Depth of cushion

Cushion front

Zip at long edge

Cushion back

Cushion cover pieces

Make sure the pattern is centred on both front and back pieces before cutting and that they match the pattern on the chair seat.

Cushion back: Measure the cushion back and add a seam allowance all around. Cut it out.

Cushion front: The front and sides are cut as one piece. Measure the depth of the cushion pad. Add this measurement to each side of the cushion front as shown. Add a 1.5cm (⅝in) seam allowance to all the outside edges and cut out. Neaten the edges of both pieces (see p.19).

To mark the placement of the zip, lay the back of the cushion cover on top of the front, with right sides facing and the pattern matching. Manoeuvre the back so that its sides align with the seam allowance of the front as shown. At both sides, measure 7.5cm (3in) along the front as shown, and 6.5cm (2⅝in) along the back. Mark with pins.

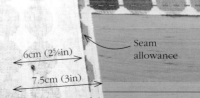

Match pattern on both pieces

6cm (2⅜in)

Seam allowance

7.5cm (3in)

2 Cut a piece of zip from the roll to the width of the cushion back. Insert the zip pull and open the zip almost to the end. Place one side of the zip, face down, between the markers on the front, with the teeth of the zip 1.5cm (⅝in) from the raw edge. Pin in place. Fold back and pin the excess tape. Stitch in place, then close the zip.

3 With right sides facing, lay the back on the front and align the other side of the zip between the markers on the back. Pin as before. Open the zip and stitch between the markers.

Stitch 1.5cm (⅝in) in from the corner

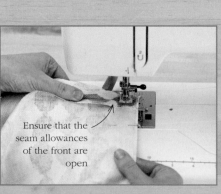

4 With right sides together, bring the two short edges of the cushion side together at each corner of the front, and pin. Stitch with a 1.5cm (⅝in) seam allowance. Repeat at each corner.

5 With right sides together, lay the front on the back. Match the corners, placing the seam allowance of the sides to the corners of the bottom so that you get a little square at each corner as shown. Pin the corners in place first, then pin all the way round to join the sides to the back.

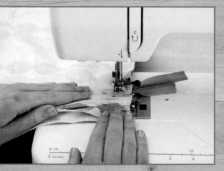

6 Starting at one end of the zip and with the zip behind the foot, stitch with a 1.5cm (⅝in) seam allowance towards the nearest corner. Backstitch at the start to secure.

Ensure that the seam allowances of the front are open

7 Pivot at the corner. Continue stitching, pivoting at each corner, to the other end of the zip. Backstitch at the end. Turn the cushion to the right side and insert the cushion pad.

Cushion 2: Seat cushion cover

Calculate the cutting sizes

Use the width (W), depth (D), and height (H) of the seat pad to calculate the sizes of the fabric pieces you must cut. Add seam allowances as below. Make a note of these measurements.

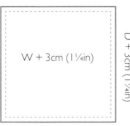

W + 3cm (1¼in)

D + 3cm (1¼in)

Seat x 2

W + 20cm (8in) + 3cm (1¼in)

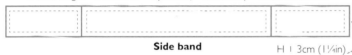

½H + 3cm (1¼in)

Zip band x 2

Overall length = Perimeter − zip band (+ difference) + seam allowances

Side band

H + 3cm (1¼in)

Top and bottom of seat

Cut two. Use the width and depth measurements of the seat pad and add 3cm (1¼in) to each, giving you a 1.5cm (⅝in) seam allowance along each side.

Zip bands

Cut two. The zip bands sit either side of the zip at the back of the cushion and should extend about 10cm (4in) around each side. Their length is W + 20cm (8in) + 3cm (1¼in) seam allowance, and their width is ½H + 3cm (1¼in) seam allowance.

Side band

The side band wraps around the front and sides of the cushion. Depending on the width of your fabric, you will almost certainly have to make it in three pieces – one long and two short. To calculate the length of the short pieces, measure the perimeter of the cushion pad. Subtract the length of the zip band. If the difference is more than the width of the fabric, you will need to add the difference as two pieces of equal length. Each piece of the band also needs 1.5cm (⅝in) seam allowance at either end.

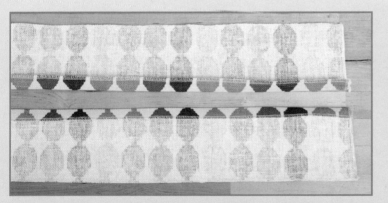

1 Cut out the pieces according to the diagram, making sure that the pattern on the top of the seat cover and the front of the side band line up with that of the seat back cushion cover. Neaten the edges (see p.19). With the zip band pieces face down, fold back and press a 1.5cm (⅝in) seam allowance along one long edge of each.

2 Cut a piece of zip from the roll slightly longer than the zip band and attach a zip pull. Open out the seam allowance of one zip band. With the zip face down and open, align the teeth of one side with the foldline. Pin in place, then stitch.

3 Lay the other zip band right side up. and open out the seam allowance as before. With right sides together, place the zip band with the attached zip on top. Pin the other side of the zip to the second band, aligning the teeth with the foldline. Pin and stitch in place as close to the teeth as possible, while leaving room for the zip to open.

4 To assemble the side band, with right sides together, align each short piece with a short edge of the long piece. The short pieces will not be visible when the seat cushion is in place.

5 Pin at each end and stitch in place with a 1.5cm (⅝in) seam allowance. Press the seams open.

6 To join the side band to the assembled zip band, with right sides together, place one short edge of the side band to one short edge of the zip band.

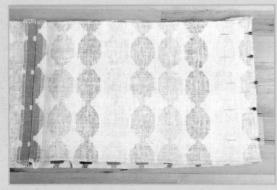
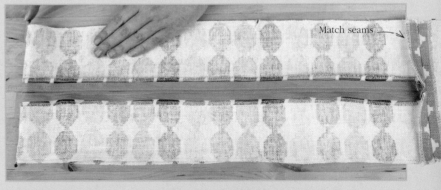

Match seams

7 Pin along the short edge and stitch together with a 1.5cm (⅝in) seam allowance. Repeat at the other end to create a continuous band. Press the seams open.

8 With the seams aligned at both ends of the zip, fold the band in half crossways. Mark the halfway points on each long edge of the zip band with pins.

9 Mark the corresponding halfway points top and bottom on the long piece of the side band. Fold the band in half again. Mark the quarter points.

10 Fold the top and bottom of the seat cover in the same way to mark their half and quarter points.

11 With right sides together, match the halfway pin on the long piece of the band to the halfway pin at the front edge of the top of the seat cover. Carefully match the pattern on the band to the pattern on the top.

12 Pin along the front edge, taking care that the pattern matches all the way along. Use plenty of pins to hold the pattern in place.

13 Match the quarter pins and the remaining halfway pin, then pin along the three sides, easing in any excess fabric as you go.

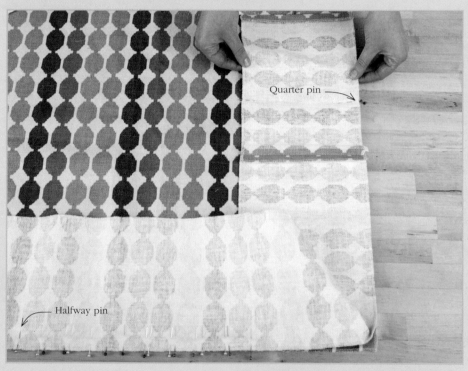

Quarter pin

Halfway pin

14 Starting at the front, sew with a 1.5cm (⅝in) seam allowance. Check that the pattern matches and adjust if needed. Clip into the seam allowance at the corners so the fabric lies flat.

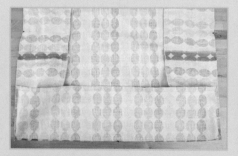

15 Open the zip. Attach the band to the bottom of the seat cover in the same way. Take care to align the corners at the same points.

16 Turn the cover inside out and insert the cushion pad. Put the finished slipcover over the chair and add the cushions.

Tub chair **COVER**

A tub chair, with its smooth curves and low lines, is the twenty-first century's take on a traditional armchair. Adding a slipcover will ring the changes without the need for reupholstery. Start by making a calico pattern that follows the curves of your chair. Then you're ready to cut the fabric and sew the pieces together.

 YOU **WILL NEED**

Materials

- *Calico*
- *5m (16½ft) furnishing fabric*
- *Matching thread*
- *Velcro fastening tape*
- *Roll zip and 2 zip pulls*
- *Piping cord*

Tools

- *Fabric tape measure* • *Pins*
- *Scissors* • *Tailor's chalk*
- *Sewing machine* • *Staple gun*

Before you start
When making a slipcover, it is always best to follow the original seams of the chair. Begin by taking a look at your chair and identifying the pieces it is made up of.

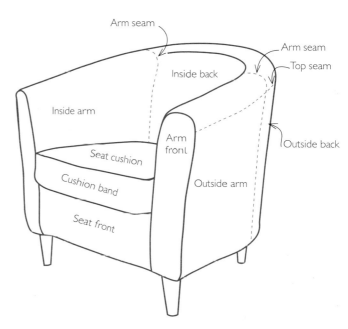

Making the calico pattern

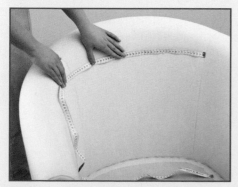

1 Using a tape measure, find the centre point of the inside back, between the seams. Mark with a pin.

2 Continue measuring between the seams and placing pins to mark the centre line along the inside back.

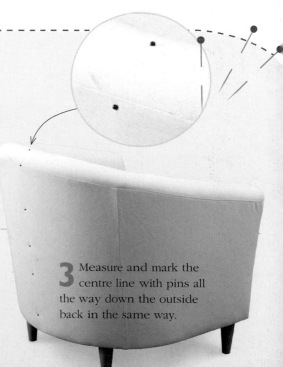

3 Measure and mark the centre line with pins all the way down the outside back in the same way.

4 Align the selvedge of a large piece of calico along the pinned line at the inside back. Cut away enough of the excess calico to allow you to lay it smoothly over the curve but leave about 15cm (6in) overhanging the seam.

5 Clip along the edge of the 15cm (6in) overhang, stopping at the seam. Clipping will allow the calico to follow the curve of the chair. Fold the clipped edge back, following the seam exactly. Crease the calico along the seam, then cut along the crease.

6 Lay a second piece of calico over the inside arm. Ensure its grainline runs vertically, that the calico covers all seams, and that it overlaps the arm front. Pin at the front edge. Smooth the calico across the inside arm so that it falls naturally, keeping the grainline vertical.

8 Fold the excess calico back along the top edge of the chair until it meets the seam. Crease along this line, then cut.

7 Clip along the back edge of this piece of calico to the seam as before. Pin the rest of the bottom edge in place, then fold the clipped edge back to follow the seam. Crease along this line, then cut along the crease, as before.

9 Lay a third piece of calico over the outside arm of the chair. Ensure its grainline runs vertically, that the calico covers all seams, and that it overlaps the arm front. Pin along the top edge. Smooth the calico across the outside arm and secure with a few pins.

10 Keeping the grainline vertical, continue smoothing the calico over the curve of the chair towards the side seam. Adjust the pins at the top edge if necessary. Fold the calico back along the side seam. Crease along this line and cut as before. Fold the calico back along the top edge of the chair along the seam. Crease and cut as before.

11 Returning to the calico at the inside back, fold back its top edge along the seam at the top edge of the chair. Crease and cut along the crease as before.

12 Align the selvedge of a fourth piece of calico with the pinned line down the outside back, ensuring it covers the seams at the top and side, and that it overlaps the bottom edge. Fold back the top edge along the seam at the top edge of the chair and the side edge along the side seam of the chair. Crease and cut along the crease as before. Draw a chalk line along the bottom edge of the outside back and arm pieces.

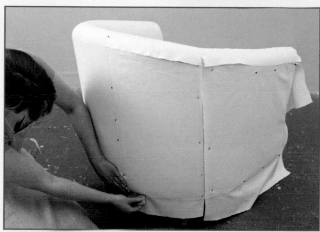

13 Returning to the arm front, trim the excess calico so it overhangs by the same amount all around. Clip along the edge of the overhang all the way around the arm front.

14 Cut a piece of calico large enough to cover the arm front and overhang the seams. Attach it with a few pins through the arm front, ensuring the grainline runs vertically. Fold back the clipped edge around the inside and outside arm pieces to meet the seam of the arm front. Pin the calico in place along both sides.

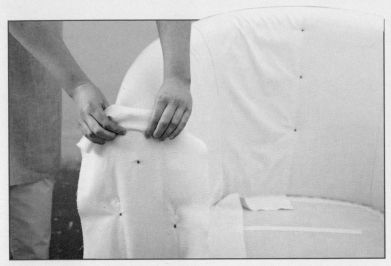

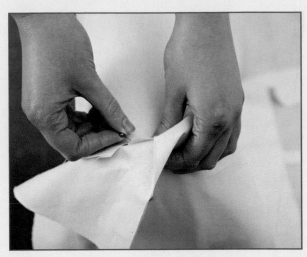

15 When you reach the top of the calico, feel for the seam in the arm front to ensure you join the calico to the inside arm piece just on top of that seam.

16 Hold the calico arm front and the inside arm piece together, exactly on top of the seam. Pin in place.

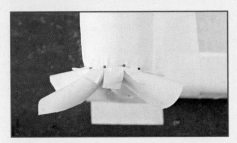

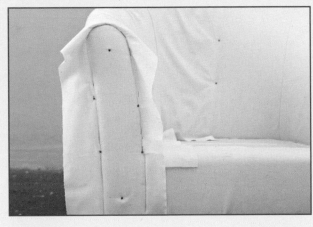

17 Pin all the way around the arm front, keeping the pieces taut. Draw a chalk line along the seam around the inside and outside arm pieces.

18 Draw a chalk line all around the arm front along the seam. Remove the pins and cut along the drawn lines to trim off the fabric on the arm front and inside and outside arm pieces. Pin the calico arm front back in place to check the fit.

Marking the pattern pieces

1 Before you take the calico pattern pieces off the chair, mark notches at the points where pieces meet. This will help you to join them again later. Also mark a notch at the point where the seat front meets the inside arm and the arm front.

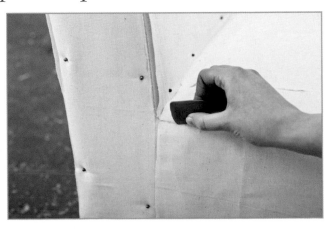

2 Mark notches all around the curve of the arm front.

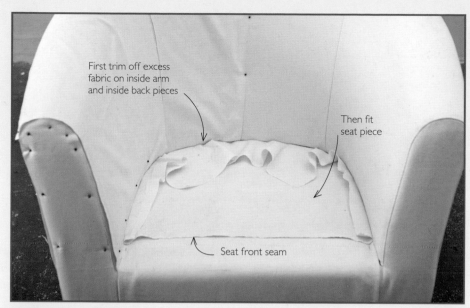

First trim off excess fabric on inside arm and inside back pieces

Then fit seat piece

Seat front seam

19 Return to the seat. Draw a chalk line around the inside edge of the seat on the inside arm and inside back pieces. Cut along this line. Lay a piece of calico on the seat of the chair, aligning its selvedge with the seat front seam. Fold the calico over so it follows the curve around the back of the seat. Crease, and cut as before. This is the pattern piece for the seat.

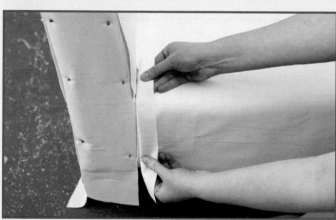

20 Lay one more piece of calico over the front of the seat. Fold it back along its edge to meet the side seams of the arm front. Crease, and cut as before. Draw along the bottom edge of the chair across the seat front.

TRADE **SECRET**

3 Mark a few notches where the inside and outside arm and the inside and outside back pieces meet. Notches are especially important for matching curved pieces correctly.

4 Finally, mark the grainlines with arrows on the calico to guide you when cutting out the main fabric.

Cutting out the fabric

I Lay the calico pattern pieces on the fabric, ensuring that the grainline of the fabric aligns with the arrows on the pattern pieces. Use the notches on the calico pieces to help match the fabric pattern on adjacent pieces. Add a 1.5cm (⅝in) seam allowance around each piece. Pieces with a hem require a 3cm (1¼in) hem allowance.

Add 1.5cm (⅝in) seam allowance to all pieces

Add a total of 3cm (1¼in) hem allowance to pieces with a hem

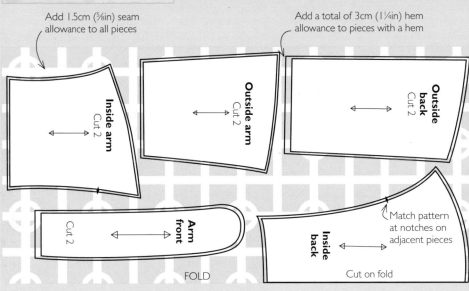

Inside arm
Cut 2

Outside arm
Cut 2

Outside back
Cut 2

Cut 2

Arm front

Inside back

FOLD

Match pattern at notches on adjacent pieces

Cut on fold

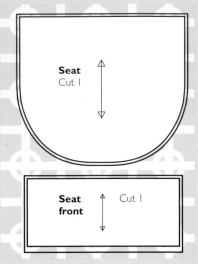

Seat
Cut 1

Seat front

Cut 1

2 Cut the seat and seat front from single fabric. Cut the inside back on a fold. To cut all the other pieces, cut out through two layers of folded fabric to make two symmetrical pieces.

3 Neaten (see p.19) the edges of all the fabric pieces.

Joining the seat and inside back pieces

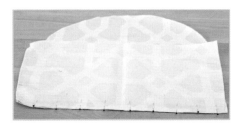

I With right sides together, align the straight edges of the seat and the seat front. Pin and stitch with a 1.5cm (⅝in) seam allowance.

2 With right sides together and carefully matching the notches, match the edge of one inside arm piece to the corresponding inside back piece.

3 Pin then stitch along this line with a 1.5cm (⅝in) seam allowance. Repeat to join the other inside arm piece and inside back piece. Press the seam allowances open as you go.

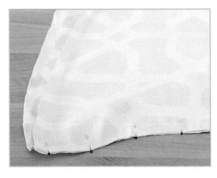

4 Lay the joined seat and seat front piece and joined inside back piece on the chair to check the fit. Adjust where necessary.

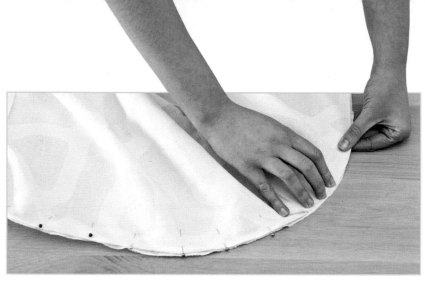

5 Fold the seat and the inside back pieces to find their centre points. With right sides together, match the centre points of these two pieces and pin. Match the notches on the seat with the notches where the seat front meets the inside arm and the arm front and pin. Ease the inside back around the curve of the seat. Pin together and stitch with a 1.5cm (⅝in) seam allowance. Check for fit.

Inserting the zip in the outside back pieces

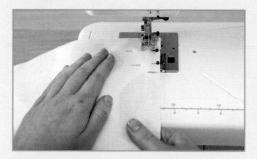

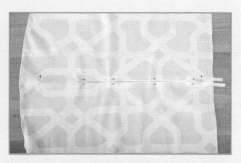

1 With the outside back pieces face down, press back a 1.5cm (⅝in) seam allowance along their centre straight edges. Make a mark 6.5cm (2⅝in) from the curved top edge of both pieces. With right sides together, stitch from the top to the mark, following the crease of the seam allowance. Backstitch at the beginning and end.

2 Press the seam open. Cut a piece of zip from the roll zip to the length of the back pieces and slip on a zip pull (see p.24). Close the zip and with the zip pull at the open (bottom) end of the back pieces, slip the zip underneath the two back pieces.

3 Position the zip along the folded edge, teeth aligned with the fold. Pin along one side of the zip. Align and pin the other side. Pin through the zip 5cm (2in) from the bottom to mark where the hemline will be. Tack (see p.20) all around the zip, through the zip tape and the folded seam allowance.

4 With the back piece face up, the presser foot aligned with the teeth of the zip, and starting from the top of the zip, stitch along one side of the zip, stopping at the pin at the hemline. Go back to the top. Sew across the zip and pivot. Sew along the other side of the zip in the same way, again stopping at the pin.

TOP TIP

Always topstitch in the same direction along both sides of the zip. This ensures that if the fabric moves, it will move in the same direction along both sides and any pattern will still match.

Assembling the slipcover

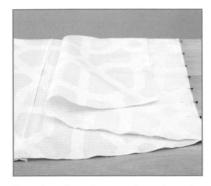

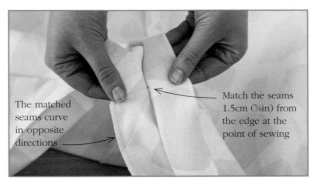

The matched seams curve in opposite directions

Match the seams 1.5cm (⅝in) from the edge at the point of sewing

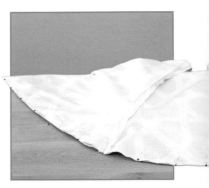

1 With right sides together, align the straight edges of one outside arm piece with the outside back piece. Pin and stitch at a 1.5cm (⅝in) seam allowance. Repeat for the other outside arm piece.

2 Fold the inside back to find its centre point and mark with a pin. With right sides together, pin this point to the centre seam of the outside back. Next match the side seams either side of the centre point. The side seams are curved, therefore ensure you match them 1.5cm (⅝in) from the edge so they are aligned at the point of sewing.

3 Ease the outside back around the inside back. Pin in place all around the curve, then stitch with a 1.5cm (⅝in) seam allowance. Press the seam allowances open.

4 Measure around the curve and long edges of an arm front. Make two pieces of piping this length, leaving the piping cord 5cm (2in) shorter than the casing at each end. This is to allow you to make a double hem later.

5 With the arm front face up, place the piping with its raw edge to the edge of the arm front. Pin together around the curve, clipping the seam allowance around the curve to allow the piping to lie flat.

6 Machine the piping to the arm front, moving the needle as far to the left as possible to stitch close to the piping cord. Repeat on the second arm front.

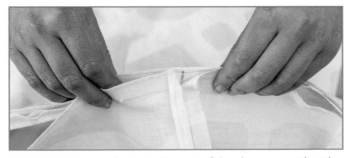

7 To join the arm fronts to the rest of the slipcover, with right sides together, match the notches along the sides of the arm fronts with the seat front-to-inside arm seams.

8 Match the notches around the curve of the arm front with the notches on the inside and outside arms. Ease the excess fabric around the curve.

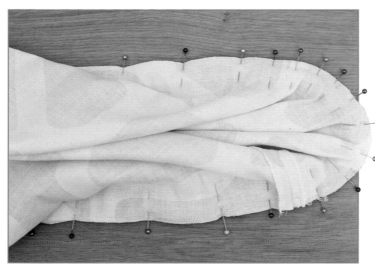

9 Continue pinning all the way around the arm fronts. Machine stitch together with a 1.5cm (⅝in) seam allowance, ensuring you hold the excess fabric out of the way so it doesn't catch under the foot as you sew.

10 Place the slipcover on the chair to check the fit.

Attaching the Velcro tape

1 Staple a length of hooked Velcro tape around the underside of the chair.

2 Open the zip at the back of the slipcover. With the cover face down, press back a 3cm (1¼in) hem all along the bottom edge, then unfold it. Fold back the excess zip tape along the pressed line. Repeat for the other side of the zip.

3 Fold the 3cm (1¼in) hem back in place along the pressed line.

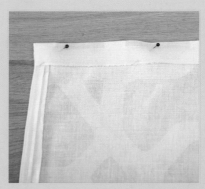

4 Align the top edge of a length of looped Velcro tape with the top of the hem, covering the raw edge, and pin in place. Stitch along one long edge, then stitch along the other, starting both lines of stitching from the same end.

Making the cushion

1 Draw around the seat cushion on a piece of calico to create a pattern.

2 Lay the calico on the fabric. Position the calico so that the pattern at the back of the piece matches the pattern on the inside back of the slipcover. Add a 1.5cm (⅝in) seam allowance. Cut out two pieces. Neaten the edges. These are the top and bottom pieces.

3 Measure all the way around the cushion. Divide this measurement by three. One-third will be the length of the zip band and two-thirds the length of the side band. Measure the depth of the cushion.

4 Use the measurements taken in Step 3 to cut out the side band and two zip bands, adding seam allowance as shown. Neaten the edges.

Length = ⅓ of cushion perimeter + 3cm (1¼in)

Zip bands x 2

Depth = ½ cushion depth + 3cm (1¼in)

Length = ⅔ cushion perimeter + 3cm (1¼in)

Side band

Depth = cushion depth + 3cm (1¼in)

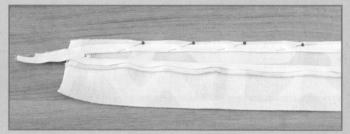

5 Cut a piece of zip on a roll to be 5cm (2in) longer than the zip band. Insert the zip pull (see p.24). With the zip face down and open, place one side of the zip along one zip band, with the teeth 1.5cm (⅝in) from the raw edge. Pin, then stitch in place using a zip foot and stitching as close to the teeth of the zip as possible.

6 Place the zip band with the attached zip on top of the second piece of casing, right sides together. Pin the other side of the zip to the other zip band, with the teeth 1.5cm (⅝in) from the raw edge. Stitch the zip in place in the same way as before. Close the zip and press on the right side.

7 With right sides together, pin one end of the zip band to one short end of the side band. Stitch together with a 1.5cm (⅝in) seam allowance. Stitch the other end of the side band to the other end of the zip band to create a continuous piece.

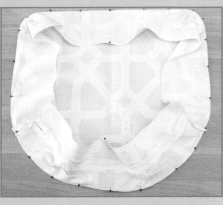

8 Fold the top and bottom pieces in half lengthwise and mark the half points with pins. Fold the band in half crosswise through the zip casing and mark the quarter points with pins.

9 With right sides together and raw edges matching, match the half point through the zip casing with the half point of the curved edge of the bottom piece and pin. Next match and pin the remaining half and quarter points.

10 Ease the excess fabric around the edge and pin all the way around. Stitch with a 1.5cm (⅝in) seam allowance. You may need to clip into the seam allowance to ease the fabric around the curves.

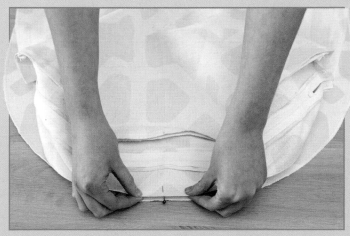

11 Join the top piece to the other raw edge of the band in the same way. Turn the cushion to the right side and insert a cushion pad. For a professional finish, ensure the seam allowances face the same way.

12 Fit the cover on the chair, ensuring the seam allowances face the same way. Fasten the cover with the Velcro tape and place the cushion on the seat.

Removable **SEAT PAD**

Upcycle an old chair with this oh-so-easy chair seat cover. All you need is a length of glamorous furnishing fabric and a staple gun. Once you have revamped one seat, you are sure to want to do more.

 YOU **WILL NEED**

Materials

- *Furnishing fabric*
- *Seat pad*

Tools

- *Scissors* • *Ruler or tape measure*
- *Staple gun* • *Hammer*

Cutting the material

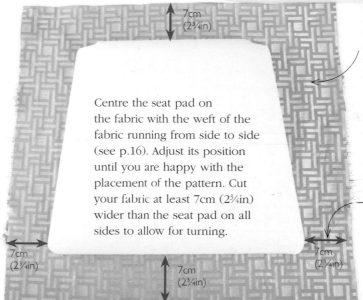

7cm (2¾in)

Check that the weft (stretch) of the fabric runs from side to side of the seat pad (see p.16).

Centre the seat pad on the fabric with the weft of the fabric running from side to side (see p.16). Adjust its position until you are happy with the placement of the pattern. Cut your fabric at least 7cm (2¾in) wider than the seat pad on all sides to allow for turning.

Leave at least 7cm (2¾in) either side at the widest point of the seat pad

7cm (2¾in)   7cm (2¾in)   7cm (2¾in)

Fitting fabric to seat pad

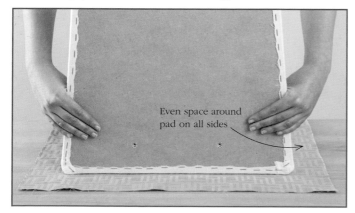

Even space around pad on all sides

1 Lay the fabric wrong side up then lay the seat pad face down on top. Make sure that the seat pad is evenly centred on the fabric. Hold the front edge of the seat pad at a right angle to the fabric and align the edge with the fabric pattern.

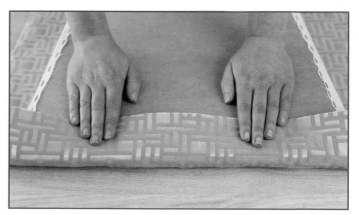

2 Grasp the edge of the fabric at the front of the seat pad and pull it gently over the base of the pad. Check that the pattern is straight and realign the fabric if necessary.

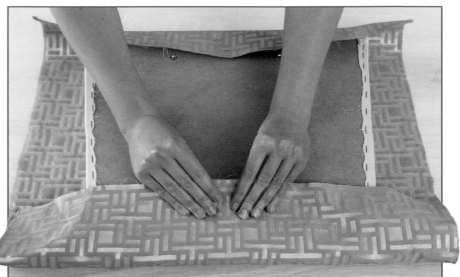

3 Place a staple in the middle of the front edge, checking that the pattern is straight.

4 Grasp the edge of the fabric at the back of the seat pad and pull it towards the centre of the seat pad. Ensure that the fabric lies taut across the pad and place a staple in the middle of the back edge.

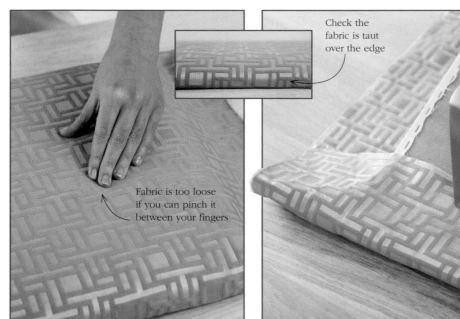

Fabric is too loose if you can pinch it between your fingers

Check the fabric is taut over the edge

5 Flip the seat pad over and check that the pattern is aligned along the straight edges and that the tension is correct. If the fabric is loose, flip the seat pad to the wrong side, remove the second staple, pull the fabric tighter, and staple again.

6 Once you are happy with the tension, flip the seat to the wrong side and place two more staples in the front edge approximately 5cm (6in) either side of the first staple. Keep all the staples in line. Before inserting every staple, check that the pattern is straight. Repeat along the back edge.

7 Repeat along the other two edges, making sure you leave enough fabric unstapled at the corners to enable you to fold them over.

Folding the corners

I When it comes to folding in the corners, your aim is to minimize the bulk. This applies whatever shape the corners are. Before you start, try out different folds at the corners until you find one that works. Always pull the fabric across tightly so it lies as flat as possible.

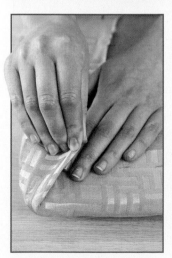

2 Holding one edge of the fabric steady with one hand, fold the fabric over the corner and pull it tight. Staple in place.

3 Make a second fold and pull it tightly across the first. Staple it in place.

4 As you go, cut away any excess fabric to help reduce bulk.

5 Make a last fold over the first two to finish the corner. Repeat for the other corners. If any staples are loose, hammer them in.

BEDDING AND HEADBOARDS

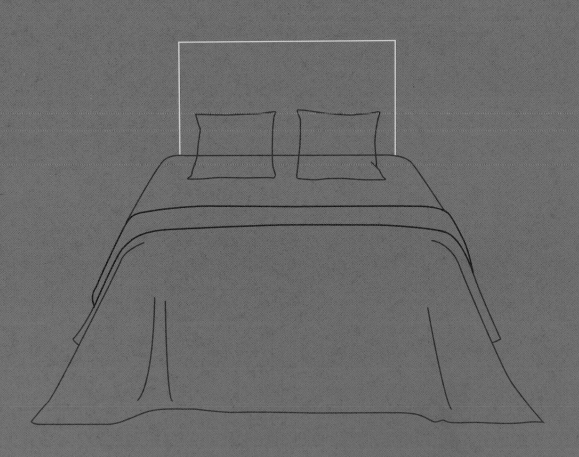

Making BEDDING

We spend so much time in our bedrooms that they should be spaces we really love. While the right paint and flooring are good starting points, soft furnishings can make all the difference between stark surroundings and sumptuous ones. Here we look at some of the lovely bedroom furnishings you could make to give your bedroom the edge.

Soft furnishings for beds

A well-dressed bed makes a bedroom feel luxurious, and having winter and summer sets of soft furnishings is a clever way to freshen up your bedroom from season to season. Failing that, simply changing the soft furnishings once in a while will give your bedroom a quick and easy style makeover. For best results, aim to keep the rest of your bedroom's décor neutral.

Bedspread drop

The drop, or overhang, of a bedspread or bedrunner is determined by its purpose and your taste. A generous, floor-length bedspread looks fabulous, but there's no point having one if you also have a valance. If that's the case, a bedspread that just overhangs the bottom edge of the mattress is a much better choice.

To calculate the finished width of your bedspread, measure the width of the mattress from side to side. Then measure from the top edge of the mattress down, to the length you'd like your bedspread to be. Multiply this drop by 2 and add it to the width measurement to get the total finished width.

To calculate the total finished length, measure the length of the mattress from top edge to bottom edge. Add just 1 drop to get the total finished length.

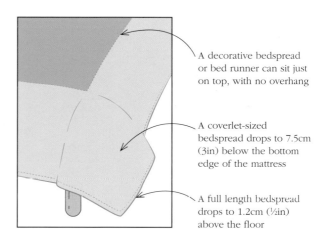

A decorative bedspread or bed runner can sit just on top, with no overhang

A coverlet-sized bedspread drops to 7.5cm (3in) below the bottom edge of the mattress

A full length bedspread drops to 1.2cm (½in) above the floor

New headboards for old

Have you got a tired old headboard or have you found an old-fashioned bargain in a second-hand shop? If so, recovering it can give it a new lease of life at minimum cost.

If the headboard padding is in good condition, you can simply get on and cover it, either with a fixed cover or a removable slipcover. Whichever type of cover you choose to make, if the padding has worn a bit thin, or your headboard is nothing more than a piece of wood, just add some wadding to pad it out and soften its corners.

If you're feeling especially handy, you can make an entirely new headboard using a piece of plywood cut to the size and shape of your choice. This option can then be padded and covered in your fabric, giving you total design freedom.

Lots of layers

Layers are the key to a well-dressed, sumptuous-looking bed. A covered headboard provides a
good starting point. As you are unlikely to change its cover frequently, either choose a fabric you
love, or go for something neutral. Next come the bedspread and bed runner – though you may
not want both. These give another opportunity to add pattern and texture. Finally, add cushions
in a variety of decorative fabrics to tie in with your décor and pull the whole look together.

Cushions

An array of decorative throw cushions adds texture and colour
to your bed dressing. For extra interest, try mixing and matching
cushions in a few different fabrics and patterns. See pages 22–65
for more information on the variety of cushions you can make.

Headboard

A covered headboard sets the stage for your bed and can look
decadent compared to a simple wooden headboard. If you
choose a headboard with a slipcover, it's an easy matter to
remove it for cleaning or if you want a change of mood.

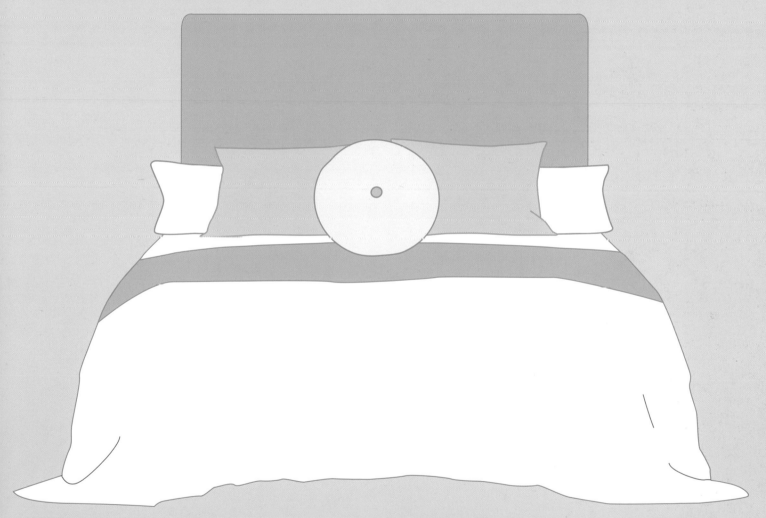

Bedspread

A bedspread adds yet another layer, and therefore an extra level
of luxury, to your bed. Bedspreads can be made to different
lengths and in different weights to suit your needs.

Bed runner

A bed runner sits across the bed and gives a contemporary,
polished look. It is a good way to add a splash of colour, texture,
or pattern to otherwise plain bedding, and does not require a
great deal of fabric.

Bed RUNNER

This lightly padded, coordinated bed runner makes the perfect finishing touch when dressing a bed, and is great for adding an extra layer of cosiness around your feet at night, too. Make sure you add borders of the same width either end so your runner is symmetrical. Our simple instructions show you how.

YOU **WILL NEED**

Materials

- *Main fabric*
- *Backing fabric*
- *Fabric in two colours for the borders*
- *Fabric for the flat piping*
- *240 x 60cm (94½ x 24in) cotton batting*
- *Matching thread*

Tools

- *Scissors* • *Pins* • *Sewing machine*
- *Hand sewing needle*

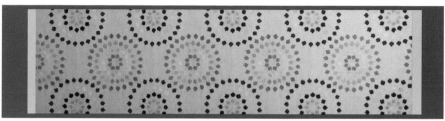

Finished dimensions
240cm (94½in) x 60cm (24in)

Cutting measurements:

Top: cut 1 rectangle, 206 x 63cm (81 x 25¼in) from main fabric
Backing: cut 1 rectangle, 206 x 63cm (81 x 25¼in) from backing fabric
Narrow border (yellow): cut 2 rectangles, 10 x 63cm (4 x 25¼in)
Wide border (pink): cut 2 rectangles, 31 x 63cm (12⅜in x 25¼in)
Flat piping: cut 2 lengths, each 243cm (48⅜in) by 4cm (1⅝in)
Cotton batting: cut 1 rectangle, 240 x 63cm (94¼ x 25½in)

Making the top

1 Place one wide and one narrow border piece right sides together, aligning their long edges. Pin, then machine stitch with a 1.5cm (⅝in) seam allowance. Repeat to join the other wide and narrow border pieces. Press the seams open.

2 With right sides together, align the narrower piece of the joined border with the short edge of the main fabric top. Pin in place along the edge.

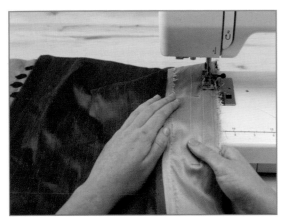

3 Stitch together with a 1.5cm (⅝in) seam allowance. Repeat along the other short edge. Press each seam towards the border.

4 With the top face down, press back 2cm (¾in) at the end of the border. Fold the border so that its pressed edge aligns with the seam joining the top to the border. Press along this fold. Repeat for the other end.

Making and attaching the flat piping

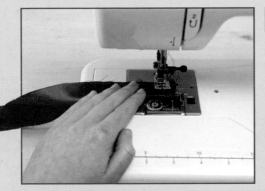

1 Fold each length of flat piping in half lengthways, wrong sides together. Press. At the ends only, turn the piping right sides together. Stitch the ends closed with a 1cm (⅜in) seam allowance.

2 Turn each end to the right side, tucking the raw edges inside.

3 Lay the top face up. Starting at the foldline in the border, align the edge of the piping with the long edge of the top, as shown. Pin in place. Repeat along the other long edge.

4 Tack (see p.20) the piping in place.

Assembling the runner

I Fold the batting and the backing fabric in half widthways to find the centre points. Mark these with a pin at either edge.

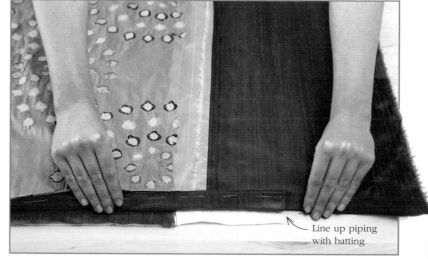

Line up piping with batting

2 Open out the batting and lay the backing fabric right side up on top, matching the centre points. Smooth out any wrinkles from the backing fabric, working from the centre outwards.

3 Place the runner top right side down on the backing, matching the raw edges. Align the end of the flat piping with the edge of the batting, as shown, ensuring that the edge of the batting lines up with the foldline in the border.

4 Tack or pin all the layers together. Machine stitch along each long edge with a 1.5cm (⅝in) seam allowance, stopping and starting at the edge of the batting.

5 Turn the runner to the right side, then lay it on the work surface with the backing face up.

6 Fold over a 1.5cm (⅝in) seam allowance along the sides of the border, then fold and press a 1.5cm (⅝in) seam allowance along the end. Re-fold the 2cm (¾in) hem at the short end.

7 Fold the border over the batting to meet the edge of the backing fabric. Pin in place.

8 Slipstitch (see p.20) the border in place, taking care not to stitch into the front of the runner. Repeat Steps 6–8 at the other end to finish.

Light BEDSPREAD

Lightweight but firm, thanks to its inner layer of batting held in place by the contrast border, this fresh-looking bedspread is perfect for warm summer nights. We have made our bedspread with finished dimensions of 240 x 260cm (94½ x 102⅜in) – the right size for a queen or double bed.

YOU **WILL NEED**

Materials

- *5m (16½ft) furnishing fabric for front*
- *236 x 256cm (94⅜ x 100¾in) sheeting fabric for back*
- *236 x 256cm (94⅜ x 100¾in) batting*
- *2.7m (108in) contrast fabric for the border*
- *Matching thread*

Tools

- *Ruler • Tailor's chalk • Set square (optional) • Iron • Scissors • Pins • Hand sewing needle • Sewing machine • Pencil*

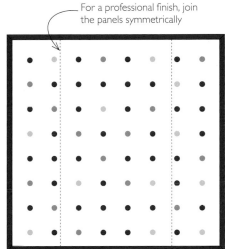

For a professional finish, join the panels symmetrically

Bedspread front

Furnishing fabric is not usually wide enough to make a bedspread for a double bed so it is made in three panels. Cut the first panel to 256cm (100¾in), then follow the instructions to cut the other two.

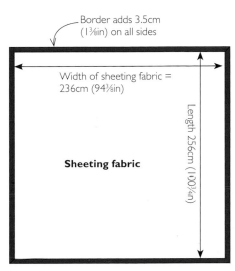

Border adds 3.5cm (1⅜in) on all sides

Width of sheeting fabric = 236cm (94⅜in)

Length 256cm (100¾in)

Sheeting fabric

Bedspread back

We have made the back from 236cm (94⅜in) wide sheeting fabric cut to 256cm (100¾in) long. If necessary, you can piece the back from narrower fabric in the same way as the front.

Cutting out the front panels

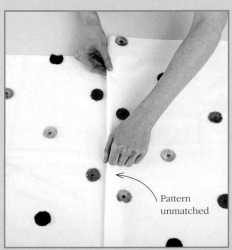

Pattern unmatched

1 Cut the centre panel of the bedspread to the required length, in this case 256cm (100¾in), using the full width of the fabric. Lay this on the work surface right side up. Before cutting the two side panels, you must match the pattern. With the right side up, fold under the selvedge of the remaining fabric and lay it so its folded edge overlaps the central panel.

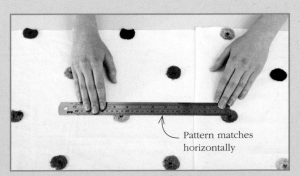

Pattern matches horizontally

2 Manoeuvre the second piece of fabric until the pattern matches horizontally across the two pieces. Then measure the distance between the horizontal pattern repeat and move the second piece of fabric until this distance also matches across the two pieces.

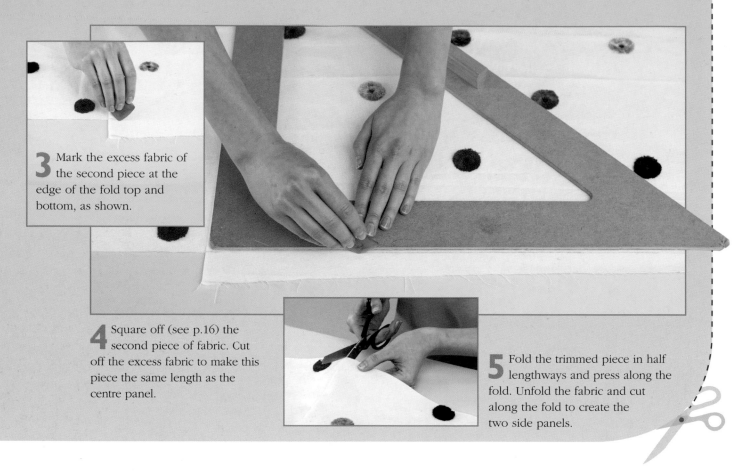

3 Mark the excess fabric of the second piece at the edge of the fold top and bottom, as shown.

4 Square off (see p.16) the second piece of fabric. Cut off the excess fabric to make this piece the same length as the centre panel.

5 Fold the trimmed piece in half lengthways and press along the fold. Unfold the fabric and cut along the fold to create the two side panels.

Joining the front panels

1 With the centre panel right side up, position one of the side panels alongside, selvedge to selvedge. Fold under the selvedge of the side panel. As before, check the horizontal alignment of the pattern across the two pieces, and check that the distance between the pattern repeat is always correct. Pin in place.

TRADE **SECRET**

2 Slipstitch (see p.20) the two panels together along the folded edge, checking that the pattern matches all the way along. Remove the pins and press on the right side.

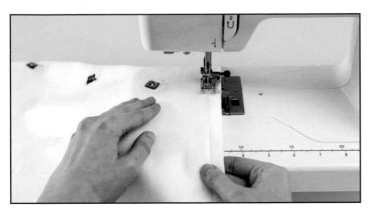

3 Fold back the side panel so that both panels are right sides together and the seam allowance is exposed. Concertina the fabric to keep it out of the way and machine stitch along the foldline from top to bottom.

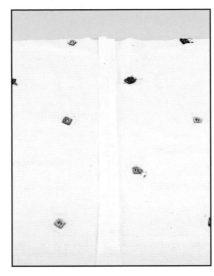

4 Align the second side panel selvedge to selvedge with the centre panel in the same way and machine stitch together as before. Press both seams open. Measure, mark, and cut the joined piece of fabric – the bedspread front – so that it is 236cm (94⅜in) wide.

Joining the layers

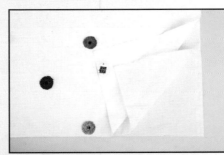

1 Lay the sheeting fabric on the work surface or floor wrong side up. Smooth out any wrinkles. Place the batting on top, then lay the bedspread front on top of that, right side up. Match the raw edges all around. Smooth out any wrinkles.

2 Tack the three layers together with horizontal and vertical rows of stitching approximately 20cm (8in) apart.

3 Pin around all four sides at regular, close intervals.

4 Using a large stitch, machine around all four sides within the 1.5cm (⅝in) seam allowance. This will stabilize the edges to allow the border to be attached with ease. Remove the tacking stitches.

Making the border

1 The border is folded in half and wraps around the bedspread. It will be mitred at the corners on top and underneath; this is a double mitre. For this you must add 5cm (2in) at both ends of each border piece, so cut two pieces, each 246 x 13cm (96⅞ x 5¼in) and two more pieces, each 266 x 13cm (104¾ x 5¼in). With right sides together, press the ends of each piece lengthways to find the centre points.

2 Unfold a 266cm (104¾in) border piece and on the wrong side, draw a 1.5cm (⅝in) seam allowance around each end. Extend the seam allowance lines along the long sides by at least 7cm (2¾in).

3 Measure 5cm (2in) down from each corner and mark the seam allowance lines at these points.

4 Align the ruler between a centre point and a 5cm (2in) mark, then join the points with a line. Repeat on the other side of the centre point. The resulting 90-degree angle marks the double mitres either end of the longer border pieces.

5 Repeat at both ends of the other 266cm (104¾in) border piece.

6 Place the end of one long border piece right sides together with the end of a short border piece. Secure with pins. Repeat to join another long piece to the free end of the short piece, then join the free end of that long piece to the second short piece. Finish by joining the two free ends to make a rectangle.

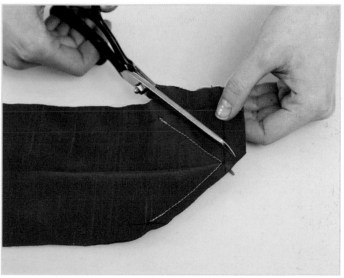

7 Machine stitch the pieces together along the 90-degree angle, pivoting at the point. Backstitch at the beginning and end of the seams to secure them. Make sure that you do not stitch inside the seam allowance.

8 Trim off the excess fabric at all four corners of the rectangle, making sure that you do not cut through the stitches.

Attaching the border

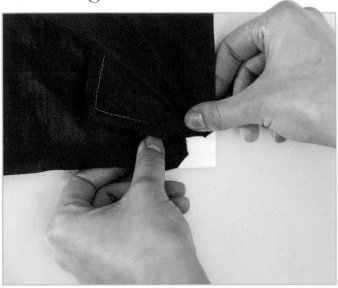

1 Lay the bedspread on the work surface. With right sides together, match the corners of the border with the corners of the bedspread. Open out and fold back the seam allowance at each corner of the border to create a tiny right angle.

2 Pin just the seam allowance of the first corner to the bedspread. Manoeuvre, or "walk", the border around the bedspread to check that it fits.

3 Secure the other three corners with pins in the same way, then pin the border to the bedspread along the sides.

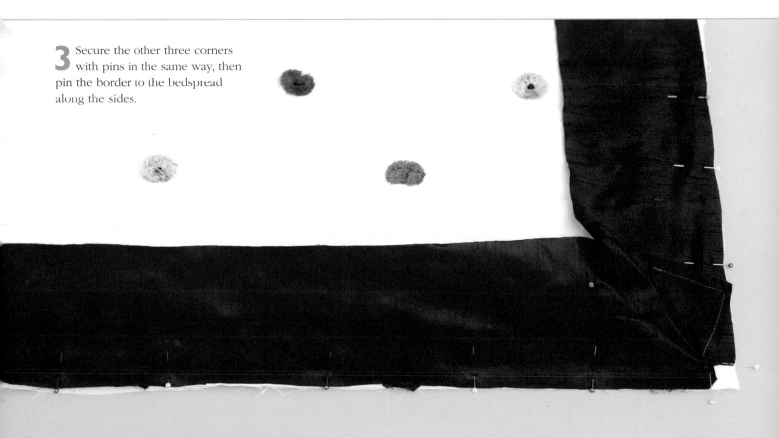

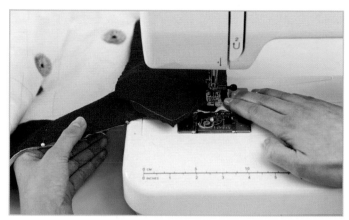

4 Machine stitch along one side with a 1.5cm (⅝in) seam allowance. When you reach the first corner, keep the double mitre out of the way, lower the needle into the fabric, and raise the presser foot.

5 Pivot the fabric, fold the double mitre out of the way to the other side, then lower the foot. Continue around the bedspread, pivoting at the remaining corners in the same way.

6 Lay the bedspread on the work surface face down. Turn the double mitres of the border to the right side.

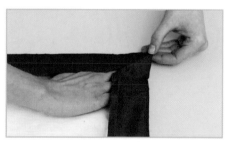

7 Push the corners out and smooth the border flat along the edges of the bedspread.

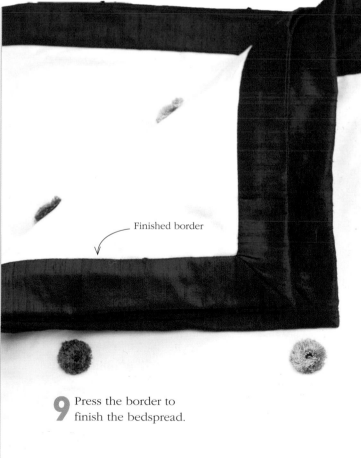

Finished border

8 Fold under 1.5cm (⅝in) along the raw edge of the border and pin in place, covering the line of stitching underneath. Slipstitch in place (see p.20) with tight, close stitches no more than 1cm (⅜in) apart. Alternatively, machine stitch in place using a hem foot.

9 Press the border to finish the bedspread.

Padded HEADBOARD

A neatly tailored, padded headboard in a fabulous bold-as-brass fabric provides the perfect focal point to a well-dressed bed. Easily made from scratch, there's no sewing required – though you may need some DIY help. This project would look just as effective in a plain fabric against a boldly patterned wall.

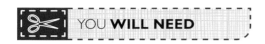 YOU **WILL NEED**

Materials

- *18mm (1¹⁄₁₆in) thick plywood, cut to size*
- *5cm (2in) thick foam, cut to size*
- *Polyester wadding (135 or 200 g/ 4 or 6oz weight)*
- *Soft furnishing fabric*
- *2 wooden battens for mounting the headboard*

Tools

- *Glue or spray mount* • *Scissors*
- *Clamps* • *Staple gun*

Before you start

Have a piece of plywood cut to the width of your bed and the desired height of your headboard. Order or cut a piece of foam that is 5mm (³⁄₁₆in) bigger all around.

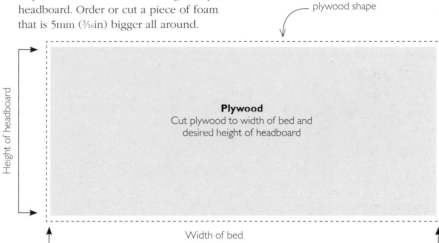

Foam cut to be 5mm (³⁄₁₆in) larger all around than the plywood shape

Height of headboard

Plywood
Cut plywood to width of bed and desired height of headboard

Width of bed

Laying out and cutting the fabric

Cut your fabric so it is 10cm (4in) larger all around than the plywood headboard. If the headboard is narrower than the width of fabric minus 20cm (8in), have the selvedges at the sides of the headboard so the fabric layout follows the lengthwise grain. If it is wider, have the selvedges along the top and bottom edges so the fabric layout follows the crosswise grain. This is known as "railroading".

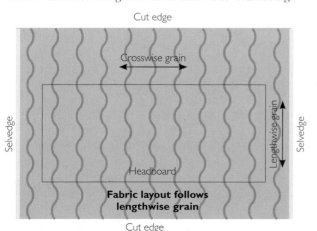

Cut edge

Crosswise grain

Selvedge

Lengthwise grain

Selvedge

Headboard

Fabric layout follows lengthwise grain

Cut edge

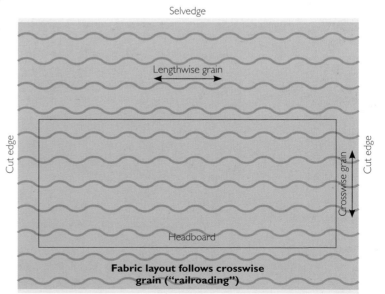

Selvedge

Lengthwise grain

Cut edge

Crosswise grain

Cut edge

Headboard

Fabric layout follows crosswise grain ("railroading")

Selvedge

Attaching the foam and wadding

  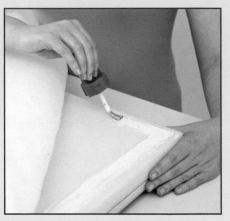

1 Lay the plywood on a table or on the floor. Position the foam on top so that it overhangs by 5mm (³⁄₁₆in) all around. Fold half the foam back and spread glue or apply spray mount on the exposed half of the plywood.

2 Lay the foam back over the glue-covered plywood and press it down to stick it in place. Fold back and glue the other half of the foam in the same way.

3 Cut a piece of wadding 10cm (4in) larger all around than the foam. Position the wadding on top of the foam so that it overhangs by the same amount all around. Glue the wadding to the foam.

Attaching the fabric

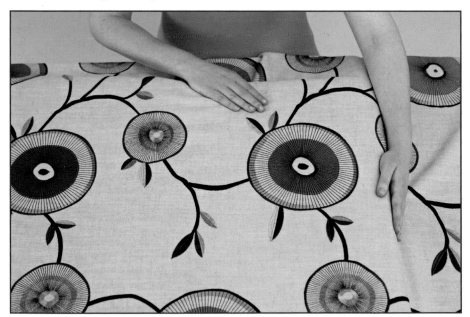 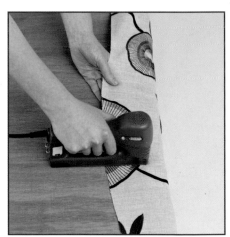

1 Lay the fabric on top of the wadding, ensuring that you are happy with the placement of the pattern. Check that the grainline is parallel to the edge of the headboard, then tuck the fabric and the wadding under the headboard all around. Clamp it in place around the edges.

2 Turn the headboard and fabric over and trim off the excess fabric, leaving approximately 10cm (4in) all around. Stretch the fabric over one short side and place a staple through the fabric and wadding into the headboard in the middle of the side, about 3cm (1¼in) from the edge.

3 Reaching underneath the headboard to stretch the fabric taut, place a staple in the middle of the opposite short side through the fabric and wadding into the headboard. Turn the headboard over to check that the fabric is taut and the pattern is still straight. If it is not, remove one or both of the staples, adjust, and staple again.

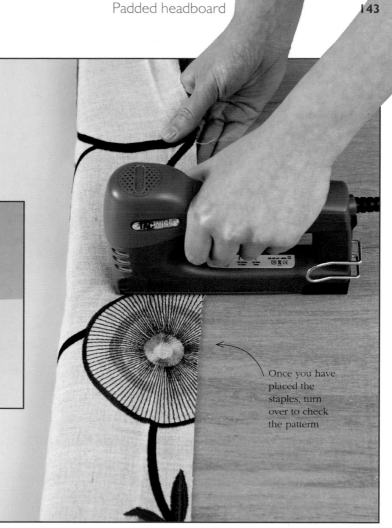

Once you have placed the staples, turn over to check the pattern

4 Staple along one short side, again 3cm (1¼in) from the edge and with the staples 4–5cm (1⅝–2in) apart. Stop 15cm (6in) from each corner. Make sure that the fabric remains taut in all directions as you staple. Repeat for the other short side.

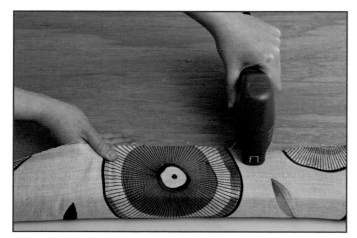

5 Pull the fabric taut on one long side and staple in two or three places. Turn the headboard over and check that the pattern is straight and the fabric flat. Again turn the headboard over, pull the fabric taut on the other long side, and attach with another two or three staples. Re-check the tension of the fabric on the right side of the headboard.

6 Staple along the long sides, with the staples 4–5cm (1⅝–2in) apart. When you are happy with the tension of the fabric, continue stapling, this time a maximum of 1cm (³⁄₁₆in) apart around all sides. Stop just before the corners.

Finishing the corners

Neatly fold
the wadding
in place first

1 Unfold the fabric from a corner. Fold the wadding back on itself towards a short side, and align the edges of the wadding.

2 Holding the edges of the wadding together, fold the wadding neatly over towards the adjacent long side. Secure in place with one staple.

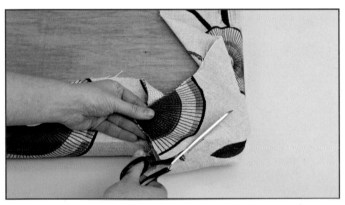

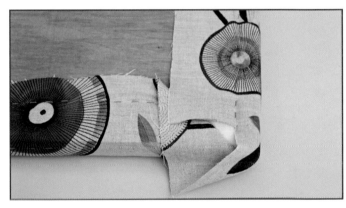

3 Fold the fabric over the corner. To reduce the bulk, cut out a square of fabric, making sure that there is plenty left to cover each edge at the corner.

4 Staple the fabric to the plywood along the short side all the way to the cut corner.

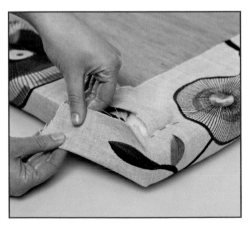

5 Pull the fabric taut across the long side.

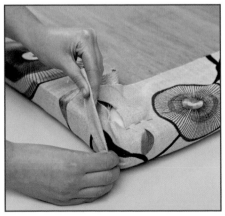

6 Start folding the fabric over the corner, tucking excess fabric under the fold.

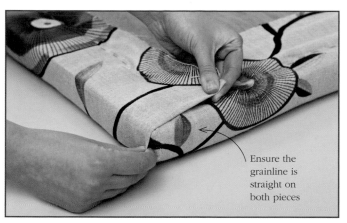

Ensure the grainline is straight on both pieces

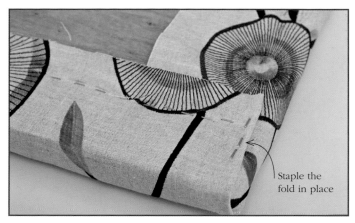

Staple the fold in place

7 Fold the fabric to meet the other edge, tucking in as much fabric as necessary to keep the grainline straight and to create a neat fold.

8 Staple the corner in place. Repeat for the other three corners.

9 Trim off any excess fabric.

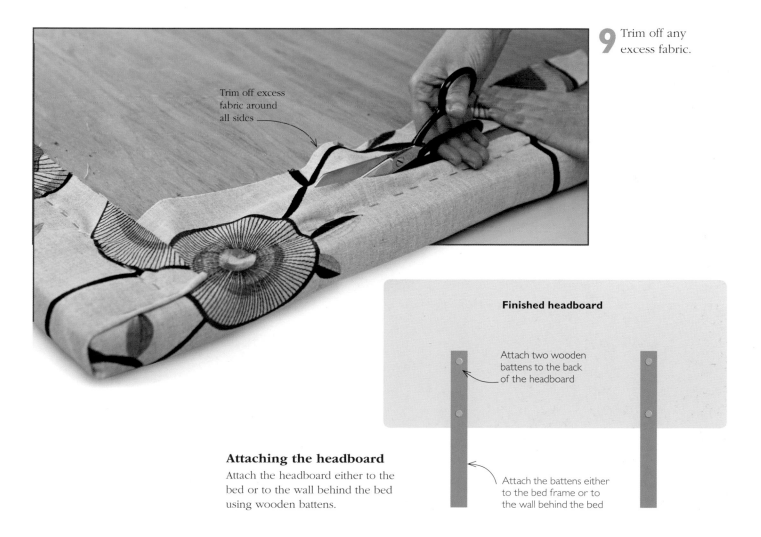

Trim off excess fabric around all sides

Finished headboard

Attach two wooden battens to the back of the headboard

Attach the battens either to the bed frame or to the wall behind the bed

Attaching the headboard
Attach the headboard either to the bed or to the wall behind the bed using wooden battens.

Headboard SLIPCOVER

A neat-fitting slipcover over a padded headboard is a quick way to update your bedroom. Our stunning cut velvet adds instant drama, but the sky's the limit when it comes to choosing your fabric.

YOU **WILL NEED**

Materials

- *Medium- or upholstery-weight furnishing fabric*
- *Matching thread*
- *Velcro fastening tape (the width of your headboard)*

Tools

- *Padded headboard* • *Tailor's chalk*
- *Pins* • *Scissors* • *Staple gun*
- *Ruler* • *Sewing machine*

Planning your headboard

You will need enough fabric to cover the headboard front plus depth plus seam allowance on all sides and an extra 7cm (2¾in) along the hem. For a wider headboard, you may need to railroad the fabric (see p.141). Make the back from the same fabric or choose a coordinating plain.

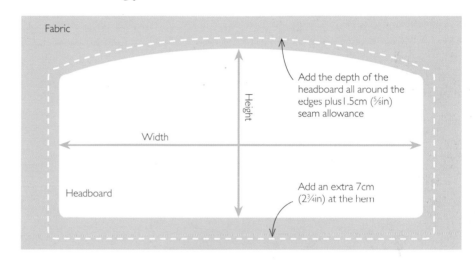

Fabric

Height

Width

Headboard

Add the depth of the headboard all around the edges plus 1.5cm (⅝in) seam allowance

Add an extra 7cm (2¾in) at the hem

Cutting out and preparing the back and front

1 Lay the fabric for the back of the slipcover, face down. Centre the headboard on top and tug gently on the fabric all around the edges to ensure that it is not wrinkled underneath. Use tailor's chalk or a fabric marker to draw around the edges of the headboard.

2 Draw a short diagonal line out from each of the upper corners of the headboard to mark a notch.

3 Lay the fabric for the front of the slipcover face down on the headboard. Starting at the centre, smooth the fabric out evenly towards the edges, tucking it around the sides.

4 Continue smoothing and tucking the fabric over the headboard until it fits perfectly. The excess fabric will gather at the corners and along the curves.

5 At each of the upper curved corners, pinch the excess fabric together to make a single fold.

6 Pin along each fold to hold it firmly in place against the curved corner. These folds will be stitched later to make darts.

7 Use tailor's chalk to mark the fabric all around the perimeter of the headboard and along the pinned folds. These will be your stitching lines.

8 Chalk along the bottom edge of the headboard. Measure 7cm (2¾in) from this line and mark another line at this point.

9 Remove the headboard and the back of the slipcover. Lay the front of the slipcover face down. Measure and mark a seam allowance 1.5cm (⅝in) from the stitching line marked in Step 7. Cut out the front of the slipcover along the seam allowance line.

10 At each of the bottom two corners of the front of the slipcover, measure and mark 6.5cm (2⅝in) up from the bottom edge and 6.5cm (2⅝in) in from the side. This is where the Velcro tape will be attached to hold the slipcover in place.

Make a mark
at this point

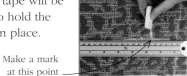

Top curve

Folded edge

11 Fold the front of the slipcover in half widthways and measure the length of the folded edge. Make a note of this measurement, which is the height of the headboard. Put the front of the slipcover to one side.

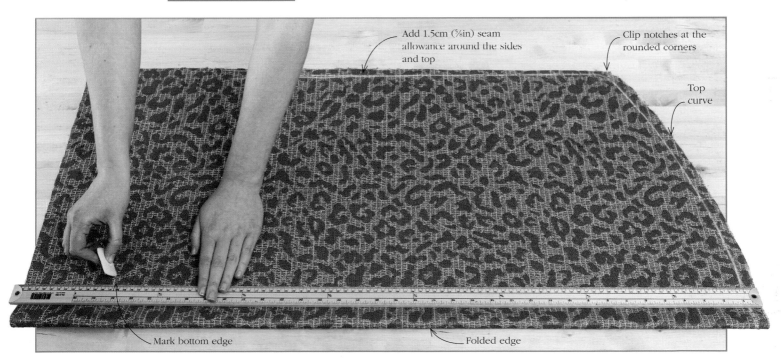

Add 1.5cm (⅝in) seam allowance around the sides and top

Clip notches at the rounded corners

Top curve

Mark bottom edge

Folded edge

12 Lay the the back of the slipcover face down. Measure and mark a seam allowance 1.5cm (⅝in) out from the line marked in Step 1, all the way around the sides and top. Cut out the back of the slipcover, extending the cutting lines all the way to the bottom edge. Clip notches into the seam allowance at the two lines drawn in Step 2. Fold the back of the slipcover in half widthways. Measuring along this fold from the top of the curve, mark the height of the front piece that you recorded in Step 11. Cut the bottom edge of the slipcover along this line.

Ease stitching and making the darts

1 Using the largest stitch possible, ease stitch (see p.19) within the seam allowance across the curve on the top edge of the front of the slipcover, from dart to dart. Fold the front in half widthways to find the centre of the curve and mark it with a pin.

2 With right sides facing, align the chalked lines, then pinch each dart together. Mark the point of the dart with a pin. Stitch along the chalked lines from the edge to the point.

Joining the back and front

1 Fold the back of the slipcover in half widthways and mark the centre of the curve with a pin. Place the front on top of the back, right sides together, with the front on top. Match the darts on the front with the notches on the back.

2 Match the centre points of the front and back and pin them together.

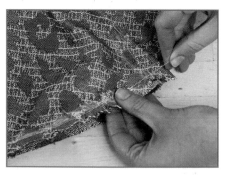

3 Use the ease stitches on the front to gather the fabric along the curve, between the darts, until the fabric fits the curve of the back of the slipcover.

4 Pin the front and back together, pinning the curve in place first and then pinning along each side.

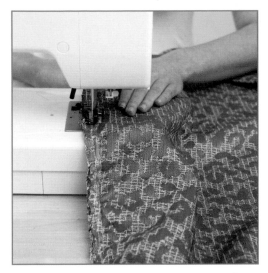

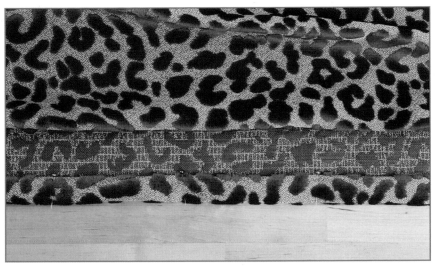

5 Stitch from a bottom corner, up one side, along the top, and down the other side to the other bottom corner. Backstitch at the start and finish of the seam to secure your stitching.

6 Turn to the right side, then turn back 2.5cm (1in) towards the wrong side all the way around the bottom edge. Then turn back another 2.5cm (1in) to make a double hem. Pin and stitch in place.

Attaching the Velcro strips

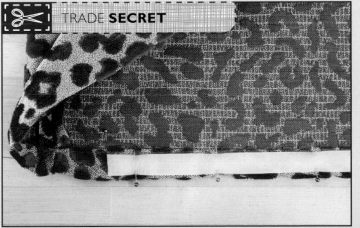

TRADE **SECRET**

1 Pin the looped strip of Velcro tape to the front of the slipcover in the middle of the turned hem, starting and finishing at the Velcro marker points. Stitch in place along both long edges of the tape.

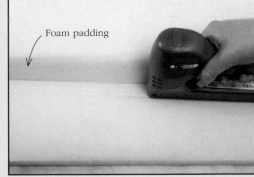

Foam padding

2 Staple the hooked strip of Velcro tape to the headboard, just below the padding. Slip the cover on and join the Velcro strips.

BLINDS

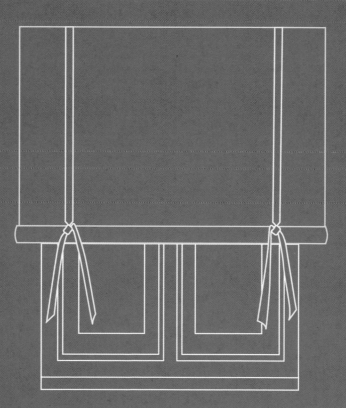

Making BLINDS

Blinds are a simple alternative to curtains for dressing a window. They use far less fabric and give a totally different effect. There are many options when choosing blinds, from the system they use for raising and lowering the blind, to the overall look they create.

Measuring

How you measure your window for a blind is determined by whether the blind is to be fixed inside or outside the window recess. A blind inside the recess is usually fixed to the top of the window frame, or to the top of the recess. When measuring for a blind fixed outside the recess, first decide where the blind will be hung from. This will be the starting point for the drop measurement. The width is determined by adding 10cm (4in) to the total window width.

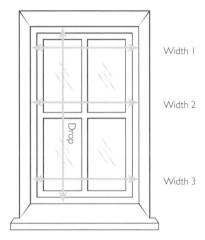

Inside the window recess

Measure the width of the recess at three points. Subtract 1cm (⅜in) from the smallest measurement to get the finished width. This ensures that the blind has room to move up and down. For the drop, measure from the inside fixing point to the windowsill.

Outside the window recess

For the width, measure the width of the recess and add 10cm (4in) to give a 5cm (2in) overlap on each side. This prevents light coming in at the sides of the lowered blind. For the drop, measure from the fixing point to just below the windowsill.

Raising and lowering blinds

What sets different styles of blind apart from each other is how they are raised and lowered. Some blinds require you to purchase a special kit to do the job, while other raising and lowering systems can be made using simple materials.

Roller blind

This is made from a kit consisting of a pole, batten, and end brackets. The brackets have a mechanism that is operated when you raise or lower the blind.

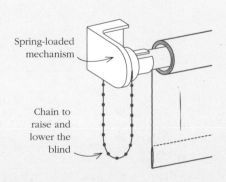

Spring-loaded mechanism

Chain to raise and lower the blind

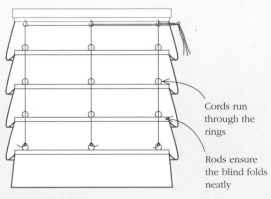

Cords run through the rings

Rods ensure the blind folds neatly

Roman blind

This operates using a pulley system of cords, rods, and rings attached to the back of the blind. The fabric stacks neatly as the blind is opened. Follow the project instructions on pages 168–177 to create the pulley system for your Roman blind.

Types of blinds

Some blinds lie flat when lowered, and some gather up into soft folds or crisp pleats.
Choose a blind according to the look you want and the way you plan to use the blind.

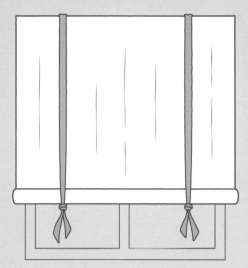

Tie blind

This is the simplest type of blind to make at home. It consists of a panel of fabric that is rolled up and unrolled by tightening and loosening a pair of ties. This blind is best in a situation where it can be left at the same drop length most of the time.

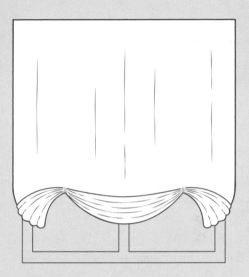

London blind

The more casual London blind is made like a Roman blind but with no lath at the bottom and without any rods. The result is a blind that gathers into soft folds when it is raised.

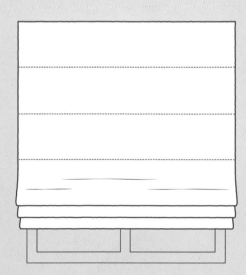

Roman blind

With its lath at the bottom and rods along its length, a Roman blind stacks into neat pleats as it is raised via its pulley system. It sits well both outside a window recess or inside, giving a crisp, tailored look to a room.

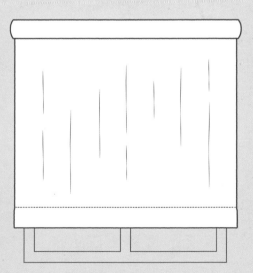

Roller blind

Roller blinds are made using a kit that automatically rolls a stiffened length of fabric around a pole. They have a simple look that is perfect for a bathroom or kitchen.

Tie **BLIND**

With its contrast lining and grosgrain ribbon ties, this roll-up blind looks fresh and pretty, and is really easy to make. Our professional technique for attaching the Velcro fastening tape at the top of the blind ensures that no stitches will be visible on the right side.

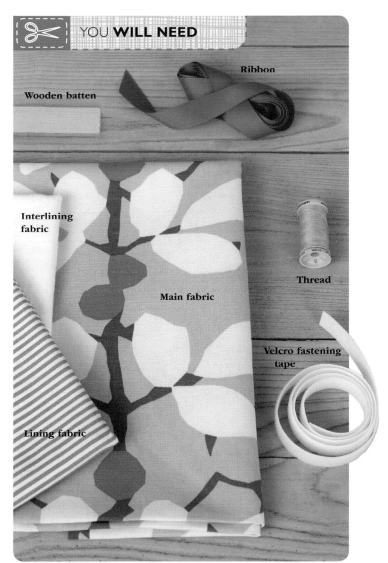

✂ YOU **WILL NEED**

Ribbon

Wooden batten

Interlining fabric

Thread

Main fabric

Velcro fastening tape

Lining fabric

Tools:

• Scissors • Set square (optional) • Pins • Iron and ironing board • Metre rule • Pencil • Staple gun

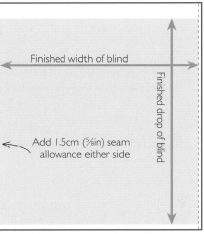

Finished width of blind

Finished drop of blind

Add 1.5cm (⅝in) seam allowance either side

Add a total of 6.5cm (2⅝in) to the overall length

Cutting measurements

Measure your window (see p.154). Add 1.5cm (⅝in) seam allowance to either side of your blind measurement. Add 6.5cm (2⅝in) to the overall drop for a 5cm (2in) turnover at the top and a 1.5cm (⅝in) seam allowance.

Cutting your fabric

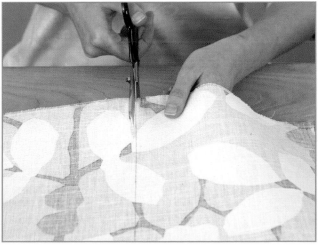

Cut the main fabric, lining, and interlining to the required size. Check that any pattern in the fabric is centred on each piece and ensure that all the pieces are exactly the same size and are cut at right angles. Use a set square if necessary.

Assembling the blind

Lining fabric on top

Main fabric
in the middle

Interlining
at bottom

1 To assemble your blind, lay the interlining on the table. Lay the main fabric right side up on top of it, followed by the lining, right side down. Make sure all three fabrics are perfectly aligned, then pin together along both vertical sides.

2 Leaving a 1.5cm (⅝in) seam allowance, stitch both vertical sides together from top to bottom, backstitching at the start and finish of each seam to secure your stitching.

Only trim
the seam allowance
of the interlining

3 Lay the tube-shaped blind flat on the ironing board and press the seams open. Make sure when you lay out the blind that all three layers of fabric are flat and you do not iron any creases into the blind. Lay the blind flat on your work surface and trim the seam allowance of the interlining fabric to 5mm (¼in).

Cut the bottom
corners, cutting
through just
the seam
allowance

4 With the blind flat and the side seams lying flat, pin together the bottom edge. Stitch the edge, leaving a 1.5cm (⅝in) seam allowance. Trim off the corners to reduce bulk but make sure you do not cut through your stitches. Turn the blind to the right side.

Roll the lining
fabric 1–2mm
(¹⁄₁₆in) away
from the blind
edge and press
it in place

5 Place the blind right side down and press along the stitched edges, rolling the lining 1–2mm (¹⁄₁₆in) away from the main fabric as you go. Turn the blind right side up and smooth out the layers, running your hand from the bottom of the blind to the top.

Making the heading

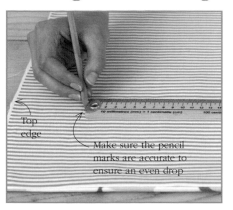

1 Place the blind right side down once again. Measure the desired length/drop at various points from the bottom edge, marking the fabric at intervals along its width with a pencil or tailor's chalk.

Top edge

Make sure the pencil marks are accurate to ensure an even drop

2 Fold over the top of the blind, lining to lining, along the marks. Press to form a crease. This fold will be for attaching the Velcro tape.

Attaching the ties and finishing

✂ TRADE **SECRET**

Fold

Raw edge

1 To determine the length of the ribbon ties, multiply the length of the blind by two and cut two pieces of ribbon to this measurement. Fold each tie in half and place a pin on the fold. Position each tie with its pin on the fold at the top of the blind and with half the ribbon on the lining side and half on the main fabric side.

2 The ties should be an equal distance from each edge of the blind. Be guided by the way it looks. Pin the ties in place.

3 With the front of the blind face up, open out the top fold and the ties. Remove the pins and lay a looped strip of Velcro tape with one edge along the fold and the other towards the raw edge. Pin in place, also pinning through the ribbon. Stitch along each of the Velcro tape's two long edges, starting each seam from the same edge of the blind. Catch the ties in the seam as you go and backstitch at the start and finish.

4 Re-fold the top fold along the Velcro tape, then fold the raw edge under 1.5cm (⅝in). Pin then slipstitch in place. Take care that your stitches do not show on the front of the blind.

5 Use a staple gun to attach the hooked side of the Velcro strip to a wooden batten the width of the blind. Attach the batten to the wall and hang your blind using the Velcro. Roll up the bottom edge and tie with the ribbons.

London BLIND

This dainty London blind creates an attractive focal point at any window. We have added additional fabric to the length to give the blind extra fullness. Normally left part-way down once its gentle folds have been arranged to best effect, it can also be unrolled for privacy.

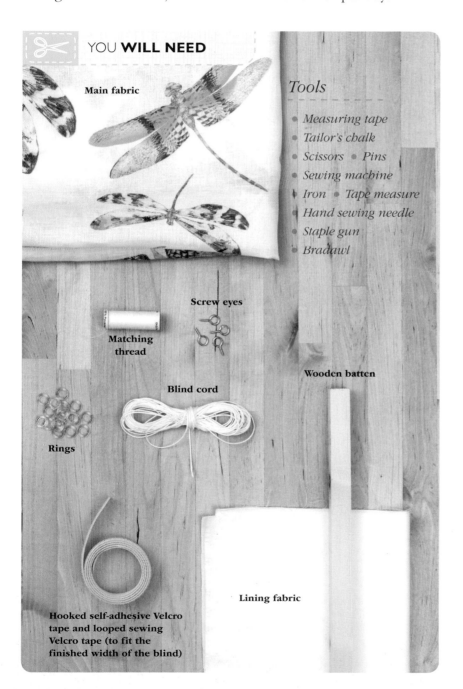

YOU **WILL NEED**

Main fabric

Tools

- *Measuring tape*
- *Tailor's chalk*
- *Scissors* • *Pins*
- *Sewing machine*
- *Iron* • *Tape measure*
- *Hand sewing needle*
- *Staple gun*
- *Bradawl*

Screw eyes

Matching thread

Wooden batten

Blind cord

Rings

Lining fabric

Hooked self-adhesive Velcro tape and looped sewing Velcro tape (to fit the finished width of the blind)

Cutting measurements

Decide whether the blind will sit inside or outside the window and measure accordingly (see p.154). Then calculate the cutting measurements for fabric and lining as below:

Main fabric
Width: Finished width of blind + 6cm (2⅜in)
Length: Finished drop (length) of blind + 14cm (5⅝in) for hem + 5cm (2in) for top + 40cm (16in) for decorative folds.

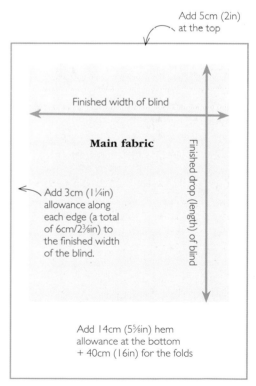

Add 5cm (2in) at the top

Finished width of blind

Main fabric

Finished drop (length) of blind

Add 3cm (1¼in) allowance along each edge (a total of 6cm/2⅜in) to the finished width of the blind.

Add 14cm (5⅝in) hem allowance at the bottom + 40cm (16in) for the folds

Lining
Width: Finished width of blind
Length: As for main fabric

Joining main fabric and lining

1 Square off the fabric (see p.16). Measure your window and cut the main fabric and lining to the dimensions on p.161. The lining will be 6cm (2⅜in) narrower than the main fabric.

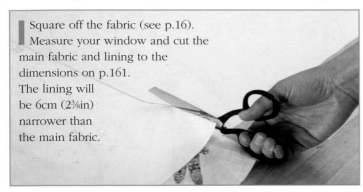

2 Fold both the main fabric and the lining in half lengthways and mark the centre points with a pin or clip with scissors.

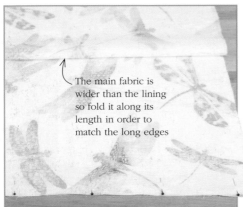

The main fabric is wider than the lining so fold it along its length in order to match the long edges

3 Place the lining and the main fabric, right sides together, matching along one long edge. Pin in place. Bring the other long edges together and pin.

4 Machine stitch with a 1.5cm (⅝in) seam allowance from top to bottom along each edge.

✂ TRADE **SECRET**

5 You now have a fabric tube. With the tube wrong side out, manoeuvre it so that the seams are not at the edges. Press each seam towards the lining along each long edge.

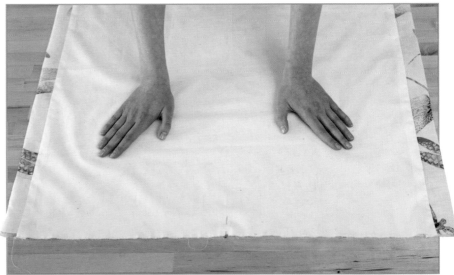

6 Turn the fabric tube right side out and, with the lining facing up, match the centre points of the main fabric and the lining top and bottom. Since the lining is narrower than the main fabric, the main fabric will roll inwards, forming a return along each edge. Smooth out any wrinkles in the lining.

Making the hem

1 Align the raw edges of the lining and the main fabric at the bottom and pin. Tack together 1cm (⅜in) from the raw edges.

2 With the lining face up, fold over the lining and the main fabric to make a 1.5cm (⅝in) hem along the bottom. Press.

3 Turn the folded fabric a second time to make a hem 12cm (4¾in) deep.

4 Pin, then slipstitch (see p.20) in place along the fold, taking care not to stitch right through to the main fabric.

Making the top

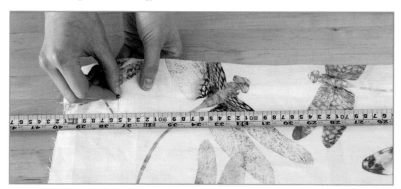

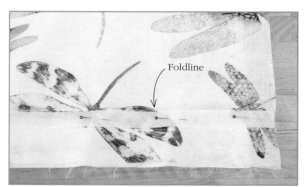

Foldline

1 With the blind face down, measure the desired drop at various points from the bottom edge upwards, marking the fabric at intervals along its width, across the top, with a row of pins. Fold the fabric along the pins towards the wrong side and press.

2 Remove the pins, open out the fabric, and with the blind lining side down, lay a strip of looped sewing Velcro tape with one edge along the foldline and the other towards the raw edge. Pin in place.

3 Stitch along each of the two long edges of the Velcro tape, sewing in the same direction each time.

4 With the blind face down, fold over the fabric right along the edge of the Velcro tape, as shown. Fold the raw edge under and pin.

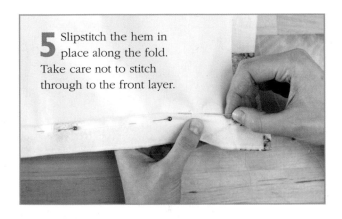

5 Slipstitch the hem in place along the fold. Take care not to stitch through to the front layer.

Attaching the rings

Placement of the rings
The rings are stitched on in two sets of two parallel lines.

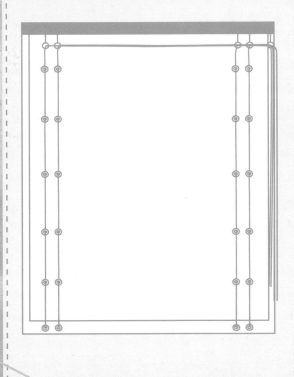

To position the first ring, with the blind face down, measure 6cm (2⅜in) from the bottom edge of the blind and 8cm (3¼in) from the side. Mark this point with crossed pins.

2 Measure from this point to the top of the blind. Divide this measurement by the number of folds you require. For a blind around 130cm (52in), you will need 6, 7, or 8 folds, depending on which number divides most accurately into your previous measurement.

Once you have found the number, measure the positions of that number of rings accordingly and mark with a line of crossed pins from bottom to top.

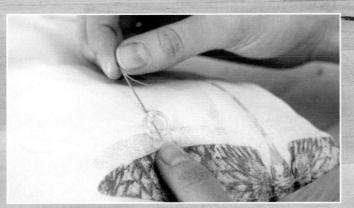

3 To attach the first ring, knot the thread in your needle and sew through the fabric at the crossed pins. Holding the ring in place, take a few stitches through it.

4 To finish, wrap the thread around the ring and take the needle through the loop to tighten the thread.

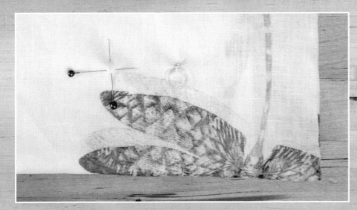

5 Repeat to sew one ring at each pair of crossed pins in the same way, ensuring that they are all parallel to the side of the blind. Pin a second line of crossed pins 4cm (1⅝in) in from the first. Sew a second line of rings at the pins in the same way.

6 Constantly checking that the lines all align vertically and horizontally, measure, mark, and sew on two lines of rings at the other side of the blind in exactly the same way.

Preparing the batten

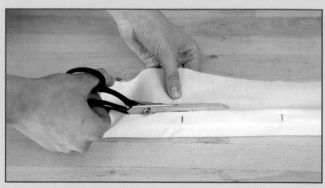

2 Wrap the calico neatly around the batten and staple in place. Trim off any excess calico.

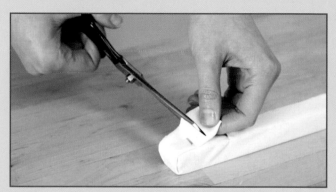

1 Cut a piece of calico longer than the batten and wide enough to wrap around it with some overlap. Staple the calico to the batten along one long edge.

3 Fold the ends together neatly over the batten. Staple in place then trim off any excess calico.

4 Peel the backing off a length of hooked self-adhesive Velcro tape, stick it to one wide face of the batten, then staple at intervals to secure.

5 Turn the batten so that a face that is adjacent to the Velcro tape is facing you. Use a bradawl to make a hole 8cm (3¼in) from the end of the batten and a second hole 12cm (4¾in) from the end.

Feed screw eye

6 Insert screw eyes into the holes. Repeat at the same distances from the other end of the batten.

7 Decide at which side of the blind you would like the pull cord to be. Add one more screw eye – the feed screw eye – about 1cm (⅜in) from the end, on that side.

8 Cut four lengths of cord, each the length of the blind, plus the length of the batten, plus another two-thirds the length of the blind. Tie the end of each cord to the bottom ring in each row, then thread it through the other rings in the row and through the screw eye at the top. Pass each cord through all the screw eyes to its right or left towards the feed screw eye. Check that the blind gathers correctly, then unthread the cords and remove the blind from the batten.

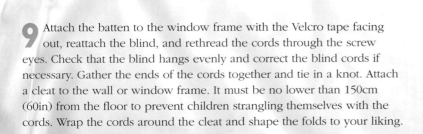

9 Attach the batten to the window frame with the Velcro tape facing out, reattach the blind, and rethread the cords through the screw eyes. Check that the blind hangs evenly and correct the blind cords if necessary. Gather the ends of the cords together and tie in a knot. Attach a cleat to the wall or window frame. It must be no lower than 150cm (60in) from the floor to prevent children strangling themselves with the cords. Wrap the cords around the cleat and shape the folds to your liking.

Roman BLIND

With its pleats supported by rods concealed in pockets at the back, a Roman blind is a neat, tailored solution for a window treatment. This project is fairly complex but the complexity lies in calculating the measurements for the pleats, so you need to hone your maths skills. The sewing is a breeze.

YOU **WILL NEED**

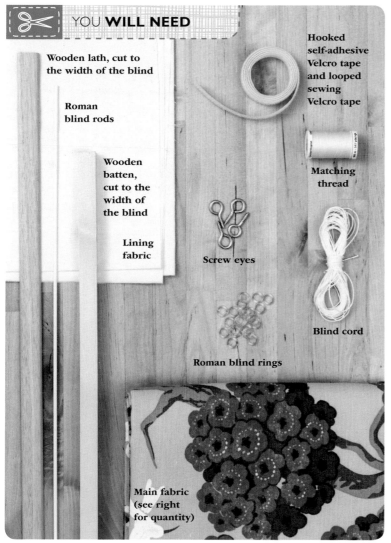

Wooden lath, cut to the width of the blind

Roman blind rods

Wooden batten, cut to the width of the blind

Lining fabric

Screw eyes

Roman blind rings

Main fabric (see right for quantity)

Hooked self-adhesive Velcro tape and looped sewing Velcro tape

Matching thread

Blind cord

Tools

- Set square (optional) • Measuring tape
- Tailor's chalk • Scissors • Pins • Iron
- Sewing machine • Metre rule
- Staple gun • Bradawl

Cutting measurements

Decide whether the blind will sit inside or outside the window and measure accordingly (see p.154). Then calculate the cutting measurements for fabric and lining as below:

Main fabric
Width: Finished width of blind + 6cm (2⅜in)
Length: Finished length (drop) of blind + 10cm (4in)

Main fabric

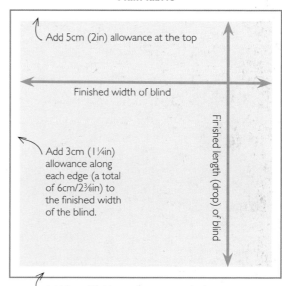

Add 5cm (2in) allowance at the top

Finished width of blind

Add 3cm (1¼in) allowance along each edge (a total of 6cm/2⅜in) to the finished width of the blind.

Finished length (drop) of blind

Add 5cm (2in) hem allowance at the bottom

Lining
Width: Finished width of blind
Length: Finished length (drop) of blind + 10cm (4in)

Cutting the fabric

1 Lay the main fabric on the work surface right side up. Square off the bottom (see p.16) and cut off the excess. Measure, mark, and cut the fabric following the instructions on the previous page.

Joining fabric and lining

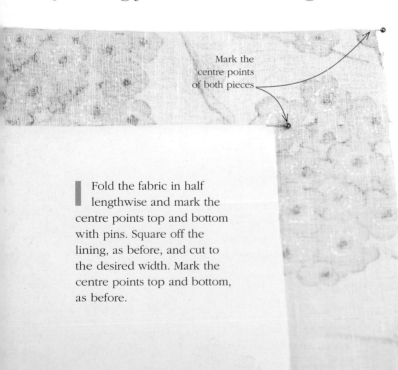

Mark the centre points of both pieces

1 Fold the fabric in half lengthwise and mark the centre points top and bottom with pins. Square off the lining, as before, and cut to the desired width. Mark the centre points top and bottom, as before.

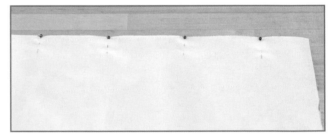

2 Lay the fabric and lining right side to right side. Match the bottom edge and one side edge. Pin together along the side edge, making sure the raw edges remain aligned.

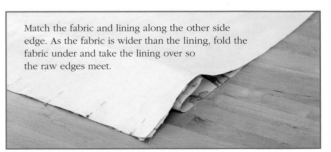

Match the fabric and lining along the other side edge. As the fabric is wider than the lining, fold the fabric under and take the lining over so the raw edges meet.

3 Pin together, then machine along both side edge from top to bottom with a 1.5cm (⅝in) seam allowance. The blind and lining now form a tube.

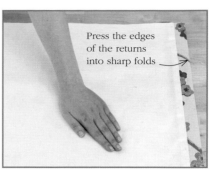

Press the edges of the returns into sharp folds

4 Lay the tube on the ironing board. Manoeuvre the seams so that they are not at the edges of the tube, then press both seam allowances towards the main fabric along both seams. This will encourage the seam allowances to lie flat when the blind is turned to the right side.

5 Turn the blind right side out and with the main fabric face down, match the centre points of the main fabric and the lining, top and bottom.

6 Smooth out the blind from the centre to the edges. Equal 1.5cm (⅝in) returns of the main fabric should now be visible along either edge and the seam allowances should lie flat under the returns.

Preparing for the lath

1 With the blind face down, fold over 1.5cm (⅝in) along the bottom edge.

3 Pin the corners of the hem in place first, ensuring they do not overhang the edge of the blind. Then pin along the hem, taking in any excess.

2 Fold over another 3.5cm (1⅜in) to make a hem. Press.

4 Using stitch length 3, bobbin thread to match the main fabric, and with the needle to the left to allow you to stitch as close to the edge as possible, machine along the folded edge. Press to set the stitches. This is the channel for the lath at the bottom of the blind.

Attaching the Velcro tape

1 With the blind face down, measure the finished length up from the bottom edge at several points across the width. Mark with a row of pins.

2 Turn the fabric over along the pinned line. Press, then draw a line 2cm (¾in) from the folded edge. Cut along the line.

3 Unfold the fabric and separate the main fabric and the lining. Re-fold the main fabric along the foldline.

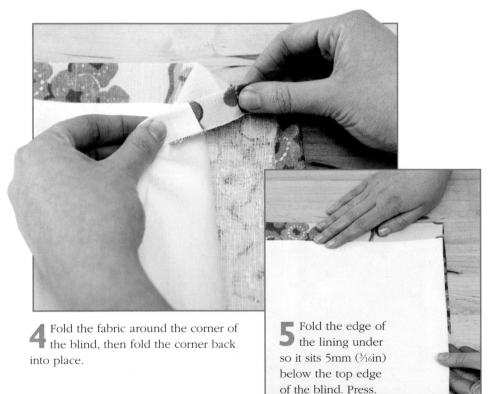

4 Fold the fabric around the corner of the blind, then fold the corner back into place.

5 Fold the edge of the lining under so it sits 5mm (³⁄₁₆in) below the top edge of the blind. Press.

TRADE SECRET

Stitch the Velcro tape in the same direction along both edges to prevent the fabric twisting

6 Cut a length of looped Velcro tape to the width of the blind. Position the Velcro tape along the top edge of the blind, approximately 3mm (⅛in) down from the edge. Pin then machine stitch the Velcro tape in place along both long edges.

Marking the pleats

1 Calculate the measurements for the pleats (see right). With the blind face down and starting from the hem, measure the depth of the half pleat along one return and mark it with a pin. Mark in the same way along the other return.

2 Check your measurements to ensure they are correct and equal on both sides. Then, using the meter rule, draw a very faint chalk line across the blind from pin to pin.

3 Measure the depth of the first full pleat from the first line and lightly mark. Again, check your measurements and mark with pins as before.

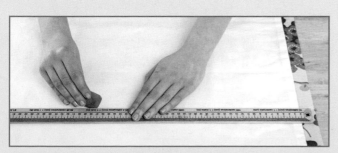

4 Lightly draw a line to join the second pair of pins. Repeat steps 3–4 to mark the positions of all the pleats.

Calculating the pleats

- A Roman blind has a half pleat at the bottom and a number of full pleats. The half pleat is made a little longer so that when the blind is up the half pleat extends further than the folded pleats.
- For blinds up to 150cm long, the optimal depth of each full pleat is 20–30cm (8–12in). For longer blinds, the optimal depth is 30–40cm (12–16in).
- Start by measuring the length of the blind from top to bottom. Deduct 5cm (2in), which is the depth of the batten, then deduct another 1cm (⅜in), which is the extra length you need for the half pleat.

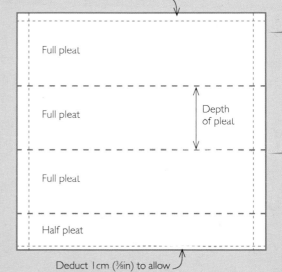

Deduct 5cm (2in) for the batten

Full pleat

Full pleat — Depth of pleat

Full pleat

Half pleat

Deduct 1cm (⅜in) to allow extra length to half pleat

- After making the deductions, divide the remaining amount by 3.5, 4.5, 5.5, or 6.5, depending on which of these calculations results in the optimum pleat size.
- Round the resulting number up or down to the nearest half centimetre (quarter inch).
- If rounding down, multiply this difference (however small) by the number of full folds there are in the blind.
- To calculate the depth of the half pleat, divide the measurement of a full pleat in two. Add the 1cm (⅜in) deducted at the beginning and add any excess you calculated in the step above.

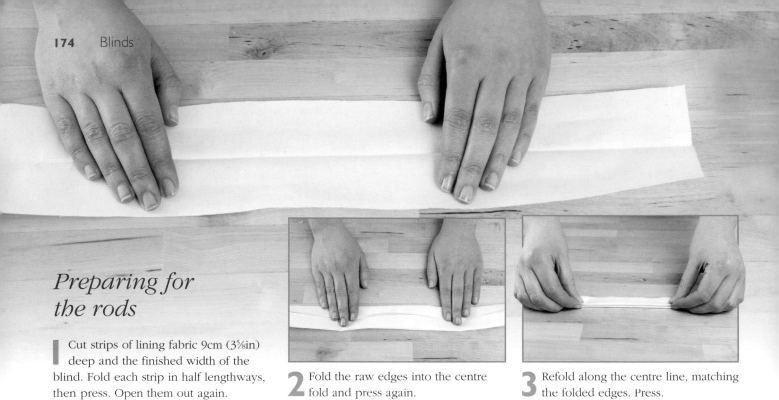

Preparing for the rods

1 Cut strips of lining fabric 9cm (3⅝in) deep and the finished width of the blind. Fold each strip in half lengthways, then press. Open them out again.

2 Fold the raw edges into the centre fold and press again.

3 Refold along the centre line, matching the folded edges. Press.

4 At one end of each strip, fold the strip right sides together. Machine stitch the end closed with a 1.5cm (⅝in) seam allowance.

5 Turn each end to the right side, tucking the raw edges inside.

6 With the blind face down and starting from the bottom edge, position a pocket along the first drawn line. Align the open edge of the pocket with the drawn line and the closed end with the left return.

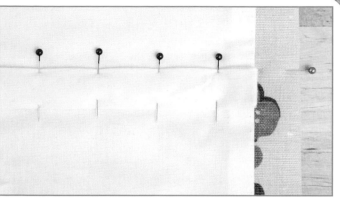

7 Pin the pocket to the blind at regular intervals. Take care to keep the tension even.

8 To neaten the open end of the pocket, first open out the pocket fold. Then turn the raw edge back towards the pocket so that the folded edge is level with the lining.

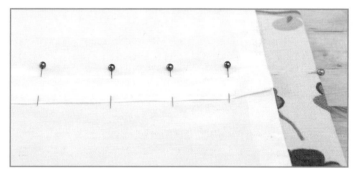

9 Fold the end of the pocket back into place and secure with a pin.

10 Pin on the remaining pockets in the same way.

11 Using bobbin thread that matches the main fabric and upper thread that matches the lining, machine the first pocket in place as close to the pinned folded edge as possible. Adjust the position of the needle if necessary to allow you to stitch closer to the edge.

12 Machine stitch the remaining pockets in place, folding the blind under the arm of the machine as you go. You now have a pocket for each rod.

Assembling the blind

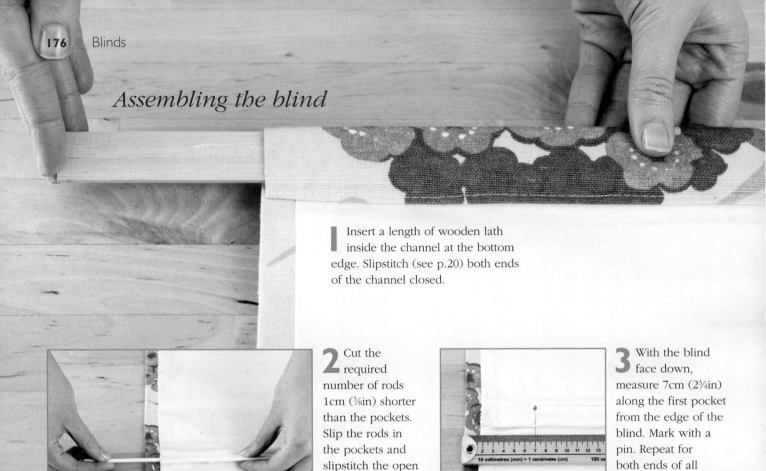

1 Insert a length of wooden lath inside the channel at the bottom edge. Slipstitch (see p.20) both ends of the channel closed.

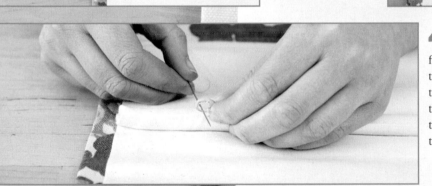

2 Cut the required number of rods 1cm (⅜in) shorter than the pockets. Slip the rods in the pockets and slipstitch the open end of each pocket closed.

3 With the blind face down, measure 7cm (2¾in) along the first pocket from the edge of the blind. Mark with a pin. Repeat for both ends of all the pockets.

4 Knot the thread in your needle and sew through the fabric from back to front at the first pin. Holding the ring in place, take a stitch through the front of the ring and back through the fabric. Repeat a few times. To finish, wrap the thread around the ring and take the needle through the loop in the thread to secure. Repeat to attach a ring at the other pins.

5 Mark the position of the rest of the rings along the first pocket between the rings at either end, first spacing them out by eye. Measure to ensure they are evenly spaced and no more than 40cm (16in) apart. Mark the position of each with a pin, then stitch on the rings at the pins as above. Sew rings to the other pockets, aligning them vertically.

Preparing the batten

1 Cover the batten with calico and attach a length of hooked Velcro tape (see p.166, steps 1–4). Turn the batten so that a face that is adjacent to the Velcro tape is facing you. Use a bradawl to make a hole 7cm (2¾in) from each end. Insert a screw eye.

2 Measure the horizontal distance between the rings on the blind and using these measurements, insert the remaining screw eyes in the batten.

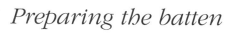

Feed screw eye

3 Decide at which side of the blind you would like the pull cord to be. With the Velcro tape facing away from you, add one more screw eye – the feed screw eye – between the end of the batten and the first screw eye on that side.

5 Thread the cord through the other rings in the row and through the screw eye at the top. Pass each cord through all the screw eyes to its right or left towards the feed screw eye. Check that the blind folds up correctly, then unthread the cords and remove the blind from the batten.

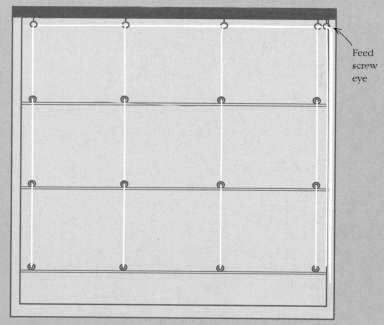

Feed screw eye

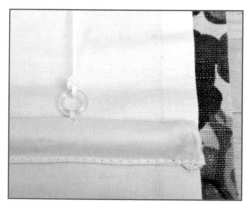

4 Calculate how much blind cord is needed by adding the length of the blind to the width plus 1m (40in). Cut one length for each line of rings. Attach a length of cord to each bottom ring, knotting it tightly.

6 Attach the batten to the window frame with the Velcro facing out, rethread the cords, and attach the blind with the Velcro tape. Tie the ends of the cords together in a knot. Attach the cleat to the wall or frame, no lower than 150cm (60in) from the floor to prevent children strangling themselves with the cords. Wrap the cords around the cleat.

Roller **BLIND**

A roller blind brings privacy to a room and is a smart, contemporary window treatment that is easy to make, thanks to commercial roller blind kits. Cutting to size, sewing the sides and a hem, stiffening the fabric, and attaching the pole are almost all you need to do for professional results every time.

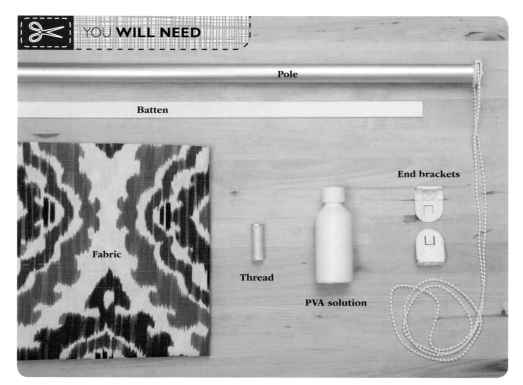

YOU **WILL NEED**

Pole

Batten

Fabric

Thread

PVA solution

End brackets

Tools

- *Roller blind kit, consisting of pole, batten, and ends brackets* • *Pins* • *Ruler* • *Tailor's chalk* • *Scissors* • *Sewing machine* • *Washing line or shower rail (optional)* • *Spray bottle (optional)* • *Bucket (optional)* • *Hacksaw* • *PVA solution*

Before you start

How you measure for a blind will be determined by whether it is to go inside or outside the window recess. Measure the finished width and drop (see pp.154–155). Following the manufacturer's instructions, cut the pole to the required length. Use the diagram, right, to determine the cutting width and length of your blind.

End bracket

Pole

Width of pole

Drop = finished length of blind

Add diameter of pole plus 5cm (2in) at the top

Cutting width: Width of pole (excluding end brackets) + 2cm (¾in) seam allowance

Cutting length: Drop of blind + diameter of pole + 5cm (2in) at the top + 6cm (2⅜in) at the bottom for the hem

Add 1cm (⅜in) seam allowance either side

Add 6cm (2⅜in) hem allowance at the bottom

Measuring and cutting out

1 Decide which part of the pattern you want at the centre of your blind. Place a pin at the centre, then add further pins in a straight line above and below this point.

2 Divide your cutting width measurement (see diagram) by two. Measure and mark this amount with tailor's chalk either side of the row of pins, the length of the fabric.

3 Decide where you would like the top of the blind to be and draw a line here. Measure the cutting length from this line and mark another line. Cut along the marked lines to cut out the blind.

Stitching the sides and hem

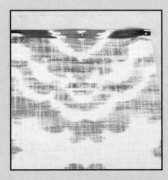

1 With the right side face down, fold over 1cm (⅜in) along each long edge of the blind. Press in place and pin. As the fabric will be treated with stiffener, it will not fray so it does not need to be folded twice.

2 Using invisible thread in the bobbin and a number 3 stitch, machine along the folded fabric as close to the raw edge as you can. Sew both edges of the blind from the same direction.

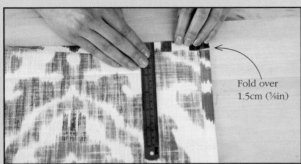

Fold over 1.5cm (⅝in)

3 With the right side still face down, fold over 6cm (2⅜in) along the bottom edge and press. Unfold the fabric then fold over 1.5cm (⅝in).

4 Refold the fabric along the 6cm (2⅜in) crease to create a channel, ensuring the sides of the fabric line up neatly. Secure with pins then machine stitch as close to the first fold as possible. Move the needle to the left if necessary.

Treating with stiffener and assembling

1 Hang the hemmed fabric on a washing line or shower rail, or ask someone to hold it. Spray with PVA solution and leave to dry. Alternatively, dip the fabric in a bucket of PVA solution and hang it up to dry.

2 Cut the batten to the finished width of the blind using a hacksaw. When the fabric is dry, insert the batten in the hem.

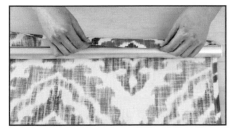

3 Following the manufacturer's instructions, remove the protective layer from the sticky tape on the roller blind pole. Wrap the top, raw edge, of the blind around the pole.

4 Attach the end bracket to stabilize the pole while you stick the raw edge to it.

5 Wrap the blind firmly around the pole. Remove the end bracket. Attach both brackets to the wall and mount the blind.

CURTAINS

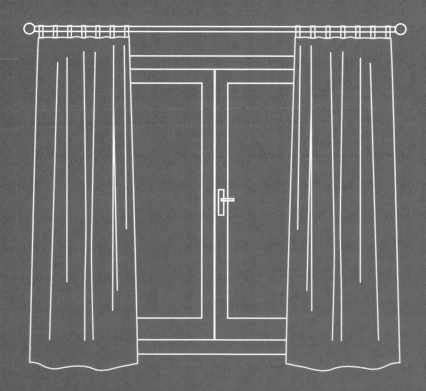

Mix and match CURTAINS

The place where you want to hang your curtains will dictate the qualities you want for them. By mixing and matching linings and heading styles, you can tailor your design to your room and your skill level.

Lining types

The lining you choose for a curtain will affect its weight, opacity, and insulating qualities, as well as how easy it is to make. Decide where your curtain will hang and what its primary use will be. For a bedroom you will probably want a lined curtain, to block light, but in a kitchen, an easy-to-wash, unlined curtain might be best.

Unlined

Made from a single layer of fabric that is hemmed around the edges, unlined curtains are easy to make and will give a room an informal look. Though less lightproof, they are cheaper and easier to keep clean than lined curtains.

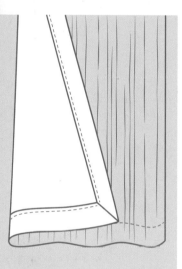

Tube lined

Making tube-lined curtains is simple and can easily be done on a sewing machine. The fabric and lining are joined together right side to right side along the long edges to form a tube. This technique is best used on smaller curtains.

Interlined

With an extra layer of material between the lining and the main fabric, interlined curtains are the thickest, heaviest option. This style involves hand sewing the lining to the main fabric along the long edges.

Lining

Interlining

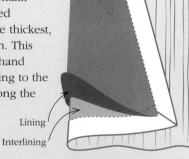

Sheer

Sheer fabrics are normally extra-wide, often 3m (3¼yds), so they are ideal for making curtains to fit wide windows. You work with the selvages at the top and bottom, and cut the fabric to fit the width of the window, thus avoiding unsightly seams.

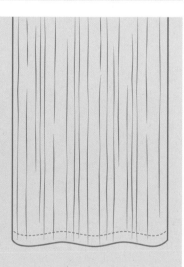

Curtain headings

Your choice of curtain heading not only affects the appearance of the top of the curtains, but also how they hang from their track or pole, and how easy they are to open and close. Some headings are more suitable for stationary curtains – those that are not opened and closed on a regular basis.

Tab top

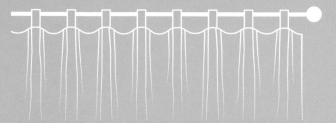

Tab tops are a simple solution to hanging a curtain on a pole. They produce a modern look, though tab-top curtains can be more difficult than others to open and close. To measure the curtain length, measure from the very top of the pole.

Eyelet

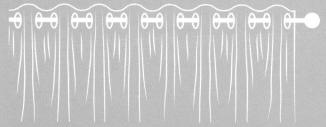

Here the curtain pole is fed through reinforced eyelets to create a modern look. To measure the curtain length, measure from the very top of the pole and add 2–3cm (¾–1¼in).

Pocket

In this style of heading, you sew a channel at the top of the curtain, into which you slide the curtain pole. The result is a gathered curtain. This heading is best for stationary curtains as the fabric can be difficult to move over the pole. To measure the curtain length, measure from the very top of the pole.

Tapes

Pencil pleat

Pencil pleat tape gives a classic, refined look to the top of a curtain. It is the most popular of the curtain tapes and works well with different kinds of fabrics. To measure the curtain length, measure from the eyelet of the curtain ring.

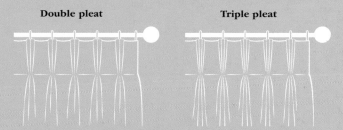

Double pleat   **Triple pleat**

Double and triple pleat

These tapes gather the curtain into evenly spaced groups of two or three pleats. Double pleats give a more relaxed look, while triple pleats add volume and formality. To measure the curtain length, measure from the eyelet of the curtain ring.

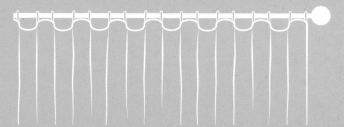

Tempo tape

Tempo tape gives a curtain an evenly undulating shape. It works both with a curtain pole or a track system to create an informal, contemporary aesthetic.

Making **CURTAINS**

In addition to the heading style and lining, there are several things to consider when planing your curtains. The length of your curtains will influence everything from the overall appearance to the way the pattern is placed on the panels.

Curtain length

Curtain lengths can usually be classified into four types: sill-length, apron-length, floor-length, and pooling. Sill-length curtains sit 12mm (½in) above the window sill. Apron-length curtains hit 5–10cm (2–4in) below the window sill. Floor-length curtains just clear the floor by 1.2cm (½in). Finally, pooling curtains bunch on the floor with 5–20cm (2–8in) extra length, depending on your preference.

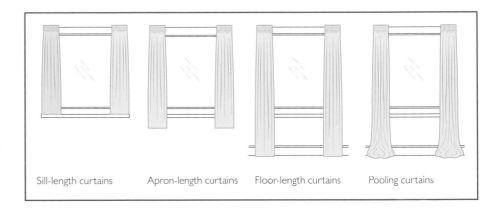

Sill-length curtains   Apron-length curtains   Floor-length curtains   Pooling curtains

Measuring for curtains

Always hang the pole or track before measuring to get an accurate measurement. The pole or track should be positioned about 15cm (6in) above the window and extend 15–20cm (6–8in) either side of the window. Hanging an extra-wide curtain, more than (10in) either side, will make a smaller window look larger.

Use a metal tape measure for the most accurate measurements. Base your width measurements on the width of the pole or track, not of the window itself. Measure the total length of the track or pole, excluding finials, to get the curtain width. Then add an additional 2.5cm (1in) to this to allow for the curtains to overlap in the centre when closed.

A curtain heading should sit slightly above a track so that the track is not visible. However, if using a curtain pole, the curtain should hang just below it so you see the pole.

For the length, decide which style you would prefer, as above. For sill- and apron-length curtains, measure from the pole or track to the window sill, then add or subtract from this measurement depending on the style. For floor-length and pooling curtains, measure from the pole or track to the floor, then add or subtract from this measurement depending on the style. If in doubt, always overestimate as you can always take up the length later.

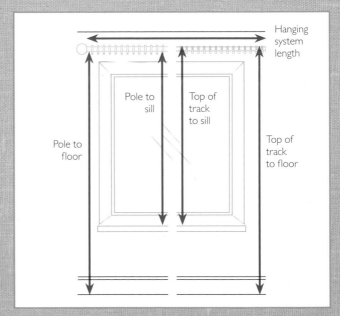

Hanging system length

Pole to sill

Top of track to sill

Pole to floor

Top of track to floor

Measuring for a pole
The spot you need to measure from will change depending on the type of curtain heading you've chosen (see p.185).

Measuring for a track
If using a track, measure from the top of the track so that the track will not be visible behind the hanging curtains.

Curtain fullness and calculating fabric

Measure the track or pole and multiply by the fullness ratio, see right, which will vary depending on the type of heading. Divide this figure by the width of the fabric to be used and round up to the next whole number. This is the number of widths of fabric required for the pair of curtains. The number of widths of lining will be the same as the fabric.

Measure the finished length required. To calculate the cut length, add 20cm (8in) to the finished length for the hem allowances. If patterned fabric is used, extra will be needed for pattern matching. The length of the lining will be the same as the fabric, minus any extra for pattern matching.

To calculate the amount of fabric, lining, and interlining required for the curtains, multiply the number of widths by the cut length of the curtains.

Curtain style	Fullness ratio
Pencil pleat	2.00
Double pleat	2.30
Triple pleat	2.20
Gathered heading	1.80
Tab top	1.25
Tie top	1.25
Eyelet	1.50
Pocket top	1.00
Flat panel	1.00

Placing and matching a pattern

All patterned fabrics have a repeat down their lengths. This is called the pattern repeat and is measured from a point in one pattern to the same point in the next pattern. If using a patterned fabric you will need to match the pattern across the curtain panels and also across the seams if joining widths.

When joining widths, cut the first length of fabric to the required curtain length. Take note of the pattern at the top and locate this start point on the next uncut length of fabric. Place a pin at this point. Finger press back the selvedge of the uncut length and manoeuvre the uncut piece until the pattern matches the first cut length at the selvedge. Mark the top and bottom of the uncut length in line with the first cut length and cut across the fabric at the marks, at right angles to the selvedge. Match the pattern across the two cut pieces along the selvedge again. Secure with pins then slipstitch along the fold. Put right sides together, then machine stitch along the fold.

Calculating amounts of fabric with pattern repeats

To calculate the amount of fabric you need, round the total cut length, as above, to the nearest pattern repeat multiple, then multiply by the number of widths. For example, if the cut length is 130cm (52in) and the pattern repeat is 25cm (10in) you will need 150cm (60in), or six pattern repeats, per width of fabric. If you need four widths you will therefore need 6m (240in) of fabric in total.

Matching across panels

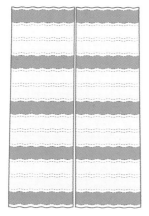

Consider how the pattern will match across the curtain panels. Make sure the pattern will match edge-to-edge when the curtains are closed. Cut out the first curtain then match the second curtain to the first.

Partial repeats

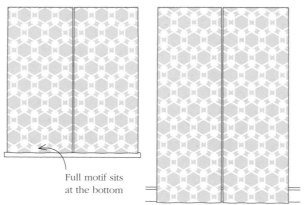

Full motif sits at the bottom

When placing a pattern it may be impossible to avoid a partial repeat at the top or the bottom. For sill- or apron-length curtains place the partial repeat at the heading. For floor-length or pooling curtains place the full pattern motif at the heading.

Placing joins

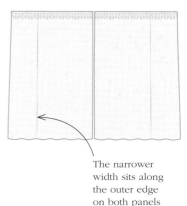

The narrower width sits along the outer edge on both panels

When joining fabric width place narrower widths on the outer sides of the panels and the full width of the fabric in the centre. Ensure you match the pattern across the join.

Cased-heading **CURTAIN**

A sheer curtain panel with an ombré effect is a modern take on a traditional window treatment. Sheer fabrics are normally 3m (120in) wide, so here you have the selvedges at the top and bottom of the curtain, while the sides start out as raw edges. Finish it off with a cased heading, one of the simplest ones to make.

 **YOU WILL NEED**

Materials

- *Sheer or lightweight fabric (see p.186 for calculating amount)*
- *Matching thread*
- *14g weighting tape (length to match the width of your curtain)*

Tools

- *Pins • Scissors • Ruler • Iron*
- *Overlocker (optional) • Sewing machine*
- *Hand sewing needle • Curtain pole*

Squaring off the first side

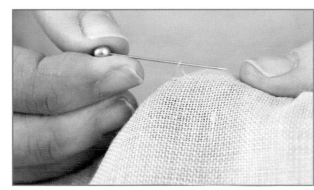

1 Start by squaring off one long edge of the fabric. This will be one side of the finished curtain. With a sheer fabric or loose weave, as here, use a pin to pick out a single thread along the long edge.

2 Gently pull the thread out completely, all the way along the long edge.

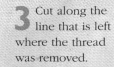

3 Cut along the line that is left where the thread was removed.

Neatening the sides

1 With the wrong side face up, fold over then press 1.5cm (⅝in) along the long, straightened edge.

2 For a straight edge on a sheer fabric, use an overlocker. Turn off the knife and overlock along the folded edge. If not using an overlocker, fold over and iron the edge a second time, then stitch close to the edge to create a double hem.

3 Trim the excess fabric from the edge. (Skip this if you have made a double hem.)

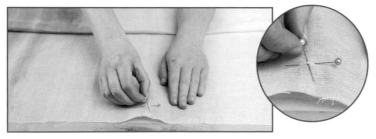

4 Measure across the fabric from the neatened edge to the width of your curtain (see p.186) and mark with a pin. Using a second pin, pull out a thread along the edge at this point. Cut along the line, then fold, press, and overlock the edge, or create a double hem.

Making the hem

1 With the wrong side face up, fold over the selvedge and press a 4cm (1⅝in) hem along the bottom.

Making the cased heading

1 Lay the curtain flat. Measure the drop from top to bottom along the edges and at points across the width. Mark with pins. Fold over to the wrong side at the pinned line and press. Remove the pins. Mark a line 8cm (3¼in) down from the fold across the width of the curtain. This makes a casing for a pole up to 3.5cm (1⅜in) in diameter. You may need to make it deeper for a thicker pole. Cut off the excess. Pin, iron, then cut along the fold.

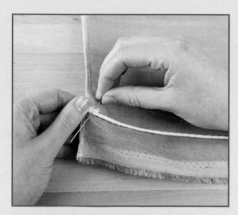

2 Unfold the hem. Remove the first few weights from the weighting tape and close the end of the tape with a few stitches. Stitch the end of the tape to one end of the foldline. Cut the tape to the width of the curtain and stitch the cut end to the other end of the foldline.

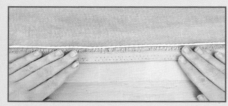

3 Fold the hem up so the selvedge meets the weighting tape. Press the hem in place.

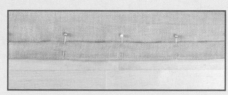

4 Turn the hem up again to make a double hem that encloses the weighting tape. Pin in place.

5 Stitch along the hem 4mm (³⁄₁₆in) from the first folded edge. Press.

2 With the wrong side face up, fold over then press a 2cm (¾in) hem along the top edge.

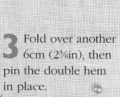

3 Fold over another 6cm (2³⁄₈in), then pin the double hem in place.

4 Stitch along the hem close to the first folded edge to create the cased heading. Insert a curtain pole through the cased heading to hang your curtain.

Tab top **CURTAIN**

Unlined and informal, a tab top curtain is simplicity itself to make. As with all sewing projects, the key is to measure, then measure again to double check. Before you start to cut your fabric, decide on the position of your pole. Placing it well above the window or door frame, as here, will make your room look bigger.

 YOU **WILL NEED**

Materials

- *Fabric*
- *Matching thread*
- *Penny weights*
- *Small piece of calico*

Tools

- *Set square* • *Tape measure*
- *Tailor's chalk* • *Scissors* • *Iron*
- *Pins* • *Sewing machine*
- *Hand sewing needle*

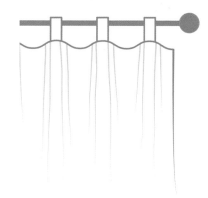

Tab top curtain

One of the easiest curtain headings to make, the tabs of a tab top heading are made in either matching or contrasting fabric and sewn to the top edge of the curtain.

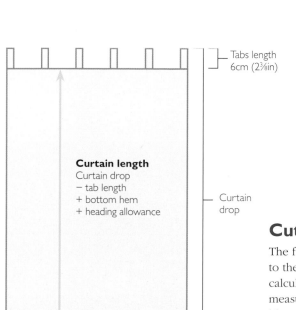

Pin double hem before stitching

Tabs length 6cm (2⅜in)

Curtain length
Curtain drop
− tab length
+ bottom hem
+ heading allowance

Curtain drop

Unlined curtain

Made from a single layer of fabric that is hemmed all around, an unlined curtain is quick and easy to make. We add penny weights to ensure the curtain hangs smoothly and looks sharp.

Cutting length

The finished tab, from the top of the pole to the top of the curtain, is 6cm (2⅜in). To calculate the cutting length of the curtain fabric, measure from the top of the pole to the required ldrop. Deduct the length of the tab from this measurement, then add 10cm (4in) for the hem and 7cm (2¾in) for the heading.

Measuring and cutting

I Lay the fabric on the work surface right side up. Square off the bottom (see p.16) and cut off the excess.

2 Use the diagram on p.193 to work out the cutting length. Measure from the bottom edge to this length and cut out.

Making the tabs

I You will need eight tabs per standard width of fabric. Cut each one 25 x 7cm (10 x 2¾in) wide. (Make the tabs longer if your pole has a large diameter.)

2 Fold each tab in half lengthways, wrong sides facing, then press. Open it out, then press a 1cm (⅜in) seam allowance towards the fold along each long edge.

3 Re-fold along the centre, matching the folded edges. Secure with pins.

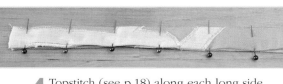

4 Topstitch (see p.18) along each long side of the tab, as close to the edge as possible. To save time, you can stitch all the tabs in one continuous chain, then cut through the stitches holding them together.

Hemming the sides and bottom

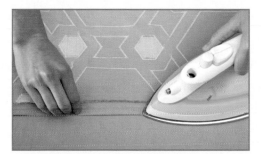

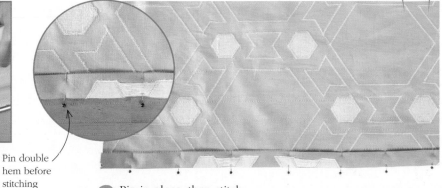

1 With the wrong side of the curtain face up, fold over then press 2.5cm (1in) along the sides of the curtain. Repeat to make a double hem.

Pin double hem before stitching

2 Pin in place, then stitch close to the folded edge.

3 With the wrong side face up, fold over 5cm (2in) along the bottom.

4 Fold over another 5cm (2in) to make a double hem. Pin in place.

5 Stitch close to the folded edge, leaving the final 2.5cm (1in) unstitched at either end. Press the side and bottom hems.

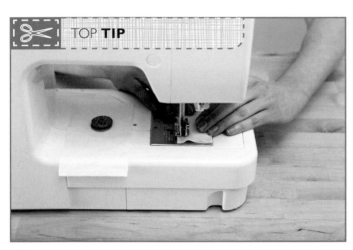

TOP **TIP**

6 Machine-made curtains sometimes pull at the corners. Compensate for this by placing one or two penny weights at each end of the bottom hem. Cut a calico rectangle to fit around each pair of weights. Fold and stitch around three sides to form a small pouch.

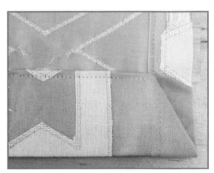

7 At each end of the bottom hem, fold in the unstitched fabric at an angle, as shown.

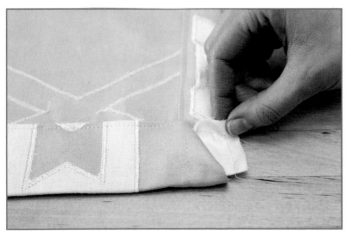

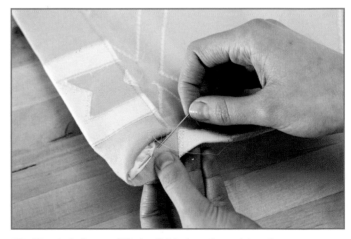

8 Tuck the covered weights into the hem, just behind the fold.

9 Slipstitch (see p.20) the fold closed, catching the calico pouch in your stitching. Take care not to stitch through to the front.

Attaching the tabs

1 Fold a tab in half crosswise. With the right side of the curtain face up, pin the raw edges of the tab at one end of the curtain's top edge. Repeat to pin a second tab at the other end. Measure the distance between the tabs and divide by seven. Measure this amount from the first tab, then from the next, and so on. Place a pin at each of these points.

2 Pin a folded tab at each of the marked points. The tabs should be equally spaced.

3 Machine stitch along the top edge of the curtain with a 1.5cm (⅝in) seam allowance, through all the pinned tabs. As you stitch, make sure the tabs remain perpendicular to the top edge. When you come to each tab, you may need to lift the presser foot and lower it again to stop the tabs being pushed out of alignment by the foot.

4 With the wrong side of the curtain face up, turn the top edge over with the tabs attached along the stitching line. Press.

5 Turn the top of the curtain over by 5cm (2in). Pin in place.

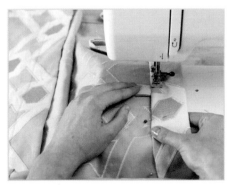

6 Stitch 1cm (⅜in) from the folded edge, removing the pins as you go.

7 Flip the tabs over the hem as shown and secure with a pin, then stitch 1cm (⅜in) from the top edge of the curtain, securing the tabs in your line of stitches. You may need to raise the foot as before. Insert a pole through the tabs to hang your curtain.

Curtain **TIEBACKS**

Complete any curtain with a tieback to hold it away from the window and allow maximum light to flood in to a room. A traditional, buckram-lined tieback like ours, looks professional and tailored. Despite this, you should be able to make a pair in just a couple of hours.

✂ YOU **WILL NEED**

Materials

- *Tieback buckram (2 x ready-made or two pieces cut from buckram using the template on pp.300–301)*
- *Main fabric (large enough for two tiebacks plus 2.5cm (1in) seam allowance all around)*
- *Backing fabric (either matching fabric or lining fabric) the same size as the buckram*
- *4 x D-rings or curtain rings, approx. 2.5cm (1in) diameter*
- *2 x tieback hooks*

Tools

- *Scissors* • *Pencil* • *Pins* • *Ruler*
- *Sewing machine* • *Hand sewing needle*

Tieback template
Use the template on pp.300–301 to create a tieback template the right size for your curtains

Deciding the size of a tieback

A tieback must be long enough to hold the curtain back without bunching it up too much, so its length is determined by the number of fabric widths in the curtain and how bulky the material is. Measure around the gathered curtain to find the ideal length. The depth of the tieback is also important; very short curtains look wrong with deep tiebacks and conversely, very long curtains look wrong if they're too narrow. Usually the width varies between 10cm (4in) and 15cm (6in).

Measuring and cutting out

1 Lay two pieces of main fabric face down on top of each other. If the fabric has a pattern, ensure that the pattern matches on both pieces. Place the tieback buckram on top, ensuring that it is symmetrical with any pattern.

2 Using a ruler and pencil, measure and mark a 2.5cm (1in) seam allowance all around the buckram. This wide seam allowance helps to support the curved edge and makes it easier when turning the tieback to the right side.

3 Remove the buckram and cut through both layers of fabric to cut out the two pieces. Cut two matching pieces from the backing fabric.

Assembling the tieback

1 Place one piece of backing fabric and one piece of main fabric right sides together.

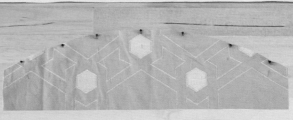

2 Pin along the curve.

3 Mark a dot 2.5cm (1in) from the long straight edge and 2.5cm (1in) from the short straight edge at each end.

4 Machine stitch from dot to dot along the curve with a 2.5cm (1in) seam allowance.

5 Cut notches into the seam allowance all the way around the curve, but make sure you do not cut through your stitches. Snip off the corners to reduce the bulk.

6 Turn the tieback to the right side. Roll the seam with your fingers to ease it to the edge and press.

7 Insert the buckram between the fabric and the backing.

8 For a smooth finish, ensure that all the seam allowance fabric is facing the tieback backing.

9 Turn the edge of the main fabric under, then fold the edge of the backing fabric under until the two edges are aligned.

10 Pin the edges in place.

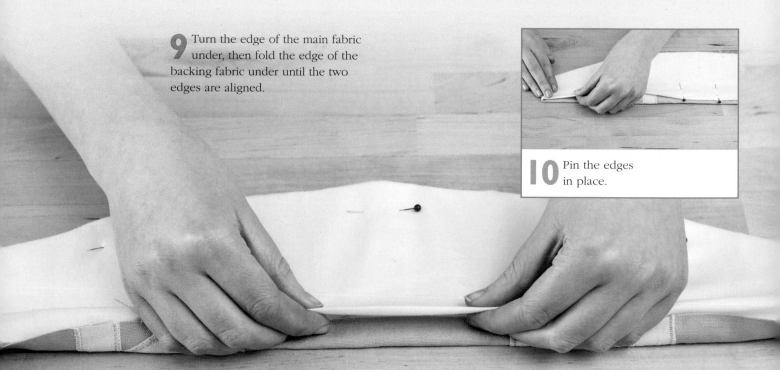

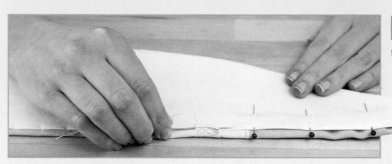

11 Slipstitch (see p.20) the edges closed. Repeat Steps 1–11 for the second tieback.

Attaching the rings

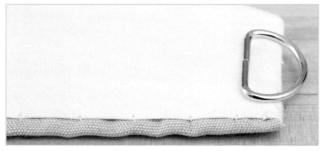

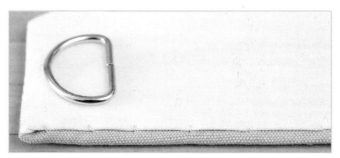

1 One short edge of the tieback will be at the front and the other at the back. For the back, position the straight edge of a D-ring 1cm (⅜in) from the edge so the curved edge overhangs.

2 For the front, position the straight edge of a D-ring 2.5cm (1in) from the edge so the curved edge is on the tieback.

3 Oversew the rings in place at two points on their straight edge.

4 Reverse the placings of the rings on the second tieback so they are a mirror image of the first tieback.

5 Position the tieback hooks at the required height either side of the window. Loop the back end of the tieback on the hook, gather up the curtain, then loop the front end on the hook.

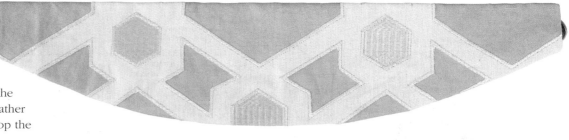

Lined eyelet CURTAIN

With their smartly contemporary, somewhat masculine look, eyelet curtains are a great choice for a room where you don't want a fussy window treatment. An added bonus is the fact that their tube-like folds do not require a lot of fabric. If using a metal curtain pole, be sure to match its finish to the eyelet rings.

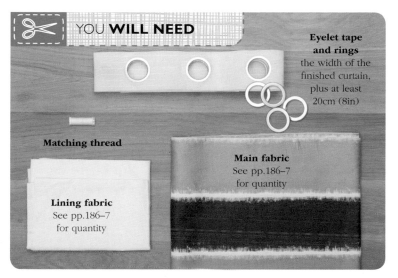

YOU **WILL NEED**

Eyelet tape and rings
the width of the finished curtain, plus at least 20cm (8in)

Matching thread

Main fabric
See pp.186–7 for quantity

Lining fabric
See pp.186–7 for quantity

Tools

- Set square (optional) • Tailor's chalk • Scissors • Pins
- Ruler • Sewing machine • Iron • Tape measure • Pencil

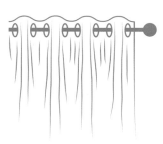

Eyelet heading

The eyelet heading tape is stitched across the top of the curtain. The eyelets are cut out and the backs of the rings are attached.

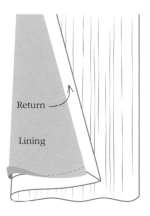

Return

Lining

Lined curtain

These curtains are "tube lined" – a technique for making lined curtains using a sewing machine in which the main fabric and lining are stitched together right side to right side to form a tube.

Cutting the main fabric and making the hem

1 Lay the main fabric on the work surface right side up. Square off the bottom (see p.16) and cut off the excess. Starting from the bottom edge, use tailor's chalk and a tape measure to measure and mark the finished drop (see p.186 for measuring the drop) plus 17cm (6¾in) at several points across the width. Join the marks and cut along the line.

2 With the fabric face down, measure and mark 14cm (5⅝in) from the bottom edge at several points across the width, as before.

3 Join the chalk marks with a line. Fold the fabric to meet the line and press the fold.

4 Fold the edge of the fabric under by 7cm (2¾in) to create a double hem and press.

5 Secure the double hem with pins

6 With the fabric face down, align the folded edge of the hem with the edge of the presser foot. Move the needle to the left. Using stitch length 3 and the foot as a guide, stitch along the hem. Backstitch at the beginning and end of the seam to secure the stitches.

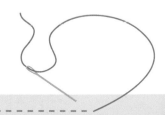

7 Fold the fabric in half lengthways, right sides together, and mark the centre points top and bottom with pins.

8 If the selvedges are very wide, trim them off. Measure the new width of the fabric.

Hemming and attaching the lining

1 Subtract 9cm (3⅝in) from the new width of the main fabric. Starting from one long edge, measure and mark this amount at several points along the length of the lining.

2 Join the marks and cut along the line. The lining is now 9cm (3⅝in) narrower than the curtain, which will create the returns (see p.203).

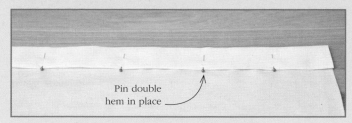

Pin double
hem in place

3 With the lining face down, start from the bottom and
measure 10cm (4in) at several points across the width. Join
the marks with a line. Fold the fabric to the line and press. Fold
under 5cm (2in) to make a double hem and press. Secure with
pins, machine stitch, then press.

Match the
stitching lines of
the two hems

4 Fold the lining lengthwise and mark the centre points top
and bottom with pins. Place the main fabric and the lining
right sides together, aligning the hem stitching lines of both
pieces. The bottom of the lining should lie 2cm (¾in) above
the bottom of the main fabric.

5 Keeping the hem stitching lines together, align one long
edge of the lining with one long edge of the main fabric.
Pin along the edge.

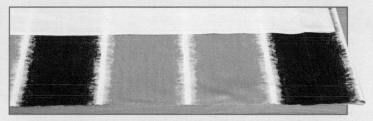

6 The main fabric will now extend beyond the other long
edge of the lining because the lining is narrower.

7 Fold the long edge of the lining back, then
make a fold in the main fabric from top to
bottom, as shown.

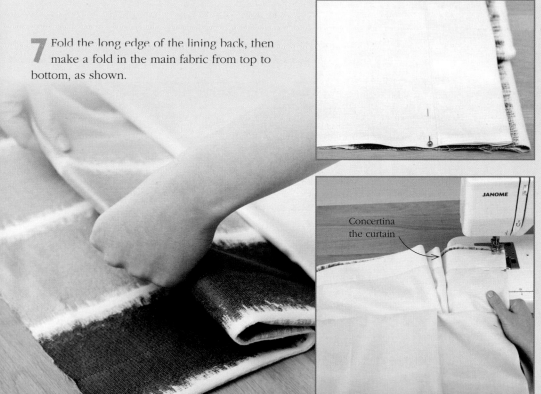

Concertina
the curtain

8 Unfold the long edge of
the lining and align it with
the long edge of the main fabric.
The fold in the main fabric will
be tucked under the lining.
Smooth out the lining, check
the hem stitching lines are still
aligned, and secure with pins
along the long edge.

9 Concertina the curtain to
make it easier to manage.
With the curtain face down, align
one long edge with the 1.5cm
(⅝in) marker on the needle plate
(see p.18). Using stitch length 2.5
and starting from the hemmed
edges, stitch the long edges
together, following the marker
and backstitching at the
beginning and end of the seam.

10 Turn the curtain over so it is face up and concertina it again. Stitch the other long edges together, again starting at the hemmed edges. The curtain and lining now form a tube.

TOP **TIP**

11 Lay the curtain tube on the ironing board. Manoeuvre the seams so that they are not at the edges of the tube, then press both seam allowances towards the main fabric along both seams. This will encourage the seam allowances to lie flat when the curtain is turned to the right side.

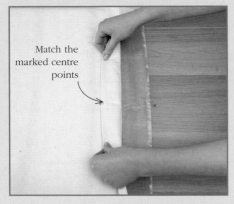

Match the marked centre points

12 Turn the curtain to the right side and place on the work surface with the main fabric face down. Match the centre points of the main fabric and the lining, top and bottom, keeping the hem stitching lines aligned. Pin together at the centre points.

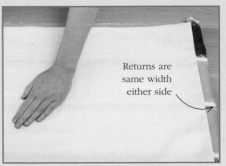

Returns are same width either side

13 Smooth out the curtain from the centre to the edges. The same width of main fabric – the returns – should now be visible along either edge and the seam allowances should lie flat under the returns. Iron the edges of the returns into sharp folds.

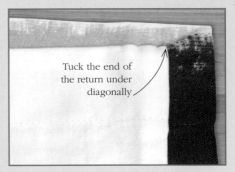

Tuck the end of the return under diagonally

14 At the bottom edge of the curtain, fold the hem of each return diagonally, tucking it under the return. This creates a half mitre. Slipstitch (see p.20) into place.

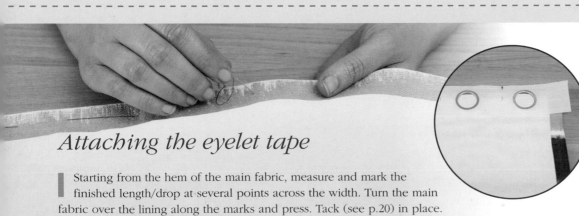

Attaching the eyelet tape

1 Starting from the hem of the main fabric, measure and mark the finished length/drop at several points across the width. Turn the main fabric over the lining along the marks and press. Tack (see p.20) in place.

2 Place the eyelet tape so its top edge is a little way beneath the top edge of the curtain and the first and last eyelets are equidistant from each long edge. Pin in place. Trim off the excess tape, leaving a 2cm (¾in) overhang at each long edge.

3 To hold the layers together, sew a line of tacking stitches through all the layers of fabric just below the eyelet tape.

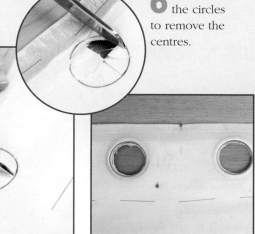

6 Cut around the circles to remove the centres.

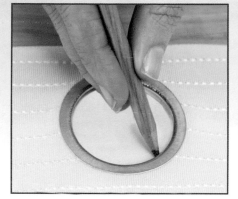

4 Using a pencil, draw around the inner circle of each eyelet.

5 Remove the eyelet tape. Using the tip of the scissors, snip into each circle and cut to the edge in both directions. Snip across at right angles to the first cut.

7 Reposition the tape and pin along its top and bottom edges. Tuck the ends of the tape under and pin.

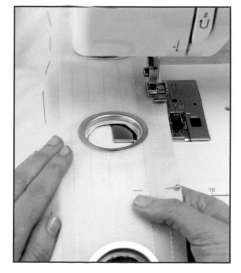

8 Stitch the tape in place through all the layers along a short edge, then pivot and stitch along a long edge. Stitch along the other long edge, then pivot to stitch the other short edge. Stitch both long edges in the same direction to avoid puckering.

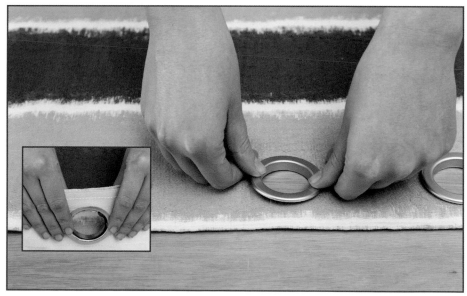

9 Insert the front of each ring through the front of the curtain and snap the front and back together. Insert your curtain pole through the rings to hang the curtain.

Pencil pleat **CURTAIN**

Crisp without being formal, pencil pleats are easily formed at the top of a curtain using the appropriate heading tape. Other heading tapes are attached in exactly the same way – see p.217 for more options. This pair of curtains is interlined as well as lined, which gives a beautiful, professional finish.

YOU **WILL NEED**

Interlining fabric
(see pp.186–7
for quantity)

Lining fabric
(see pp.186–7 for quantity)

Main fabric
(see pp.186–7 for quantity)

Curtain hooks

Pencil pleat heading tape, to fit the
width of the ungathered curtains

Penny weights

Matching
thread

Tools

- *Ruler/metre rule* • *Set square*
- *Scissors* • *Hand sewing needle*
- *Sewing machine* • *Iron* • *Pins*
- *Tailor's chalk* • *Tape measure*
- *Curtain hooks*

Pencil pleat heading

A pencil pleat heading tape is stitched across the top of the curtain to create narrow pleats.

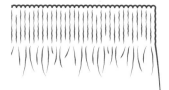

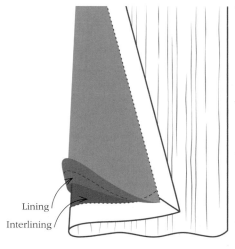

Lining

Interlining

Interlined curtain

The curtains are draught-proof and lusciously thick thanks to the interlining that is stitched to the main fabric. The lining fabric is handstitched in place along the edges of the returns.

Cutting the fabric and preparing the hem

Selvedge
of main
fabric

1 Measure the cutting size for your curtains (see pp.186–187). Square off the fabric along the bottom edge (see p.16). Cut the fabrics and interlining to the required size for each curtain. If more than one width is required, join the widths together with a flat seam. Make sure to add any half-widths at the outside edges (see p.187 for joining panels).

2 Place the main fabric on the work surface face down and lay the interlining on top. Match the raw edges along the sides and the bottom.

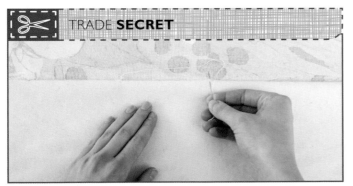

✄ TRADE **SECRET**

3 To hold the interlining in place, fold back its long edge by 20cm (8in). Using matching thread, lockstitch (see p.21) the interlining to the main fabric from top to bottom along the folded edge, spacing the stitches approx 10cm (4in) apart and stopping them approx 10cm (4in) short of the bottom edge. Repeat along the other long edge. (NB: If your curtain is more than one width wide, also lockstitch the interlining to the main fabric along each seam.)

4 Unfold the lockstitched edge then, with the main fabric still face down, fold the two fabrics over together by 5cm (2in). This is called a return. Starting 35cm (14in) from the bottom edge, herringbone stitch (see p.21) from bottom to top along the whole length of the long edge. On the selvedge, stitch through the two layers of interlining and the main fabric; below the fold, only stitch through the interlining. Ideally, use matching thread, but contrast thread will not show on the right side.

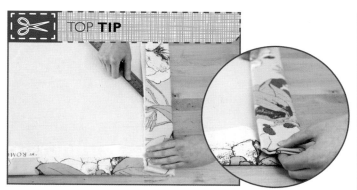

TOP **TIP**

5 Fold over the main fabric and the interfacing by 7cm (2¾in) at the bottom edge of the curtain. If the interlining moves, use a ruler to tuck it back in place.

6 Turn the two fabrics over again by 7cm (2¾in) to form a double hem.

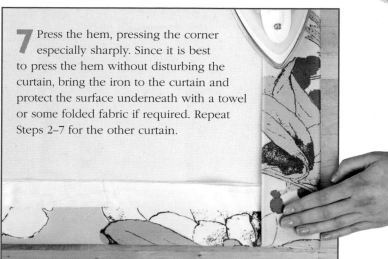

7 Press the hem, pressing the corner especially sharply. Since it is best to press the hem without disturbing the curtain, bring the iron to the curtain and protect the surface underneath with a towel or some folded fabric if required. Repeat Steps 2–7 for the other curtain.

Creating a true mitre at the corners

1 Mark the corner with a pin.

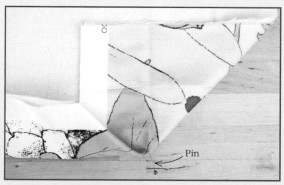

2 Unfold both fabrics at the corner then bring the tips of both fabrics back towards the body of the curtain until the pin is at the corner, as shown.

Pin

3 Unfold the main fabric. Cut the interlining along the fold from the raw edge towards the pin, as shown.

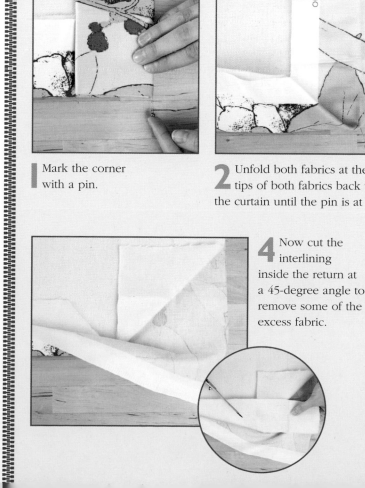

4 Now cut the interlining inside the return at a 45-degree angle to remove some of the excess fabric.

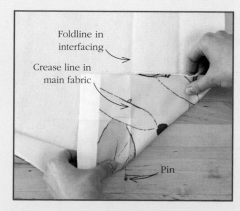

Foldline in interfacing

Crease line in main fabric

Pin

5 Fold the main fabric back again so the pin is once more at the corner. To check everything is straight, the crease line in the main fabric should lie on top of the foldline in the interlining.

6 Cut a calico rectangle to fit around the penny weight. Fold and stitch around two sides to form a small pouch. Slip in the weight and sew closed. Place the penny weight on the main fabric in the return but above the hemline. Stitch in place taking care not to stitch through to the main fabric.

Penny weight

7 Fold the return back over the weight to create the first 45-degree angle of the mitre.

8 Fold the double hem along the first pressed line.

9 Fold the double hem along the second pressed line. The hem and the side will meet at the second 45-degree angle, hiding the weight and creating a true mitre.

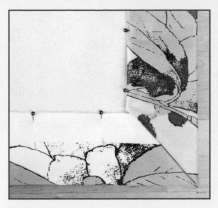

10 Pin partway along the hem and the return to secure the mitre. Repeat Steps 1–9 at the other bottom corner. Pin along the other return and the remainder of the hem.

11 Ladder stitch (see p.21) the mitred corners closed.

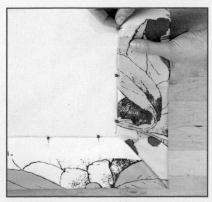

12 Slipstitch (see p.20) along the edge of the double hem. Repeat Steps 1–12 on the other curtain.

Making the lining

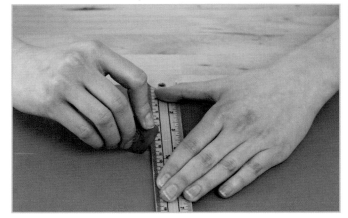

Measure and mark a line 10cm (4in) from the bottom of the lining.

2 Turn up the bottom raw edge to meet the line.

3 Turn up the hem again to create a double hem. Secure with pins.

✂ TRADE **SECRET**

4 Fold the lining in a concertina to make it easier to manage, leaving the pinned hem accessible.

5 Concertina the curtain the other way, again leaving the pinned hem accessible.

6 Stitch the hem as close to the fold as possible, unfolding the concertina as you go. Keep your fabric as flat and neat as possible.

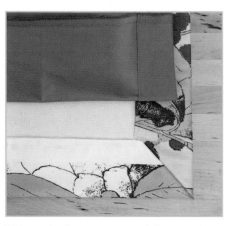

7 Lay the lining on top of the curtain, wrong sides together, aligning the stitching lines of the two hems.

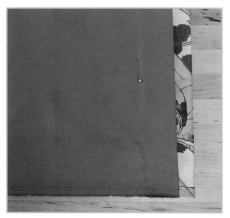

8 Making sure the long sides are also aligned, place a couple of pins along the aligned stitching lines to hold the lining in place. Smooth out the lining.

9 Starting at the bottom hem, turn under the long raw edge of the lining to meet the mitre.

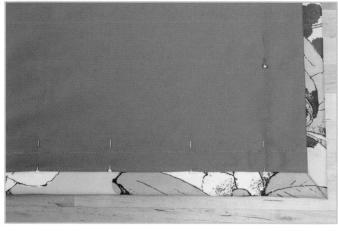

10 Turn under the rest of the raw edge from hem to top by the same amount. Pin in place.

11 Stitch the lining to the curtain by making a few tight slipstitches (see p.20) at the hem end. Continue with a ladder stitch (see p.21) all the way up the long side.

12 Double-check the final length of the curtain. Starting at the hem, measure and mark this length at various points along the width of the curtain.

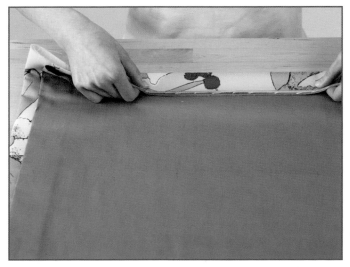

13 Fold over the top – the main interlined fabric and the lining – at the marks and press.

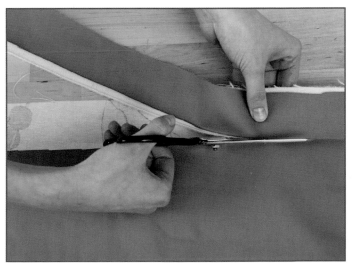

14 Unfold the fabrics then cut the lining and interlining along the foldline. Fold the main fabric back over the lining.

Attaching heading tape

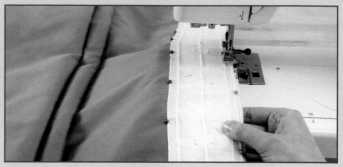

1 Cut the heading tape the width of the curtain plus 6cm (2⅜in). Knot the cords at one end of the tape on the wrong side. With the tape face up, place it close to the top edge of the curtain. Turn the knotted end of the tape under and pin in place. At the other end, free the cords from the tape until you can turn under the end to meet the other edge of the curtain. Pin along the top and bottom edges of the tape.

2 Concertina the fabric as before. Using a bobbin thread that matches your main fabric and a cream or white top thread, stitch the heading tape along a short edge, then pivot and stitch along a long edge, through all the layers. Stitch along the other long edge, then pivot to stitch the other short edge. Stitch both long edges in the same direction to avoid puckering.

3 Take care not to sew over the loose ends of the cords. Remove the pins.

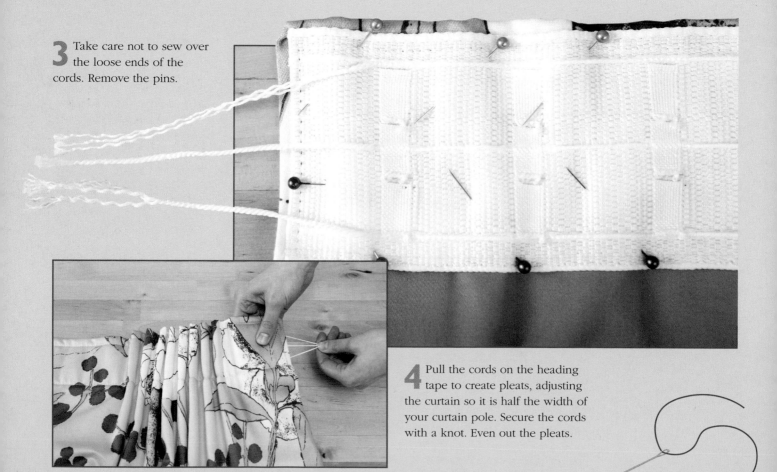

4 Pull the cords on the heading tape to create pleats, adjusting the curtain so it is half the width of your curtain pole. Secure the cords with a knot. Even out the pleats.

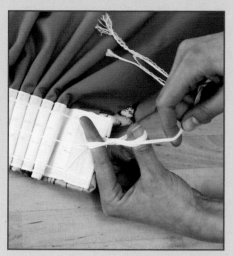

5 Create a figure-of-eight with the end of the cord.

6 Tuck the figure-of-eight under the knot to keep it out of the way. Insert curtain hooks into the heading tape and hang the curtain. Repeat Steps 1–6 to attach heading tape to the other curtain.

Different heading tapes

Create very different looks by choosing a different heading tape to top your curtains. Other tapes are attached in exactly the same way as the pencil pleat heading tape, but produce different looks ranging from formal to modern.

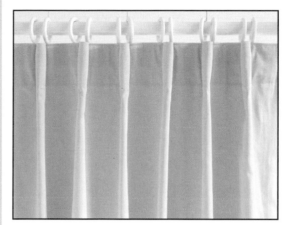

Cartridge tape

Cartridge tape forms small, rounded pleats separated by a flat panel. These can be pushed close together to give fullness to the curtain.

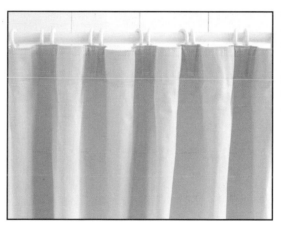

Tempo tape

Tempo tape is a relatively new heading tape which guides the top of the curtain to form an S-shaped curve. It is best used on curtains that hang on a pole rather than a track to give the "S" plenty of space at the back.

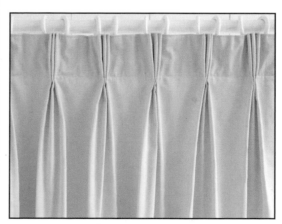

Pinch pleat tape

Stylish and formal pinch pleats are made using a tape that creates groups of two or three pleats separated by a flat panel. Give the pleats additional structure by taking a few small stitches at the base of each group of pleats.

ACCESSORIES

Drum LAMPSHADE

With its clean, simple lines, a drum lampshade in a fabric that coordinates with your interior adds a cool, contemporary accent. Lampshade-making kits are readily available and come in all shapes and sizes. Start with a drum lampshade for guaranteed first-time success.

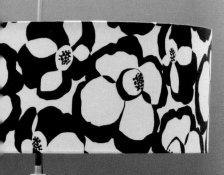

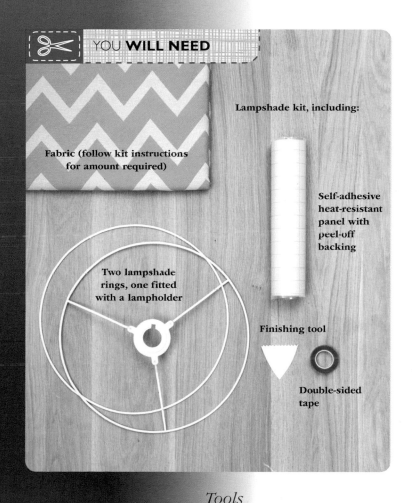

YOU **WILL NEED**

Fabric (follow kit instructions for amount required)

Lampshade kit, including:

Two lampshade rings, one fitted with a lampholder

Self-adhesive heat-resistant panel with peel-off backing

Finishing tool

Double-sided tape

Tools

- *Iron* • *Pins* • *Tailor's chalk*
- *Ruler* • *Scissors*

Planning your lampshade

If your fabric has a directional print, you need to decide in advance whether you use your lampshade as pendant or table lamp. Position the rings according to the instructions below.

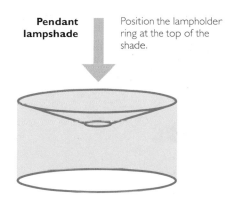

Pendant lampshade — Position the lampholder ring at the top of the shade.

The lampholder ring must always point to the centre of the shade.

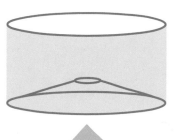

Table lamp or floor lamp — Position the lampholder ring at the bottom of the shade.

Preparing the fabric

Press your fabric to remove any creases, then place it on the work surface right side up. Choose the area of fabric that you would like to see on the lampshade and position the self-adhesive panel accordingly. Mark the position of the four corners of the panel with pairs of pins through the fabric, as shown, and add a few pins to mark the edges.

Mark corners with pins

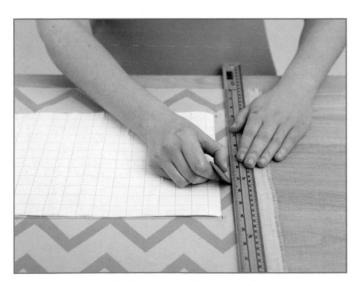

2 Remove the self-adhesive panel and turn the fabric over. Reposition the panel on the fabric according to the marker pins. Using tailor's chalk, draw around the two long edges and one short edge of the panel. Add a 1cm (⅜in) seam allowance parallel to the other short edge and mark it with a line.

Stick down 10cm (4in) at a time

3 Peel off the first 10cm (4in) of the panel backing and position the panel, adhesive side down, within the marked lines on the fabric. Stick the first 10cm (4in) of the panel to the fabric, pushing the fabric away from you to ensure there are no creases or air bubbles. Repeat to stick the rest of the panel to the fabric, peeling off the backing and smoothing the panel down as you go.

4 Cut the fabric along the edges of the panel including the 1cm (⅜in) seam allowance along the short side.

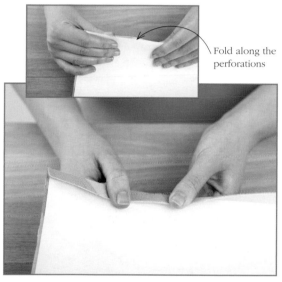

Fold along the perforations

5 The panel is perforated 1cm (⅜in) along the long edges. Fold and unfold the edges a few times to break the perforations.

6 Remove the strips of panel above the perforations, leaving 1cm (⅜in) of fabric free at the top and bottom edges.

Preparing the join

Apply double-sided tape

1 With the fabric right side down, apply a strip of double-sided tape along the 1cm (⅜in) seam allowance of the short side.

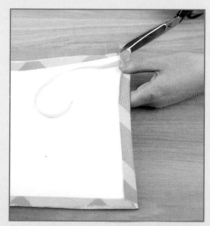

2 Peel off the backing from the double-sided tape. Fold the seam allowance over the edge of the panel and stick it down. Clip the corners of the folded seam allowance diagonally, as shown.

3 Apply a second strip of double-sided tape along the folded seam allowance.

Joining fabric and lamp rings

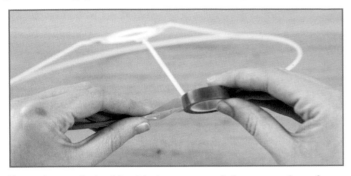

1 Firmly attach double-sided tape around the outer edge of both lampshade rings.

Place ring against panel edge

2 Remove the double-sided tape backing paper from one of the rings. Place the ring carefully on the fabric against the edge of the panel. Remove the backing paper from the second ring and place it against the other edge of the panel.

3 Slowly roll both rings along the edges of the panel, keeping them parallel to each other.

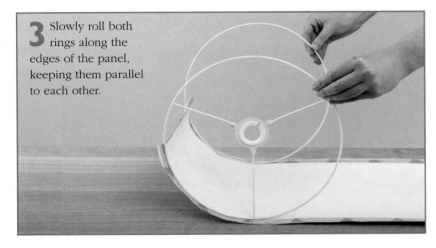

4 When you reach the end of the fabric, remove the backing paper from the tape along the seam allowance and stick the two edges together, producing a 1cm (⅜in) overlap.

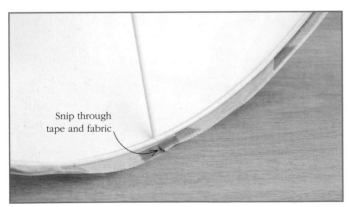

Snip through tape and fabric

Use finishing tool to tuck away excess fabric

5 Place a small piece of double-sided tape at each of the spokes in the rings and snip through the tape and fabric at these points.

6 Use the serrated edge of the finishing tool to help you fold the excess fabric over the rings at the top and bottom of the lampshade; use the smooth edge to tuck away the raw edges. At the spokes, remove the tape backing paper and stick the fabric down either side of the spokes.

Square storage **BASKET**

You can never have too much storage space – especially if there are children in the house. These super-sturdy storage baskets in contemporary graphic prints are just the job for stowing toys, clothes, nappy-changing essentials, and towels. Mix and match to suit your room and make a real talking point.

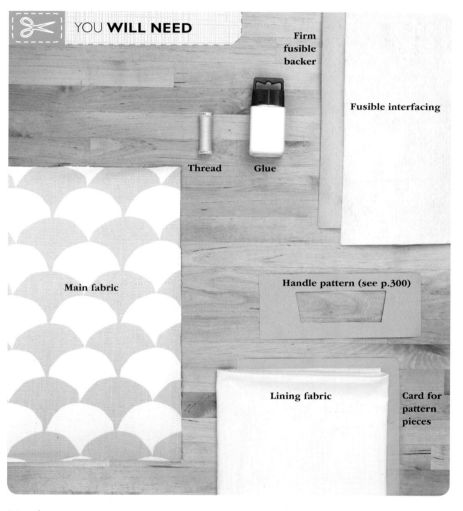

✂ YOU **WILL NEED**

Firm fusible backer

Fusible interfacing

Thread Glue

Main fabric

Handle pattern (see p.300)

Lining fabric

Card for pattern pieces

Tools

- Ruler ● Pencil ● Scalpel and cutting mat ● Scissors
- Iron ● Sewing machine
- Pins ● Bulldog clips

Making the pattern pieces

You need to cut three pattern pieces – a handle, a master pattern, and a fabric pattern. The handle template can be found on p.300. The fabric pattern is the same as the master pattern but with a seam allowance added to all sides.

Master pattern
29 x 29cm
(11½ x 11½in)

Fabric pattern
(Master pattern + seam allowance)
32 x 32cm
(12¾ x 12¾in)

Trace and transfer the handle template on p.300 to card and cut it out.

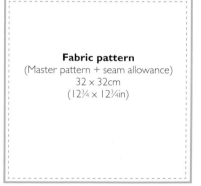

Handle

Cutting the pieces

Use the template to cut a handle pattern

1 To make the master pattern, draw a square on card or sturdy paper to the required size of the basket, in this case 29 x 29cm (11½ x 11½in). Fold it in half exactly by matching the sides and corners.

2 Trace the handle template onto card to make the handle pattern.

3 Fold the handle pattern in half crosswise and place on the master pattern so that its folded edge is aligned with the folded edge of the master pattern. Position the top of the handle pattern 3.5cm (1½in) from the top edge of the master pattern, as shown.

Cutting mat

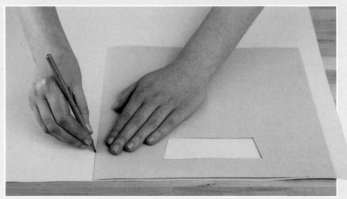

4 Draw inside the handle cutout, then use a scalpel to carefully cut a handle cutout in the master pattern.

5 Lay the master pattern on a piece of backer, draw around the outline, and cut a square of backer. Repeat to cut a total of five squares of backer and five squares of interfacing.

6 Still using the master pattern, mark and cut a handle cutout on two of the squares of backer and on two of the squares of interfacing. Using the handle pattern, cut two handles from the backer.

2 x handles cut from backer

2 x interfacing squares with handle cutout

3 x interfacing squares without handle cutout

2 x backer squares with handle cutout

3 x backer squares without handle cutout

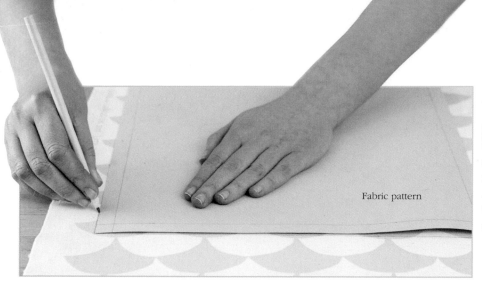

Fabric pattern

Preparing the pieces

I Draw around the master pattern onto card and add a 1.5cm (⅝in) seam allowance all around. Cut this out to make your fabric pattern. It will measure 32 x 32cm (12¾ x 12¾in). Use this pattern to cut five squares from the main fabric and five squares from the lining fabric.

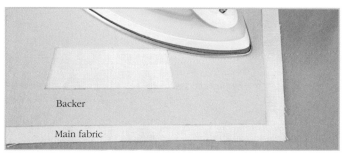

Backer

Main fabric

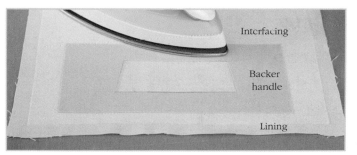

Interfacing

Backer handle

Lining

2 With a main fabric square face down, place a backer square with a handle cutout on top, centering it on the fabric. Press to fuse the backer to the fabric. Repeat to make another matching piece. Then fuse the three remaining main fabric squares to the three remaining backer squares.

3 Lay an interfacing square with a handle cutout on a lining square, centering it on the fabric. Iron to fuse, then align a backer handle with the handle cutout on the interfacing. Iron to fuse again. Repeat to make another matching piece, then fuse the three remaining interfacing squares to the three remaining lining squares.

4 Use a craft knife to cut a 9cm (3½in) slit across the centre of a handle cutout. Then, using the ends of your scissors, cut into the corners at a 45-degree angle, as shown.

Spread glue and fold the edge over

5 Glue thoroughly around the edges of the opening, then stick the fabric down. Take special care that the corners are well glued. Repeat for the other three handle cutouts.

6 Fold the fabric back around the opening making sure it folds neatly at the corners. Check on the right side and cut into the corners a little more if necessary.

7 Topstitch (see p.18) around the edges of each of the four handle cutouts. Repeat Steps 4–7 for the lining.

Joining the lining pieces

1 Place an interfaced lining square right sides together with an interfaced lining square with a cutout. Align the edges and pin. Stitch from the very top of the fabric to the bottom of the interfacing, stopping at the 1.5cm (⅝in) seam allowance.

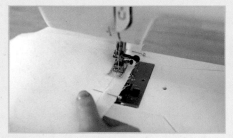

2 Stitch another cutout interfaced lining square to the free edge of the plain square. Add the remaining plain square to the free edge of the first cutout square, thus joining all four pieces. Iron open the seams.

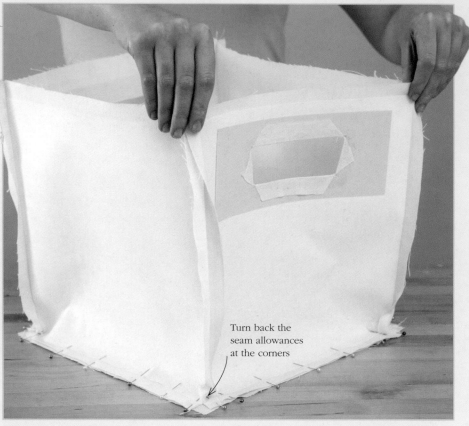

Turn back the seam allowances at the corners

3 Pin the four joined pieces to the remaining plain interfaced lining square – the base of the basket – matching the corners and seam allowances. Turning back the seam allowances at the corners, stitch around the base, pivoting at the corners and squashing the body as needed to fit it under the presser foot.

Constructing the storage basket

1 Join the four backed fabric pieces in the same way as the lining pieces. Clip the excess fabric away at the corners.

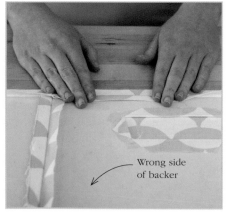

Wrong side of backer

2 With the fabric face down, press back the seam allowance along the top edge to meet the wrong side of the backer. Glue in place.

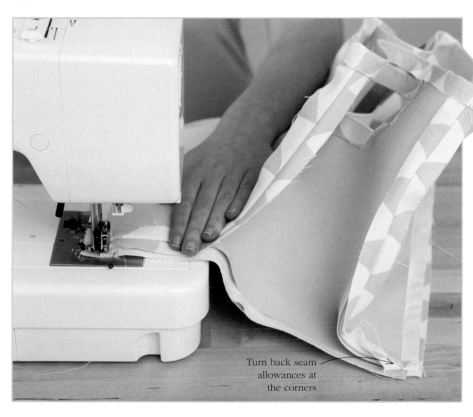

Turn back seam allowances at the corners

3 Pin the remaining fabric square – the base – as for the lining. Stitch around the base, clearing the edge of the backer by about 1–2mm (¹⁄₁₆in). Turn the storage basket to the right side so the main fabric faces outwards.

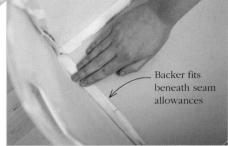

Backer fits beneath seam allowances

4 The backer sometimes comes loose during turning, so use an iron to reattach the backer where necessary. Push out the corners of the basket. Lay the remaining backer square inside the basket, glue-side down, lifting up the seam allowances to make room. Press to fuse the backer to the fabric.

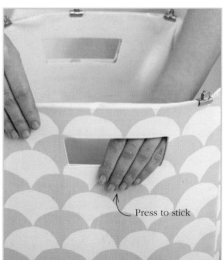

Press to stick

5 Fit the lining inside the fabric basket, matching the handles and seams. Turn under a 1.5cm (⁵⁄₈in) seam allowance along the top edge of the lining. Roll this seam allowance up or down until its folded edge aligns with the top of the fabric. Secure in place using bulldog clips.

6 Undo the clips at each end of the handles and carefully glue around the handles on both the lining and the fabric. Leave 1–2mm (¹⁄₁₆in) free of glue along the top edge but glue right up to the corners of the handles. Press together to stick.

7 With the clips still attached and the lining facing you, position the edge of the basket under the presser foot. Topstitch around the top of the basket, 4mm (³⁄₁₆in) from the edge. Press again if required.

Round storage BASKET

A round, taller version of the square storage basket (see pp.226–231) is ideal where floor space is limited, for example in a bathroom or hallway. If you have already made the square storage baskets, you won't be surprised to see the same techniques in use again; if you haven't, you'll soon get the hang of things.

✂ YOU WILL NEED

Materials

- Main fabric
- Lining fabric
- Firm fusible backer
- Matching thread

Tools

- Pencil • Measuring tape
- Scissors • Ruler • Handle template (see pp.300–301)
- Card • Scalpel and cutting mat • Compasses • Pins
- Iron • Glue
- Sewing machine
- Zip foot
- Bulldog clips

Finished dimensions
This basket has a finished height of 51cm (20⅜in) and a diameter of 32cm (12⅝in).

Cutting out the backer pieces

1 Cut a rectangle 51 x 100cm (20⅜ x 40in) from fusible backer.

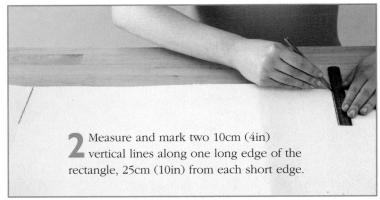

2 Measure and mark two 10cm (4in) vertical lines along one long edge of the rectangle, 25cm (10in) from each short edge.

3 Trace the handle template onto card to make the handle pattern (see p.300). Fold the pattern in half crosswise to mark its centre. Open out the pattern and place it 1.5cm (⅝in) from the long edge of the rectangle, matching its foldine with one of the vertical lines. Draw inside the handle cutout. Repeat at the other vertical line.

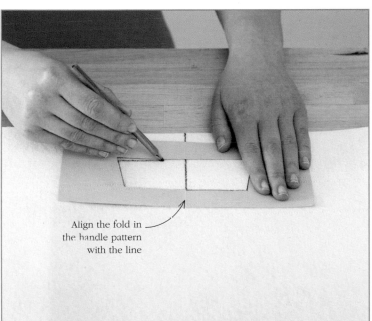

Align the fold in the handle pattern with the line

4 Using a scalpel, cut both handle cutouts.

5 Lay the handle pattern on a spare piece of backer and draw around the pattern and inside the cutout. Cut the shape out of the backer including the cutout to make a backer handle. Repeat to make a second one.

6 Set your compasses at 16cm (6¼in) and draw a circle on another piece of backer. Cut out the circle.

Cutting out the fabric pieces

1 Place the lining face down. Using the backer as a template, mark a 1.5cm (⅝in) seam allowance all around it. Remove the backer and cut out the lining rectangle. Don't cut out the handles at this stage.

2 Place the main fabric face down with the backer rectangle on top. Make sure any vertical or horizontal lines in the fabric pattern are aligned with the edges of the backer rectangle. Draw the handles on the wrong side of the fabric.

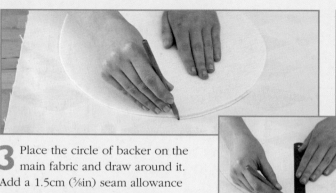

3 Place the circle of backer on the main fabric and draw around it. Add a 1.5cm (⅝in) seam allowance all around the circle on the fabric. Cut out the fabric circle for the base of the basket.

4 Pin the circle of main fabric onto the lining fabric. Cut around it to cut out a matching circle to make the lining base.

Making the base and the lining body

1 With the fabric base face down, place the backer circle on top, within the seam allowance. Flip the two circles over, holding the backer in place, so that the fabric is face up. Press to fuse the backer to the fabric. This completes the base of the basket.

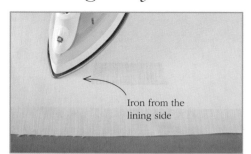

Iron from the lining side

2 Cut the lining fabric to about 5cm (2in) bigger all around than the backer rectangle. Place the backer rectangle on the work surface, glue side up, then place the lining on top, right side up, so that the lining overlaps the backer equally all around. Press the lining to fuse it to the backer.

3 Turn the fused pieces and with the backer on top, mark a 1.5cm (⅝in) seam allowance all around on the lining. Mark and trim off 5mm (³⁄₁₆in) from each short edge of the backer rectangle. Cut out the lining along the drawn lines to make the lining body.

Making the handles

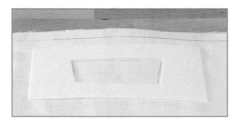

1 With the fabric rectangle face down, match a backer handle to a handle drawn on the fabric. Keeping them together, turn them over and iron to fuse. Repeat to fuse the other backer handle to the fabric.

2 With the fabric face down again, cut a 9cm (3½in) slit across the centre of the handle cutouts, then clip into the corners at a 45-degree angle.

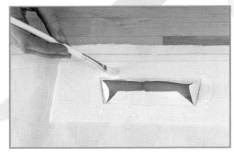

3 Fold the fabric back and glue around the edges of the opening.

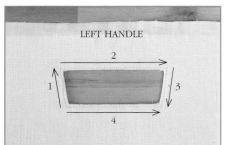

4 Stick the fabric down.

5 Topstitch (see p.18) around the edges of both handle cutouts. You now have the fabric body.

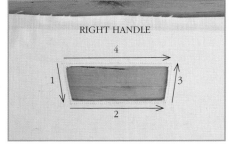

LEFT HANDLE

RIGHT HANDLE

6 Cut and glue the handles in the lining body in the same way. The lining is very stiff so the handles must be topstitched in stages. For the handle to the left of the body, start at the bottom left and stitch sides 1, 2, and 3, as shown. Re-position the piece to stitch side 4.

7 For the handle to the right of the body, start at the top left and stitch sides 1, 2, and 3 as shown. Re-position the piece to stitch side 4.

8 With the lining body face down, spread glue along the entire top edge. Turn over the 1.5cm (⅝in) seam allowance and glue in place.

Assembling the basket

Staystitch (see p.19) around the lining base within the 1.5cm (⅝in) seam allowance.

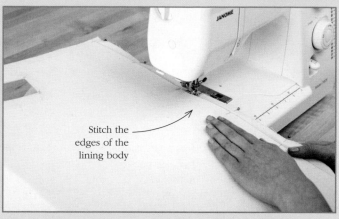

Stitch the edges of the lining body

2 Fold the lining body along its short edge, lining side to lining side. Use a zip foot and a 1.5cm (⅝in) seam allowance to stitch the edges together. Backstitch at the start and finish to secure the stitches. Press the seam open.

3 Fold the fabric body right side to right side. Stitch from top to bottom with a 1cm (⅜in) seam allowance. Backstitch at the start and finish. This smaller seam allowance makes the fabric body slightly bigger than the lining, which helps when assembling the basket. Press the seam open.

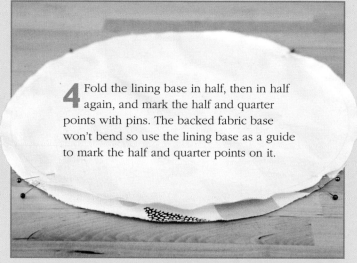

4 Fold the lining base in half, then in half again, and mark the half and quarter points with pins. The backed fabric base won't bend so use the lining base as a guide to mark the half and quarter points on it.

5 Fold the fabric and lining bodies in half lengthwise, then in half again. Mark the half and quarter points with pins along the bottom edge.

6 Snip into the seam allowance along the bottom edge of the fabric and lining bodies.

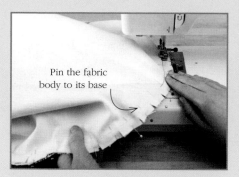

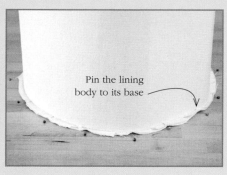

Pin the fabric body to its base

Pin the lining body to its base

7 With right sides together, pin the bottom edge of the fabric body to the fabric base at the half and quarter points. Ease the remaining fabric around the base and pin, then stitch together. Turn to the right side.

8 With right sides together, pin the bottom edge of the lining body to the lining base in the same way. The backed body will be difficult to machine stitch and will need some manipulating. If the lining and backer separate during sewing, iron to reattach.

9 Place the lining body inside the fabric body, matching the handles but with the side seams at opposite sides. Push the lining in place until lining and fabric fit together snugly. Carefully glue around the handles on the wrong side of the lining and fabric bodies. Stick together securely.

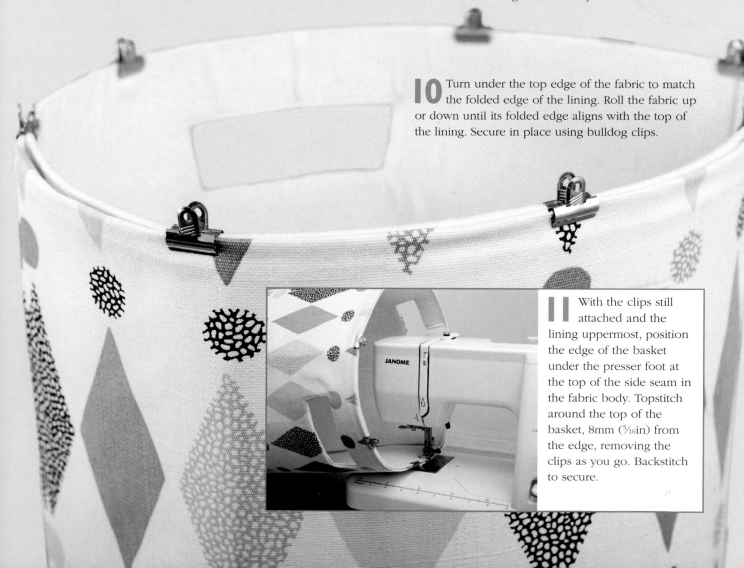

10 Turn under the top edge of the fabric to match the folded edge of the lining. Roll the fabric up or down until its folded edge aligns with the top of the lining. Secure in place using bulldog clips.

11 With the clips still attached and the lining uppermost, position the edge of the basket under the presser foot at the top of the side seam in the fabric body. Topstitch around the top of the basket, 8mm (⁵⁄₁₆in) from the edge, removing the clips as you go. Backstitch to secure.

Piped POUFFE

This pouffe with attitude features a fabulous modern fabric and zingy contrast piping. The zip is hidden away underneath the pouffe and is inserted in a similar way to the zip in the Oxford cushion (see pp. 34–37), but because sitting on the pouffe puts strain on the zip, some extra strengthening is required.

 YOU **WILL NEED**

Materials

- Calico for pattern plus extra (optional) for lining
- Main fabric
- Matching thread
- Contrast fabric for piping
- Contrast thread
- Piping cord
- Filling (3–4 round cushion pads or feathers, polystyrene beads, or polyfibre cushion filling)

Tools

- Ruler • Pencil • Masking tape
- Compass or string • Scissors
- Pins • Sewing machine • Iron
- Fabric pen • Zip foot • Zip, 6cm (2⅜in) shorter than the diameter of the pouffe

Calculating the size

The diameter of your pouffe should be the same as the diameter of your cushion pads. Work out the circumference by multiplying the diameter by π (3.14). Decide the height according to the thickness of your filling.

Radius
Diameter
Circumference = diameter × π (3.14)
Height

Making a pattern and cutting out

Measure from the folded centre point

I Fold a square of calico in half then in half again. Calculate the radius of your pouffe (half the diameter) and add a 1.5cm (⅝in) seam allowance. Measure and mark this distance on two adjacent sides of the calico, starting at the folded centre point.

Ensure that the string stays taut and the pencil upright

2 Tape the folded calico to the work surface. Use a compass to draw an arc from point to point or tie a pencil to a piece of string. Hold the pencil at one of the marks and, holding the string taut, pin the other end of the string to the folded centre point. Hold the pencil upright at one mark and draw an arc to the second mark. Cut along the arc to cut out the pattern piece.

Transfer notches
to fabric

Snip notches

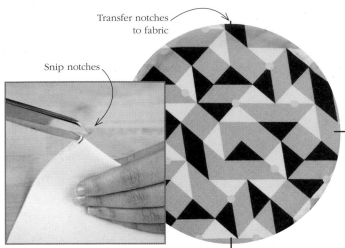

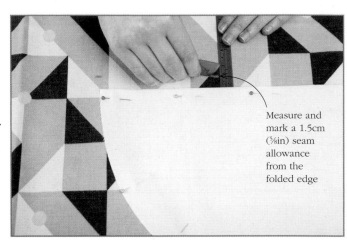

Measure and
mark a 1.5cm
(⅝in) seam
allowance
from the
folded edge

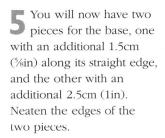

3 Cut along the arc to make the calico pattern piece.
With the calico still folded, snip notches at the half and
quarter points. Open the pattern piece and lay it on the main
fabric. Pin and cut out, then transfer the notches to the fabric.
Neaten the edges of the fabric circle (see p.19). This is
the top of your pouffe.

4 For the base of the pouffe, fold the pattern piece in half and
place on the fabric. Measure and mark 1.5cm (⅝in) from the
folded edge at several points. Join the marks. Cut the fabric out
around the pattern piece, cutting the straight edge along the new
line. Repeat to make a second base piece, but this time add
2.5cm (1in) along the folded edge. Mark and cut out as before.

5 You will now have two
pieces for the base, one
with an additional 1.5cm
(⅝in) along its straight edge,
and the other with an
additional 2.5cm (1in).
Neaten the edges of the
two pieces.

Half circle plus 2.5cm
(1in) for zip casing

2.5cm (1in)

1.5cm (⅝in)

Half circle plus 1.5cm
(⅝in) for zip

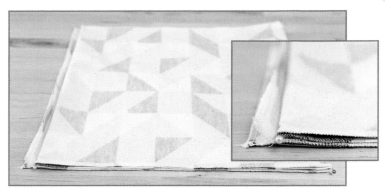

6 For the body of the pouffe, cut a fabric rectangle with its long sides equal to the circumference of your pouffe, plus two 1.5cm (⅝in) seam allowances, and with its short sides equal to the height of your pouffe, plus two 1.5cm (⅝in) seam allowances. Neaten all the edges.

7 With right sides together, join the two short sides with a 1.5cm (⅝in) seam allowance to create a cylinder. Press the seam open. Fold the fabric cylinder in half and mark the half points with pins at the top and bottom edges. Fold in half again and mark the quarter points with pins.

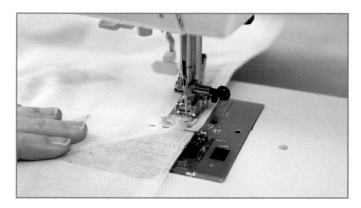

✂ TOP **TIP**

8 Stitch a line of ease stitching (see p.19) within the seam allowance and between the half and quarter markers on the body of the pouffe, stopping and starting at each pin. This will help you to ease in any excess fabric when you come to assemble the pouffe.

Inserting the zip

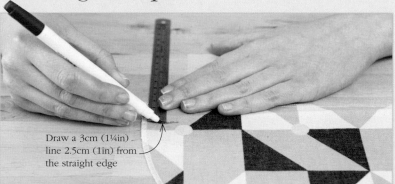

Draw a 3cm (1¼in) line 2.5cm (1in) from the straight edge

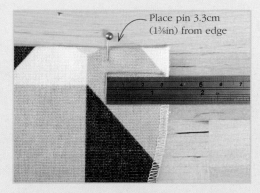

Place pin 3.3cm (1⅜in) from edge

1 With the smaller base piece face down, turn back then press the 1.5cm (⅝in) seam allowance. Turn the piece face up and unfold the seam allowance. Using a fabric pen, draw a 3cm (1¼in) line parallel to the foldline and 2.5cm (1in) from the straight edge. Repeat at the other end of the foldline. This is where the two base pieces will be stitched together.

2 Re-fold the 1.5cm (⅝in) seam allowance. Mark with a pin on both ends of the foldline at 3.3cm (1⅜in). This is where the zip will go.

3 With the larger base piece face down, turn back then press the 2.5cm (1in) seam allowance. Unfold the seam allowance and on the wrong side of the fabric, draw a 3cm (1¼in) line along the foldline from one end. Repeat at the other end of the foldline. Where the lines end, mark the right side of the fabric with dots.

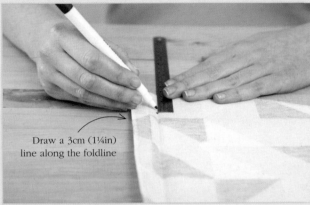

Draw a 3cm (1¼in) line along the foldline

4 Place the smaller base piece face up. With the zip face down and open, place one side of the zip between the marks made in Step 2. Pin in place with the teeth just overhanging the foldline. Using a zip foot and adjusting the needle so it is as close to the teeth of the zip as possible, stitch the zip in place.

Pin in place

3cm (1¼in) line

5 With the smaller base piece right side up, close the zip and place the larger piece on top, right side down. Align the dot on the larger piece with the line on the smaller piece. Unfold the seam allowance of the larger piece and pin together along the line.

Align the dot and the line

Tack the zip
in place with
contrasting thread

Machine along
the marked lines

6 Machine along the foldlines to join the two base pieces at either end of the zip. Press the seam open.

7 Open the joined base piece flat and lay it wrong side up. Match the second side of the zip to the neatened straight edge of the larger base piece. Tack the zip in place through all the layers.

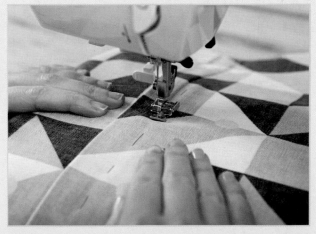

8 Working from the right side and using stitch length 3, stitch the zip in place. Starting at the closed end of the zip and backstitching to secure the thread, machine across the short end of the zip until the foot has cleared the teeth. Leave the needle down, lift the foot, and pivot to sew along the tacked side of the zip.

9 Sew along the length of the zip, keeping the edge of the foot along the edge of the teeth. Stop at the end of the zip, then pivot again and stitch along the other short end. Backstitch to secure.

Attaching the piping

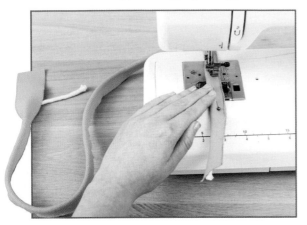

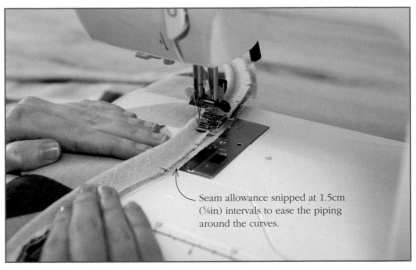

Seam allowance snipped at 1.5cm
(⅝in) intervals to ease the piping
around the curves.

1 Make two lengths of piping (see pp.40–41) from the contrast fabric, at least 4cm (1⅝in) longer than the circumference of the pouffe. Leave 10cm (4in) of each end unstitched. Snip the seam allowance at 1.5cm (⅝in) intervals to ease the piping around the curves.

2 With right sides together, align the raw edge of the piping with the edge of the top of the pouffe. Using a zip foot, stitch as close to the piping cord as possible. Leave 10cm (4in) unstitched at the start and finish.

✂ TRADE **SECRET**

3 To join the ends of the piping, place the pouffe top right side up, with the unstitched ends of the piping lying on top of each other. Measure and mark the casing to give an overlap of 4cm (1½in). Snip off the excess casing.

4 Open out each end of the piping casing and hold the ends with the wrong side of each facing you. Leaving the left-hand end where it is, twist the right-hand end away from you so the right side of the casing is now facing you.

5 Holding the ends in this position, overlap them, left over right, so that the short end of the left-hand piece lines up with the long edge of the right-hand piece, and the corners match up. Pin from top to bottom, as shown.

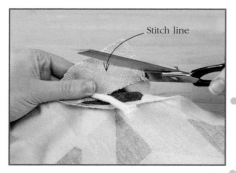

Stitch line

6 Machine stitch the two ends together across the pins. Remove the pins and trim the raw edges of the seam to 1cm (½in).

7 With the casing opened out, overlap the ends of the piping cord and cut them level. Avoid cutting directly on top of the seam in the casing as it leads to too much bulk.

8 Tuck the ends of the cord inside the casing, then bring the raw edges of the casing together and machine stitch them closed. Repeat to attach piping to the bottom of the pouffe.

Assembling the pouffe

✂ TRADE **SECRET**

Match pins to notches

1 With right sides together, match the notches in the top of the pouffe to the pins at the half and quarter points of the body. Pin at these four points first, then gently pull the ease stitches to ease the body to match the curve of the top of the pouffe.

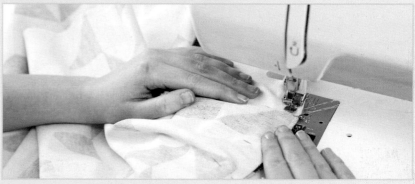

2 Pin in place then stitch along the seam allowance, as close to the piping cord as possible. Fold the bottom of the pouffe in half, then in half again and mark the half and quarter points with pins. Open the zip. Repeat Steps 1 and 2 to attach the bottom piece to the body.

3 Turn the pouffe cover to the right side.

4 Either fill with a stack of round cushion pads or make a calico lining consisting of two top pieces and one body piece. Fill the lining with feathers, polystyrene beads, or polyfibre cushion filling, and slipstitch closed.

JUST FOR KIDS

Making soft furnishings
FOR KIDS

Creating a space for kids can sometimes be a challenge. At times it can feel that there is no common ground between looking cartoonish and too adult, but by choosing the right colours and fabrics, and by adding touches of fun and whimsy, you can make a space that both you and your child will love.

Adapting soft furnishings for kids

• Nearly all of the projects in this book can be made child-friendly simply by choosing an appropriate fabric and by altering the size of the item if necessary.

• Be bold! When choosing fabrics for children, you can opt for bright accent colours and loud prints that you might not pick for yourself. These don't always need to be juvenile though: a bold, bright stripe can be just enough sometimes.

• Choose child-friendly fabrics. Think about whether stains will show, and how the fabric will wash and wear. It is a good idea to pick heavy, machine-washable, fabrics – and remember that a busy pattern will hide stains better than a simple one.

• Involve your child in the design choices, if possible. Letting her pick the fabric for a project can make it that little bit more special. She may not like the same patterns or colours that you like, but involving her could make all the difference between an item being beloved or rejected.

• When making blinds, curtains, or bed coverings, choose naturally flame-retardant fabrics, such as those made from natural fibres. Position soft furnishings away from radiators and other sources of heat, such as lights.

Fun with pattern

Layer fabrics in co-ordinating colours, a variety of patterns, and with differently scaled prints for a sophisticated bedroom that your child won't tire of overnight.

A headboard slipcover can easily be removed for washing

A bedspread in a large-scale, colourful print packs a punch

Add some comfy places to curl up with a book or toy

Cushions in fun prints can liven up a bed and easily be swapped for others as your child grows

A place of their own

Your child's bedroom is the one place that's their very own. Be sure to include some special spots where your child can curl up, hide away, and just be himself.

Bean **BAG**

Sassy stripes give a modern twist to a comfortable, squashy bean bag that is just as at home in the living room as in a child's bedroom. Thanks to its neat, sturdy handle, you can easily carry it to wherever you happen to need some extra seating. As a bonus, the zipped cover can easily be removed for cleaning.

 YOU **WILL NEED**

Materials

- *3m (120in) light- or medium-weight furnishing fabric*
- *3m (120in) calico for lining bag*
- *2 x 450g (1lb) bags of polystyrene fire-retardant beads for filling*
- *Matching thread*

Tools

- *Paper or calico for pattern* • *Photocopier* • *Pencil*
- *Fabric marker* • *Pins* • *Scissors* • *Sewing machine*
- *Zip foot* • *Large piece of card to use as a funnel*

Bean bag construction

The bean bag is made up of five equally-sized sections. The handle is attached to a five-sided panel stitched to the top.

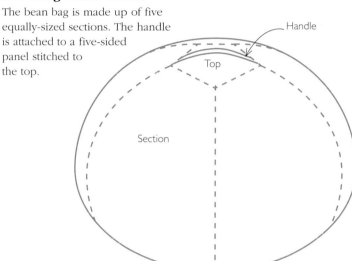

Making the pattern pieces

Turn to pp.298–299 for the templates for the bean bag pieces. Photocopy or trace the template for the top and cut it out. Enlarge the bean bag section on the photocopier. Cut out the enlarged pieces and tape them together. You may choose to trace around the taped piece onto calico or pattern paper to make a more versatile pattern piece. Don't forget to transfer any dots or notches to your pattern piece.

Top
Cut 1

Bean bag section
Cut 5

Preparing the bean bag sections

Lay the pattern on your main fabric to make the most of the fabric's design. Here we align the point of the pattern with the middle of a stripe. Pin then cut out. Repeat to make five bean bag sections, then repeat to make five lining pieces.

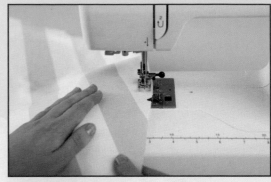

2 Transfer the notch and dot markings from the template to each bean bag section.

3 Stay stitch (see p.19) 1cm (⅜in) from the edge between the first and last notches on each fabric piece to prevent the fabric from stretching along the curve. Neaten the edges (see p.19).

Making the handle

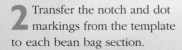

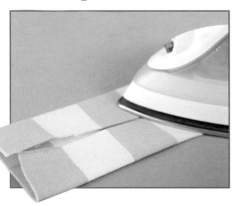

1 Cut out a rectangle 31cm (12⅜in) long and 16cm (6⅜in) wide for the handle. Fold in half lengthways, wrong sides facing, then press. Open it out, then fold the raw edges into the centre fold and press again.

2 Refold along the centre line, matching the folded edges. Secure with pins.

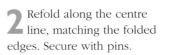

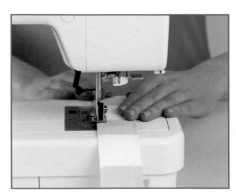

3 Using stitch length 3, topstitch (see p.18) along each long side of the strip, as close to the edge as possible. Press again to set the stitches.

4 Pin the pentagon-shaped template for the top to another piece of fabric and cut it out.

5 Fold then press a 1cm (⅜in) seam allowance to the wrong side all the way around. Tack (see p.20) in place.

Inserting the zip

1 Lay one bean bag section right side up. Centre the zip in the middle of one curved side. Mark the fabric at the beginning and end of the zip.

2 Lay another section on top, right sides together and matching the notches. Transfer the zip markings to the right side of the second section. Fold under then press a 1.5cm (⅝in) seam allowance between the notches.

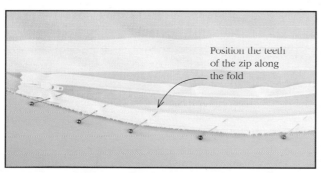

Position the teeth of the zip along the fold

3 With the fabric right side up and the zip face down and open, place one side of the zip along the edge, between the zip markings, with the teeth aligned with the fold. Fold back and pin the excess zip tape, then pin and stitch the zip in place using a zip foot. Stitch as close to the teeth of the zip as possible.

4 Lay the zipped section on top of the other section, right sides together. Align the teeth of the unattached side of the zip with the fold in the second section. Fold back and pin the excess zip tape, then pin and stitch the zip in place as before.

5 With the zip open, lay the two sections, right sides together with notches matching. Pin together along the seam allowance, starting from the marked dot and finishing at the zip. Repeat at the other end of the zip.

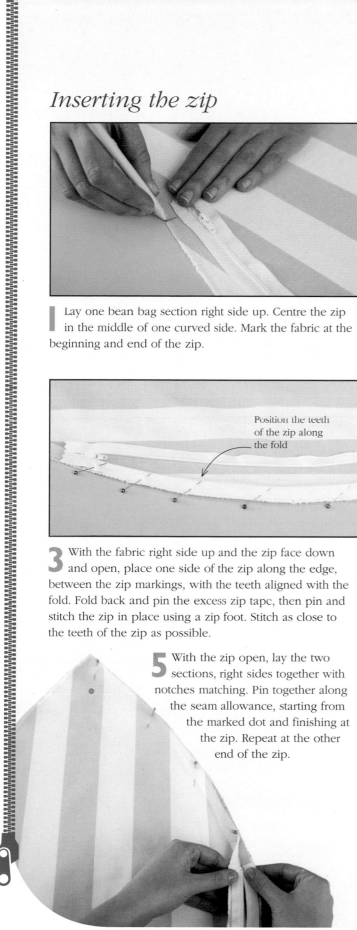

6 Stitch along each pinned edge with a 1.5cm (⅝in) seam allowance, starting at the dot at each end. When you reach the end of the zip, pull the end of the zip towards the seam allowance, then sew as close as possible to the end of the zip. Press the seam allowance open.

Joining the sections

1 With right sides together and notches matching, lay the edge of a third section along the free edge of the second section. Pin at the notches then along the whole edge.

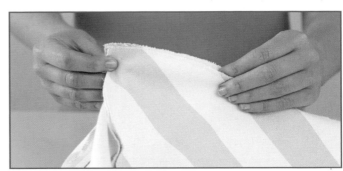

2 Check that the sections are aligned at the top and bottom. Pin and stitch, starting and ending at the dots. Ensure that you are only stitching through two sections at a time and that any other fabric is held out of the way. Continue joining the sections in the same way, until you have joined all five.

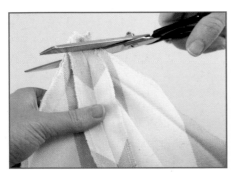

3 Trim off the seam allowances at the point to reduce bulk, but make sure you do not cut through your stitches.

5 Turn the bean bag to the right side and lay it out so that the point where all five sections meet is lying as flat as possible. This can be tricky as you are trying to lay a spherical shape flat. Place the pentagon on top, right side up and matching its points to the five seams. Pin at each point.

4 Fold the ends of the handle under then pin and tack the ends to the right side of the fabric pentagon, as shown. Leave some slack in the handle so there is room to hold it.

6 Pin the pentagon to the bean bag along all five sides, easing the fabric of the bean bag so it fits between the five pinned points.

7 Using a number 3 stitch, topstitch the pentagon in place, as close to the edges as possible and pivoting at the points. Ensure that the fabric does not bunch up underneath the needle, and that the seam allowances on the wrong side of the bean bag lie flat.

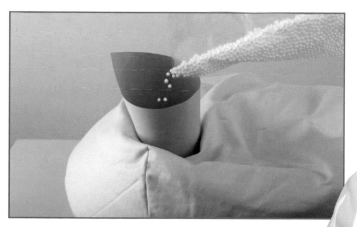

8 Make a lining bag using the lining pieces and joining them as in steps 1–3. When you join the last section to the previous one, leave a gap between the 2nd and 4th notches. Make a wide funnel from a piece of stiff paper or card, insert it in the gap and use it to fill the bag with polystyrene beads.

9 Topstitch the opening closed. Place the filled lining bag inside the bean bag cover and close the zip.

Teepee **TENT**

It's Wild West time in the playroom thanks to this unique, home-crafted teepee. It even boasts a window for watching out for baddies. Make one of these in a few hours and let your child's imagination do the rest.

Making the pattern piece

To make the most of your fabric, plan your panels so that the maximum width of each panel is half the width of the fabric. Start by drawing a line 140cm (56in) long in the centre of a piece of pattern paper. Measure and mark 9.5cm (3¾in) either side at the top of this line. Draw a line to join these two points.

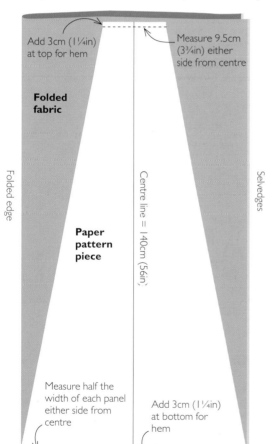

Add 3cm (1¼in) at top for hem

Measure 9.5cm (3¾in) either side from centre

Folded fabric

Folded edge

Centre line = 140cm (56in)

Selvedges

Paper pattern piece

Measure half the width of each panel either side from centre

Add 3cm (1¼in) at bottom for hem

At the bottom of the centre line, measure and mark either side of the line half the maximum width of each panel. Draw a line to join these two points. Using a long stick, join the ends of the line at the top to the ends of the line at the bottom. Measure and mark an extra 3cm (1¼in) top and bottom for the hems. Cut out the pattern piece.

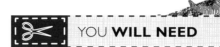
Cutting out

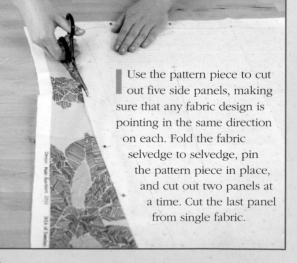

Use the pattern piece to cut out five side panels, making sure that any fabric design is pointing in the same direction on each. Fold the fabric selvedge to selvedge, pin the pattern piece in place, and cut out two panels at a time. Cut the last panel from single fabric.

2 To make the doors, fold the pattern piece in half lengthwise and fold the fabric in half lengthwise as before. Place the folded pattern piece on top and pin in place. Make several marks 3cm (1¼in) from the folded edge of the pattern piece. Join the marks with a line. Cut along this line through both layers of fabric.

3 Cut a notch in both layers of fabric 35cm (14in) from the top of the pattern piece along the edge you have just cut. This is where the two doors will meet. Cut around the rest of the pattern piece through both layers of fabric to cut out two doors.

Assembling the doors

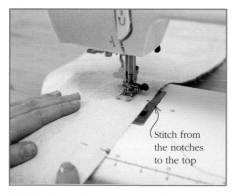

Stitch from the notches to the top

1 With right sides together, pin then stitch the doors from the notches to the top with a 3cm (1¼in) seam allowance.

Then fold under to create a 1.5cm (⅝in) double hem

First press back a 3cm (1¼in) hem

2 With the doors face down, press the seam open then press back a 3cm (1¼in) hem along each edge. Fold each hem under to create a 1.5cm (⅝in) double hem.

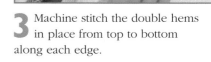

3 Machine stitch the double hems in place from top to bottom along each edge.

Making the ties

1 Cut two strips the full width of the fabric and 6cm (2½in) wide for the ties. Press in half lengthways, wrong sides facing. Open them out, then press the raw edges into the centre fold and press again.

Press the raw edges into the centre fold

2 Refold along the centre line, matching the folded edges. Secure with pins, then machine stitch as close to the open edge as possible. Cut each strip in half to make four ties.

3 Lay the doors right side up on the table. Fold under the raw edge of a tie and position it about one-third down one of the doors. Secure with pins, ensuring that the tie goes in the direction of the other door. Pin a second tie about two-thirds down the door in the same way.

Topstitch around the ends of the ties

4 Pin the remaining two ties to the other door, making sure they line up with the first two ties. Topstitch (see p.18) each tie in place, stitching through the two layers of the tie and the edge of the teepee door (inset).

Making the window

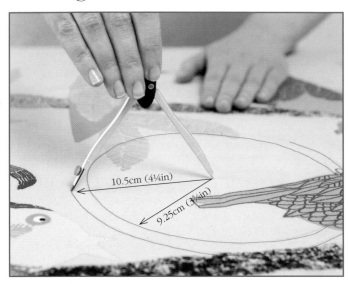

I Choose one panel as the back of the teepee and place it right side up. Decide on the position of the window. Set the compasses to 9.25cm (3⅝in), place its point at what will be the centre of the window, and draw a circle for the cutting line. Reset the compasses to 10.5cm (4¼in) and draw a second circle using the same centre point.

2 Stay stitch (see p.19) around the outer circle to help keep the circle in shape.

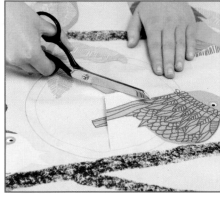

3 Make a snip into the middle of the circle, then cut four or five times from this point to the cutting line.

4 Cut out each section along the cutting line to make a hole in the centre. Then snip at regular intervals from the cutting line to the line of stay stitches, but make sure you do not cut through the stay stitches.

Snip from cutting line to stay stitches

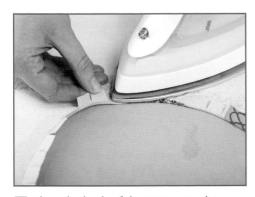

5 Place the back of the teepee on the ironing board, right side down. Pull back the snipped seam allowance until you can see the line of stay stitches. Press the snipped fabric, making sure to pull the stay stitching to the wrong side, otherwise it will be visible from the front of the tent.

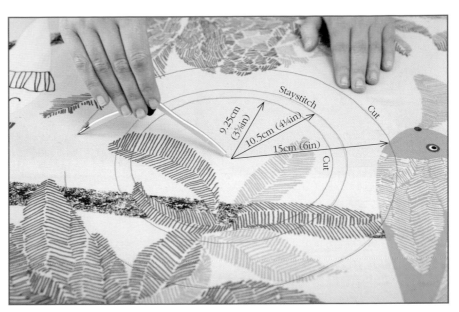

6 For the facing for the window opening, lay a piece of fabric right side up. Set the compasses to 9.25cm (3⅝in) and draw a circle as before. This is the inner cutting line. Using the same centre point, reset the compasses to 10.5cm (4¼in) and draw a second circle for the stay stitch line using the same centre point. Now reset the compasses to 15cm (6in) and draw a third circle for the outer cutting line.

7 Stitch around the stay-stitch line as before, then cut out the middle of the circle along the cutting line as before. Snip at intervals to the stay-stitch line as before, then press the snipped seam allowance to the wrong side. Cut out the facing along the outer cutting line. Neaten the outer edge (see p.19).

Cut facing out along outer cutting line

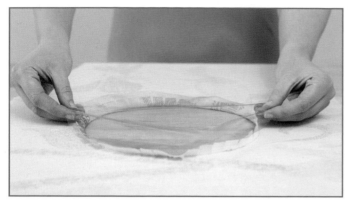

8 Cut a circle of clear plastic table covering for the window using the facing as a template. Lay the back of the teepee right side down, then place the circle of plastic over the hole for the window.

9 Lay the facing right side up on the plastic, matching the facing's pressed edge to the window opening. Take care to keep the plastic still. Pin in place, ensuring that the pressed edge of the facing stays just outside the plastic and doesn't show through on the right side.

10 With the teepee right side up, increase your stitch length to 3 and topstitch the facing and plastic in place around the window as close to the edge as possible.

11 On the wrong side, the facing will now be in place, holding the plastic window in position.

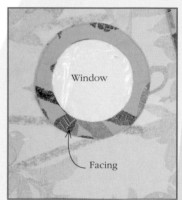

Window

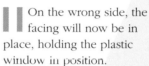

Facing

Assembling the teepee

1 With right sides together, pin a side panel to each edge of the back piece (this is the window piece). Machine stitch in place with a 1.5cm (⅝in) seam allowance. Add the two remaining side panels, one on each side. You should now have a back piece with two side panels on either side. Press the seams open as you go.

Pin the panels together along the sides

The bottom edges of all panels should line up

2 Attach the doors in the same way to each of the outer side panels to complete the circle.

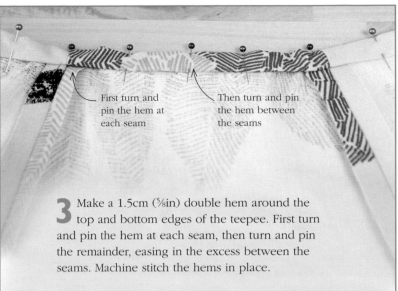

First turn and pin the hem at each seam

Then turn and pin the hem between the seams

3 Make a 1.5cm (⅝in) double hem around the top and bottom edges of the teepee. First turn and pin the hem at each seam, then turn and pin the remainder, easing in the excess between the seams. Machine stitch the hems in place.

Hemmed bottom edge

Side seamline

4 To create the channels for the dowels, bring two adjacent panels together wrong sides facing. Bring the seamline right to the edge, then pin the two layers of fabric together to hold them in place.

5 Stitch 3.5cm (1⅜in) from the seamline, working from the top to the bottom, to create a channel.

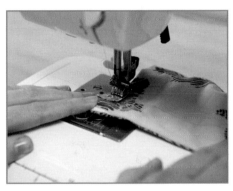

6 At the bottom of the channel, leave the needle in the fabric, raise the presser foot, and pivot the fabric. Sew the bottom edge of the channel closed. Repeat to make a total of six channels.

7 Insert a dowel through the top of each channel. Spread out the dowels to stand the teepee up.

Spread out the dowels at the top

Hanging play TENT

A bunting-trimmed play tent suspended from the ceiling makes the most wonderful fairytale hideaway for a child's room. Created in just a few hours, and with the simplest materials, this tent is sure to become a family favourite.

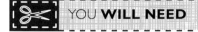

YOU **WILL NEED**

Materials

- 9m (10 yards) lightweight cotton fabric for the tent
- Embroidery hoop or hula hoop (we used an embroidery hoop with a 47cm (18¾in) diameter)
- 150cm (60in) ribbon
- Matching thread
- White thread
- 1m (40in) fabric for the bunting
- 1.5m (60in) Velcro fastening tape

Tools

- Pencil • Ruler • String
- Masking tape (optional) • Scissors
- Pins • Sewing machine • Iron
- Ceiling hook

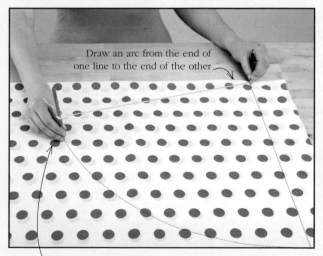

Hoop diameter

Tent top
To calculate the size of the tent top, measure the diameter of the hoop and add a 1.5cm (⅝in) seam allowance.

Selvedge

Tent top

Cutting the pieces
Once you have cut out the tent top, divide the rest of the fabric in three, giving you three panels for the tent body.

Selvedge

Making the tent top

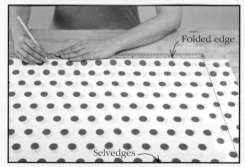

Folded edge

Selvedges

Draw an arc from the end of one line to the end of the other

Keep the string taut and the pencil upright

1 Fold the fabric in half selvedge to selvedge, right sides together. Add a 1.5cm (⅝in) seam allowance to the diameter of the hoop. Draw a line this length from the folded edge towards the selvedges. Draw a second line the same length along the folded edge from one end of the first line.

2 Use a pencil tied to a piece of string the length of the line. Pin the string to the point where the lines meet. Hold the pencil upright and draw an arc from the end of one line to the end of the other. Keep the string taut. It may help to tape the fabric to the work surface with masking tape to stop it slipping.

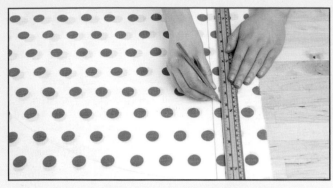

3 Measure and mark a 1.5cm (⅝in) seam allowance along the first line. Cut through both layers of fabric to cut out the tent top.

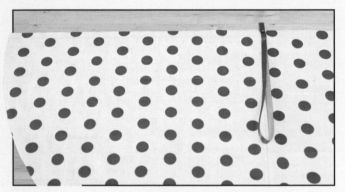

4 Open out the semicircular tent top, right side up. Cut a 50cm (20in) length of ribbon and fold it in half. Place the raw edges of the ribbon at the centre point, as shown. Pin in place.

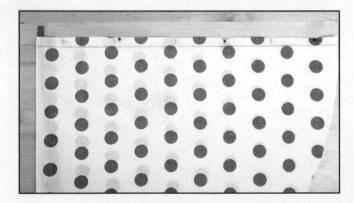

5 Fold the tent top right sides together with the ribbon tucked inside. Pin along the open straight edge. Sew along the edge, starting at the ribbon, stitching over it, and backstitching a few times at the start to ensure the ribbon is stitched firmly in place. Press the seam open.

Making the tent body

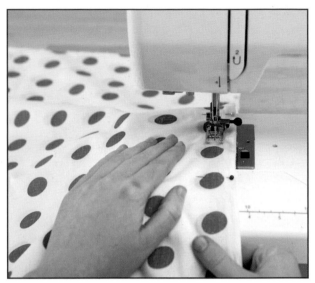

I Cut the remaining fabric into three equal full-width pieces for the tent body. Place two pieces selvedge to selvedge and right sides together. Pin and stitch with a 1.5cm (⅝in) seam allowance. Press the seam open. Attach the third piece to the other two in the same way. You now have three joined pieces with a selvedge on both long edges.

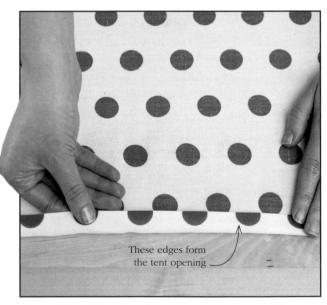

These edges form the tent opening

2 With the fabric face down, turn over a 1.5cm (⅝in) double hem along the two selvedges. Pin, then machine in place as close to the edge as possible. Press to set the stitches. These edges form the tent opening.

Fold the corner diagonally

3 With the fabric face down, turn over a 3cm (1¼in) double hem all the way along the bottom of the three pieces. At each end, mitre the corner by folding it diagonally. Pin and stitch in place. Press to set the stitches.

Turn over 1.5cm (⅝in)

Turn over another 1.5cm (⅝in) to make a double hem

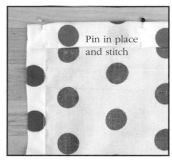

Pin in place and stitch

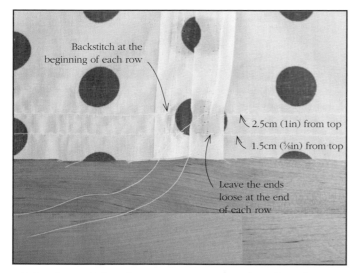

Backstitch at the beginning of each row

2.5cm (1in) from top

1.5cm (⅝in) from top

Leave the ends loose at the end of each row

4 Set the stitch length to its maximum length and machine two rows of gather stitches along the top of each panel, stopping and starting at each seam. Stitch the first row 1.5cm (⅝in) from the top and the second 2.5cm (1in) from the top. Backstitch at the beginning of each row but not at the end.

5 Now you will need to gather the fabric. To do this, hold the pair of loose threads at the end of the row in one hand. With the other hand, push the fabric away from you.

6 Gather the top of each panel so that the fabric fits around the hoop to give an overlap at the front of the tent. Start by multiplying the diameter of the hoop by π (3.14) to give the circumference. Add 10cm (4in) to this measurement, then divide this by three (the number of panels). You can round up or round down slightly if required. Following the instructions in Step 5, gather the top of each panel evenly until it fits this measurement.

7 Secure the ends of the gather stitches on each panel by wrapping them around a pin in a figure of eight.

TRADE SECRET

8 Cut a length of looped Velcro tape to match the hoop's circumference. Place the gathered fabric under the machine foot, right side up. Lay the Velcro tape on top, aligning its top edge with the upper row of gather stitches, as shown here. Stitch the Velcro tape in place along its top edge, ensuring that the gathers remain even and keeping them at a right angle to your stitches. Stitch along the bottom edge of the Velcro tape, starting from the same end as before.

9 Cut five lengths of ribbon 30cm (12in) long and mark the middle of each. Lay the gathered tent body face down. Space the ribbons out evenly along the gathered edge and pin in place through the middle of each ribbon. Hand or machine stitch in place.

Joining top and bottom

1 Stay stitch (see p.19) around the bottom edge of the tent top. With wrong sides together, lay the tent top flat with the seam to one side. Mark the side opposite the seam with a pin. This is the centre front of the tent.

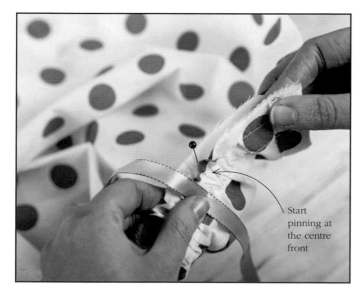

Start pinning at the centre front

2 With right sides together, pin the body of the tent to the top. Starting at the centre front of the top, pin the body so it overlaps the centre front by 5cm (2in).

3 Pin all around until you reach the beginning. The front edges of the body will overlap each other.

4 Machine the body to the top, holding the ribbons out of the way of the needle.

Making the bunting

Mark lines at top
and bottom

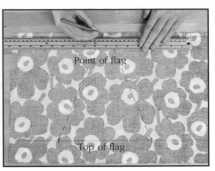

Point of flag

Top of flag

1 Cut two strips of bunting fabric, each 30cm (12in) deep and long enough to fit the circumference of the hoop. If necessary, make each strip from two pieces joined right side to right side along the short edge. Place the two long strips right sides together. Draw a line 1cm (⅜in) from the bottom edge and a second line 5cm (2in) from the top edge.

2 An ideal width for what will be the top of a flag is 20cm (8in). Calculate how many times this will fit around your hoop. Adjust the width until it divides into the circumference of the hoop evenly. Mark the width of the first flag along the line. Mark the same amount for the next flag and so on until you reach the end.

3 Mark the points of the flags on the bottom line. Starting at the bottom left-hand edge, mark 10cm (4in) along the line, then a further 20cm (8in), followed by 20cm (8in) each time until you reach the end.

5 Measure and mark a 1.5cm (⅝in) seam allowance along the outer edges of each flag, as shown.

4 To mark the outlines of the flags, start at the left-hand edge and join the end of the top line with the first mark on the bottom line. Continue joining marks diagonally. Then join them in the other direction.

6 Pin or tack both layers together. Cut out through both layers around the seam allowances, removing the excess fabric as you go.

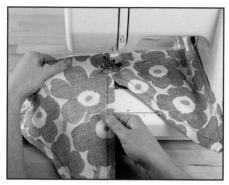

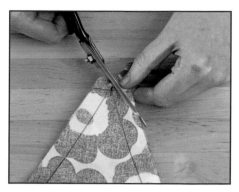

7 Sew along the seam allowance lines in one continuous seam, pivoting at the corners.

8 Snip between the flags close to the seam allowance but make sure you do not cut through your stitches.

9 Trim off the seam allowance around the points of the flags as close as possible to the stitching.

10 Turn the flags to the right side one by one, pushing the points of the flags out using a pointed but blunt tool such as a pencil.

11 Lay the bunting flat on the table, finger-pressing the seams to the sides. Check that the joins between the flags lie flat, clipping into the seam allowances a little more if necessary. Press the bunting.

12 Fold over 1cm (⅜in) at the top of the band.

13 Lay a length of hooked Velcro tape, right side up, on the folded band. Pin then stitch the Velcro tape along its top edge, then along the bottom edge, starting from the same end as before.

14 Tie the hoop inside the tent using the ribbons around the body. Attach the bunting to the outside using the Velcro tape. Hang the tent up from a ceiling hook.

Use white top thread and bottom thread to match fabric

PUTTING IT
ALL TOGETHER

DEFINE *your style*

Is your home a true reflection of your taste? Is it filled with things you've carefully chosen over the years or have you yet to work out what works and what doesn't? Or maybe you've just bought your first home and simply don't know where to start? Follow our guide to discovering – and perfecting – a look that's right for your home, and you.

2 Look for inspiration

Finding inspiring photos is a great place to start when defining your own personal style. Look through magazines and pull out photos that you like – whether it's just one item or the entire room – then lay them out on the floor or tack them to the wall and look for consistencies in terms of the styling, colours, patterns, or materials used.

What's your property's style?

When choosing a style for your home's interior, take a moment to think about whether it will fit the architecture, proportions, and period of the property. Is your home modern with clean lines or a period property with historical features?

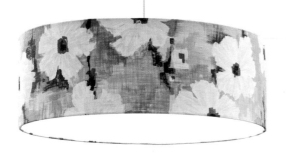

4 Make a scrapbook

Make an online scrapbook of looks you like, taking photos of friends' rooms or simply of ideas you see when out and about. Again, look for consistencies in colour and style that will help you understand what appeals to you and why. Is it the colour, shape, or material? Be prepared to upcycle, recycle, sell, or give away items you don't like to clear the way for future purchases.

Try mixing two or three styles you like to create a more personal look.

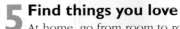

5 Find things you love

At home, go from room to room and make a list of the things that you love and the things you'd like to change. As before, consider what you like about these items – colour, shape, or perhaps material?

3 Create an individual look

You may find you're attracted to more than one look. This is fine – part of defining your own style is to try not to stick to a theme. If you realize that you can mix and match different styles to make them work, you will end up with a more individual look that's personal to you.

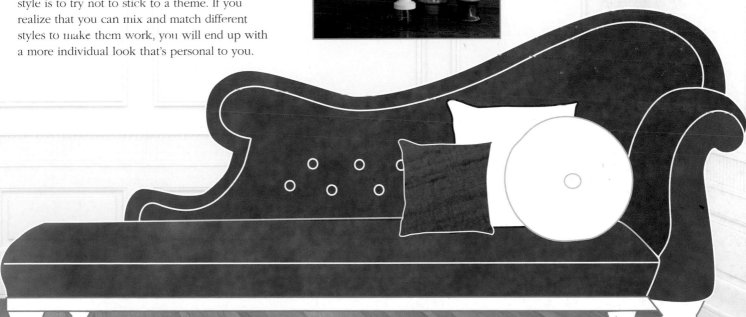

PLANNING *your space*

When it comes to planning your space, the size and shape of your room is always the first consideration. However, you also need to think about how you want to use the room and whether it will work from a practical point of view – there's no point in making a style statement if you can't watch the TV or eat comfortably.

Daylight matters

Consider how light changes during the day and how it falls in different areas of the room. While a spot that gets the sun in the afternoon might be perfect for reading or afternoon napping, it won't be practical for working or watching TV. Televisions and computers should be placed away from windows and sunlight to avoid poor visibility.

2 Zone the room

Consider separating a large room into several areas for reading, conversation, and dining. This can be accomplished with colour, distinct furniture groupings, and area rugs.

3 Create focal points

Each room should have an interesting place for the eye to settle on – this could be a fireplace, a large piece of furniture (a beautiful sofa, for example), or maybe a large painting. Once you've identified your focal point, place your furniture to draw attention to it.

4 Where to work

Think about where setting up a work zone will create the least disruption. A kitchen or dining room table, or a desk in an alcove or corner of a living room or bedroom would all work well.

Dual-purpose furniture is perfect when you have only a small, shared space for work and play.

An out-of-the-way radiator improves the floor plan

6 Rework to make it work

If a large radiator or even a second entry door is preventing your preferred layout, think about making a change. Consider having a radiator moved to a different part of the room or closing off a door that's not used.

5 Hide the clutter

Family living rooms or dining rooms that double as play areas for children require plenty of storage for toys and games. Consider pretty storage baskets or a sideboard or chest of drawers that won't look out of place, but will provide plenty of stashing space.

Baskets slot into a cube storage system.

7 Find versatile pieces

What kind of furniture will allow you to fit in everything you need? A small space may require furniture with storage and versatility, such as a media cabinet with shelves, a hall bench with baskets, or an ottoman at the foot of a bed.

Using **COLOUR** *and pattern*

Using colour and pattern is a great way to add style and personality to a room, but, it's not as easy to get right as you might think. Follow our expert tricks below, though, and you'll get a successful scheme effortlessly.

Watch your rooms come alive when you introduce colour and pattern.

2 Keep a colour scrapbook Keep a record of colours and colour combinations you like, as well as swatches of fabric or wallpapers that catch your eye. Then, when you want to add character to a room, you can use those as inspiration.

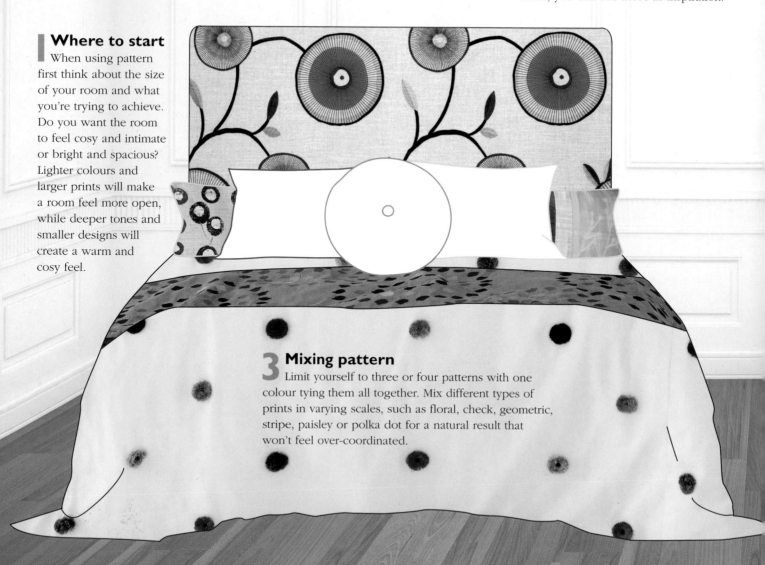

Where to start
When using pattern first think about the size of your room and what you're trying to achieve. Do you want the room to feel cosy and intimate or bright and spacious? Lighter colours and larger prints will make a room feel more open, while deeper tones and smaller designs will create a warm and cosy feel.

3 Mixing pattern
Limit yourself to three or four patterns with one colour tying them all together. Mix different types of prints in varying scales, such as floral, check, geometric, stripe, paisley or polka dot for a natural result that won't feel over-coordinated.

Ribbon
ties

4 Working together
Keep adjacent rooms in mind when decorating, and think about how the colours and patterns you are using will work together. They don't need to match – but they should harmonize or coordinate with other rooms – and shouldn't clash.

5 Choosing a wall colour
The main wall colour will set the tone for the whole room, so if you're choosing paint, get exactly the right shade – a tone lighter or darker can make a difference. Buy samples of colours, paint large pieces of paper, and tack them onto the walls you're planning to paint. Then, see how the colour looks in different lights.

6 Add pattern in fabrics
Cushions and even a rug are a great way to add instant colour and pattern, and a patterned blind or curtains in an otherwise plain room will make your scheme pop. Block colours create a lively contrast.

Choosing FURNITURE

The furniture you choose needs to be comfortable and functional, as well as reflect your taste and the style of your home. Since it is a major investment, before you buy, think about what will fit into your space, what you need, and how much you want to spend.

Where to start?
Work out exactly what you need first. Make a list detailing the seating, surfaces, and storage that will make the room practical for you and the way you live.

Measure several times to ensure furniture will fit.

Pendant lighting accents an area such as a dining table.

2 Choose materials carefully
Dark wood can make a small room feel crowded and more formal. Furniture made of glass and pale-coloured wood will give a room a feeling of space, and a lighter, airier look.

Straight back chairs look lighter, so are ideal for a small room.

60cm

3 Leave space
When planning the placement of furniture, keep in mind how people will move around in the room, leaving at least 75cm (30in) to 1m (40in) for pathways. Behind dining and desk chairs, leave a minimum of 60cm (24in) so that people can comfortably pull the seats back to sit down.

Cover dining chairs to harmonize with the room.

4 Will it fit?
Laying out newspaper the actual size of the piece of furniture will help you to see how it works in the room's layout and how it will affect the way you use the room. Ensure you leave enough space for people to walk around, and bear in mind that the furniture's height will have an impact, too.

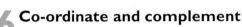

5 Easy care?

When choosing sofas and armchairs think about how the room will be used and the amount of maintenance needed. Feather and down cushions on seating are soft, but will need plumping regularly, while foam-filled cushions tend to look smarter. Check if seat cushions move forwards when you're sitting on them.

Furniture should be welcoming and fit comfortably into the available space.

6 Co-ordinate and complement

Pieces of furniture needn't match or be part of a suite, but they should work together. Look for items that create a harmonious blend of textures, colours and styles.

7 Short on space?

Look for flexible furniture that serves more than one function: a basic table can be used for both eating and working, sofa beds fulfil a double purpose, and stools function as side tables as well as additional seating.

8 Scan your home for swaps

Furniture from elsewhere in the house may work well in another room. Equally, items that have traditionally been in a certain room don't necessarily need to stay there.

9 Be restrained

Overcrowding a room with too much furniture will make it feel small and cluttered. If your needs outstrip the room's size, look for lower, light coloured furniture that will be less bulky visually..

CREATING
lighting effects

You can both update a room and improve how it feels with good lighting. To get the best from a space, this will mean investing in a combination of different lighting types. Ambient lighting – usually overhead – provides general illumination, accent lighting is used to highlight special features, and task lighting is for close-up work, such as reading.

1 Planning
When choosing your lighting, consider the rest of your decoration choices. Dark and textured finishes absorb light more than paler, glossier ones.

3 Highlight key features
Draw attention to key features in your room, such as a piece of artwork, beams, or architectural features like plasterwork or panelling, with uplighters or by positioning spotlights or wall lights nearby. The more effective the result, the higher the room's ceiling will feel.

Try a pendant instead of a table lamp

2 Location
Pendant lights don't have to be hung in the centre of a room. Position them in a corner to illuminate a reading area, over a kitchen island for practical task lighting, or either side of the bed as bedside lamps.

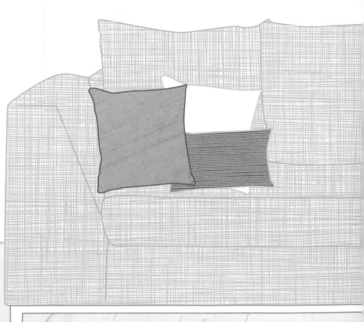

Mix patterns
and sizes

4 Group pendant lights

Hang a group of pendant lights together to create a dramatic statement. You can mix and match the shades, too. Darker colours will pool light more than paler tones.

5 Choosing bulbs

Make sure you choose a light that is going to be bright enough for your room, and that you are using the correct bulb. Nothing makes a room feel more unwelcoming and dated than bad lighting.

7 Choosing a shade

Measure the height and width of your lamp base – to appear balanced, the shade you choose should be a similar width to the height of the base, and its height should be approximately two-thirds of the height of the lamp base. The shade should also be wider than the widest part of the lamp base.

6 Install plug sockets

Plug sockets fitted in the floor allow floor and table lamps to be added centrally in a room without having to trail leads from wall sockets.

IDEAS *for small spaces*

Make the most of a small room by being clever with your furniture and decorating choices. Every bit of space can be used to your advantage. Here's how.

1 Be clever with colour
Painting walls in dark colours can make a room feel smaller, but used sparingly, such as on a door, you can still create a dramatic effect without it dominating the room.

Search for pieces that can multi-task, such as a table that can be used for dining and as a desk.

3 Reflect space
A mirrored wall is a great way to open up a small space. The reflective surface creates an optical illusion of doubling the size of the space. It also picks up and reflects light from various sources in the room, especially at night.

4 Create space
Two armchairs offer a more versatile seating option than a sofa in a small room because you can move them around to create space when needed. Add a footstool so that you can stretch out.

5 Use lighting cleverly
Place lights at different levels to highlight various areas or features in the room, making it look intimate and cosy, or open and spacious.

2 Choose folding furniture
A gate-leg table can be easily stowed away or moved into another room. Folding chairs can be stored in a cupboard or made a feature of by being hung on a wall when not in use.

6 Fit handy shelves

Shelves fitted in unused spaces, such as above your bed, window, or door frames, provide extra storage for books and knick-knacks, and are great for displaying pictures or mirrors, too.

8 Streamline your rooms

Swap bulky curtains for a more streamlined window dressing such as shutters or blinds. This is also a great way to add colour or pattern to a small room.

Light up dark corners

Use bold patterns as a feature

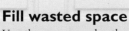

7 Fill wasted space

Use the space under the stairs to house a cloakroom, store coats and shoes, display a large object, or fill with shelves lined with storage boxes or baskets. Need a home office? It could fit here, too.

9 Use visual tricks

Wallpaper with vertical stripes or patterns can make a low-ceilinged room feel taller. Similarly, floor-to-ceiling cupboards make the most of space as well as giving the illusion of height. If you prefer plain walls, try floor-length curtains on poles set higher than the window to create a similar effect.

CREATING *light and airy spaces*

Rooms that don't receive much natural light can feel dark and unwelcoming. While you might not be able to change the size of the room you can transform it with these clever tricks to give it a light and airy feel.

Choose your wall colour

As a general rule, the closer to white the paint, the more reflective it will be. Light colours such as pale grey, yellow, and blue make a room look larger; while darker colours make a room look smaller.

2 Use mirrors to reflect light

Placing a mirror adjacent to a window will reflect light around the room. The taller the mirror, the more effective the result and the higher the room's ceiling will feel.

Capture more light with a well-placed mirror.

3 Avoid heavy, dark furniture

Instead, use pale wood, white painted, mirrored, perspex, or glass pieces that will reflect the light and appear to take up less space. Going for upholstered pieces? Choose light colours – just make sure the covers are easy to clean.

Light wood gives a spacious feeling.

4 Hang sheer curtains

Curtains can absorb light, so swap heavy curtains for light or sheers. Fit a blackout roller blind or shutters behind the curtains if you need to block out artificial light at night, or need privacy at any time.

5 Choose high-gloss flooring

Hardwood and laminate, tiled, resin, and concrete flooring with a high-gloss finish will bounce light upwards into a room, with lighter colours giving the best results.

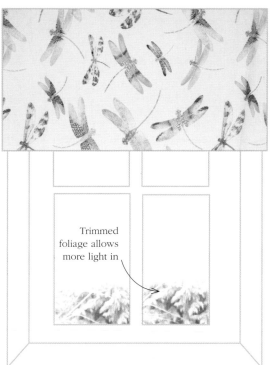

Trimmed foliage allows more light in

6 Outside matters

Trim trees or bushes outside windows that could be blocking light entering the room.

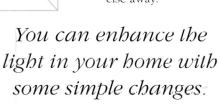

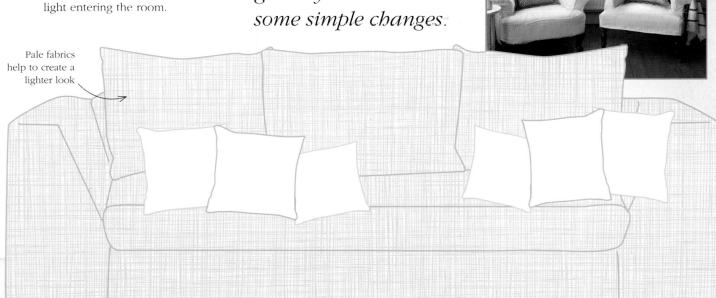

Pale fabrics help to create a lighter look

8 Swap the doors

Change solid interior doors for those with glazed panels. You could also consider putting a fanlight over a door.

Glass makes the most of natural light

7 De-clutter the space

Clutter absorbs light so keep surfaces as clear as possible. Only display what you really love, storing everything else away.

Keep sills free of clutter

You can enhance the light in your home with some simple changes.

9 Choose raised furniture

Dark, heavy furniture can absorb a lot of light. For a lighter feel, choose sofas and beds that have clear space underneath. If the floor is also a pale colour, the light will bounce around the space, adding to the light, airy appearance of the room.

CREATE *a room that grows with your child*

It's amazing how quickly your child's tastes and needs change as they grow, so when you're designing a bedroom for them, keep this in mind. Follow these tips that will take toddlers right through to their teens – with minimal redecorating and outlay on your part.

❙ Find versatile furniture

Don't buy furniture for toddlers – look for teen furniture you can adapt now to save yourself money in the future. For example, open shelving allows easy access for toddlers and, a few years down the line, will provide ample storage for study folders or DVDs.

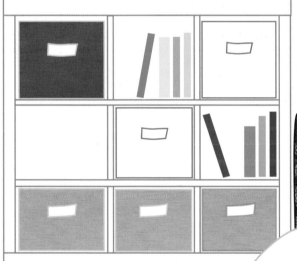

If your headboard slipcover is a strong colour, try neutral bedding accented with that colour.

2 Make a slipcover

Want to change the room's look every few years without buying a brand new bed? A headboard slipcover is a great way to completely change its look, turning it from cute to grown up quickly and cheaply.

3 Find furniture that grows

Look for furniture that grows with your child. A toddler bed that can turn into a single bed, for instance, or a wardrobe that has shelves (for baby clothes) and hanging space (for when their clothes are big enough to put on hangers).

4 Update the look with bedding

If you keep the backdrop (walls and floor) neutral, you can easily update the look of the room with new bedding.

5 Look for hidden storage

Small children's and teenagers' bedrooms need more than just open storage – there are things you'll want to hide away (such as past school work or clothes that don't fit yet). Look for storage space that's under-used. Beneath the bed is the most obvious place. A bed with built-in storage will be invaluable as they grow.

6 Seating for friends

Teenagers will want to use their bedroom to entertain friends. If space allows, provide beanbags or pouffes covered in washable fabrics. If space is tight, extra cushions and even a fitted loose cover can turn a single divan into a trendy daybed.

You can tailor your square storage baskets to fit neatly onto open shelves.

7 Invest in hard-wearing floors

Modern, man-made carpets are often chemically cleanable, so are the perfect choice for children's rooms. Rubber flooring is also a good choice and will allow you to be really creative with your colour choices. Or, throw a colourful but inexpensive rug over painted or varnished wooden floorboards for a look that can be updated regularly and affordably.

Tips *for* RENTERS

Finding non-permanent ways to update a rental property can be tricky. However, with a little imagination and a few decorating tricks you can make it feel like home.

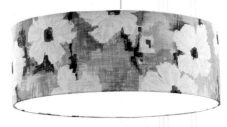

1 Get better lighting

Good lighting can transform a room, so if yours is dark and dingy, use floor and table lamps to highlight the room's nicest features and to create a warmer, welcoming atmosphere. You can then take them with you when you leave.

2 Swap the shade

Changing a boring or worn lampshade can give a pendant or table light a new lease of life. Can't find one you like? Make one yourself in a fabric of your choice.

3 Disguise a chair

A simple slipcover will hide an ugly armchair or dining chairs. Make them in a washable fabric or even from woollen blankets.

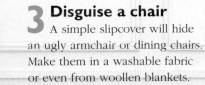

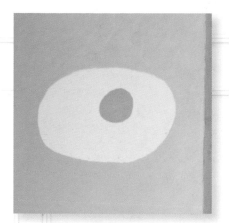

Got some spare fabric from your cushions? Why not frame it and hang it on the wall?

4 Hang some prints

Create a picture wall of photos and prints you love. Cover canvases or wooden frames with fabric that has a bold, artistic, or colourful print to add personality to an otherwise plain wall. If you can't nail into the wall use wall stickers or hooks (ensuring you use the right ones for the your picture's weight), or Velcro strips.

5 Seating to go

Bean bags are great for extra seating and pouffes can double up as a table top as well as an extra spot for someone to perch. They also have the added bonus of being easy to move from room to room.

6 No nails? Lean instead

If you'd prefer not to fix anything to the walls, lean large prints or canvases, and even large mirrors against the wall for instant impact. Either sit them directly on the floor, or on a sideboard, chest of drawers, or console table.

7 Cover up

Large rugs can help to define spaces, add warmth and most importantly, cover up unattractive floors. Invest in one you love as you can take it with you when you leave.

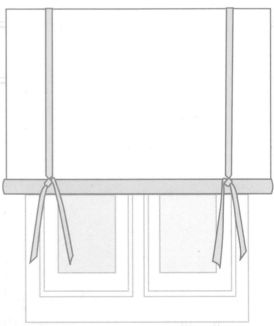

8 Rework the floorplan

Would rearranging the existing furniture make the room feel more comfortable and welcoming? Sometimes just changing the layout of furniture can give a room a fresh or more practical feel. Or, perhaps you could also consider moving a piece of furniture from one room to another to get the look (and storage) you need.

9 Wallpaper a panel

Removable wallpaper can be used on any dry, smooth, clean surface, and fixing it in place couldn't be easier – just peel off the backing and stick it on. It can be trimmed and shaped to fit any space, and can even be removed and reused – so you can change your colour scheme as often as you want. Alternatively, wallpaper large MDF or plywood panels and lean them against walls.

10 Get some privacy

Window film is ideal for overlooked rooms and can be used in place of old-fashioned net curtains. Easy to put up (some soapy water and a helping pair of hands are all you need), they can be removed when you leave.

11 Paint the furniture

Want to add colour but can't paint the walls in your rental home? Then why not paint a large piece of (your own) furniture? Painting a headboard, bedside tables, chest of drawers, wooden chairs, or a cupboard will add just as much impact as a colour on the walls.

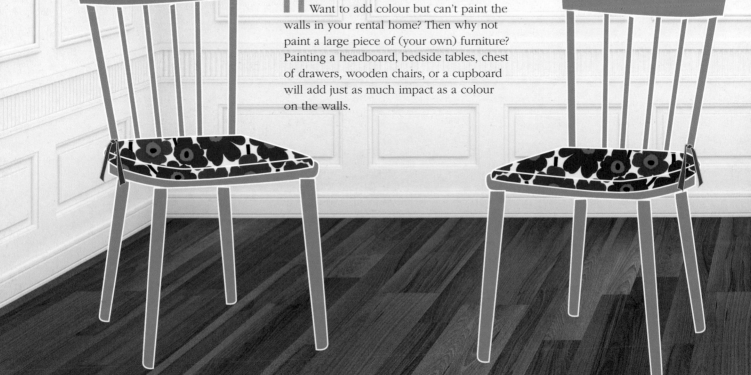

*Match your
curtain colour
with your cushions
or seat pads.*

12 Transform a sofa

A large throw, or two or three smaller throws, can hide an ugly sofa. Cushions in your favourite colours will also help to make it your own.

13 Treat the windows

Hanging new curtains will make a big difference to a room, and if you choose curtains with the same headings or fixings, they won't take long to change. Or, invest in temporary blinds, which are easy to fix into place, can be cut to fit, and taken with you when you move.

FINISHING *touches*

You've painted, decorated, and furnished your space, so now you can add the finishing touches. Paintings, books, and plants will all add life to your room.

▌ Add layers
A bedspread or blanket in either complementary or contrasting colours is a good opportunity to add some texture as well as colour and pattern to your bed.

Soft furnishings in your bedroom create a cosy, relaxing space.

3 Create groupings
Group accessories such as vases and frames in odd numbers – either groups of three or five – and in varying heights. Link random objects by either colour, theme, or size.

2 Add cushions
Finish off by adding interest with cushions in both plain and patterned fabrics. Pile on the cushions, and don't shy away from mixing patterns. Combine large prints with small ones, florals with geometrics.

5 Plants and flowers

A simple potted plant or flowers set on a coffee table, bookshelf, on top of a cabinet, almost anywhere, adds instant life and colour.

Flowers add fresh colour to any room.

6 Shelving

Use open box shelving to provide a neat border in which to display collections and mementos. Create depth by placing objects from the back of the shelf to the front instead of in a straight line.

4 Seasonal changes

Use cushions, decorative objects, frames and vases to make seasonal changes in your room. In summer opt for fresh colours such as sky blue and yellow, and in winter change them for purples and deep reds.

Add interest to a seating area with embellished cushions.

7 Give it an edge

Adding a trim – lace, bobble, tassel, or beading – will instantly update cushions, curtains, hand towels, and lampshades. Use coordinating or contrasting colours.

Fabric suppliers

Supplier websites

Bemz: www.bemz.com
Bluebellgray: www.bluebellgray.com
Borovick Fabrics: www.borovickfabrics.com
Clarke & Clarke: www.clarke-clarke.co.uk
Fermoie: www.fermoie.com
Harlequin: www.harlequin.uk.com
Ikea: www.ikea.com
Kirkby Design: www.kirkbydesign.com

Marimekko: www.marimekko.com
Osborne & Little: www.osborneandlittle.com
Romo: www.romo.com
Scion: www.scion.uk.com
Vanessa Arbuthnott: www.vanessaarbuthnott.co.uk
Villa Nova: www.villanova.co.uk
Voyage: www.voyagedecoration.com

Bean bag (pp.250–255)

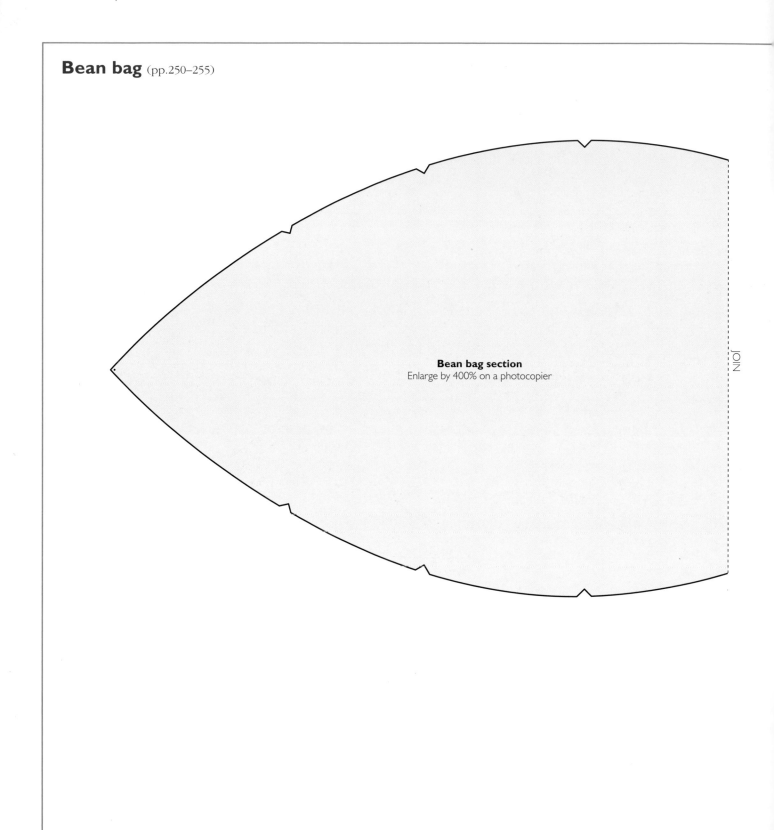

Bean bag section
Enlarge by 400% on a photocopier

JOIN

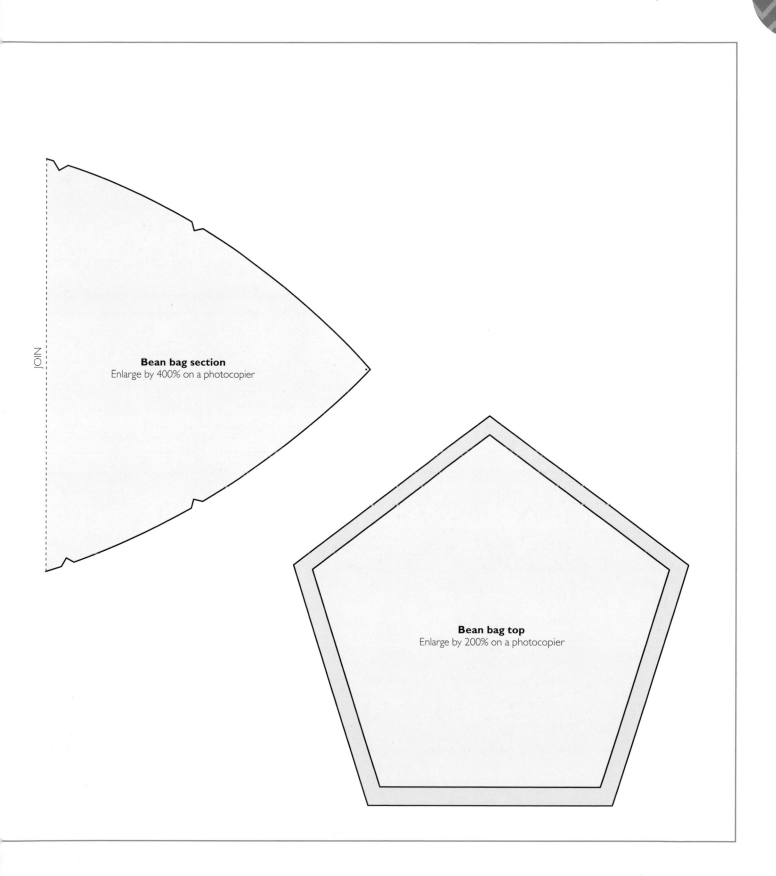

JOIN

Bean bag section
Enlarge by 400% on a photocopier

Bean bag top
Enlarge by 200% on a photocopier

Square storage basket (pp. 226–231)
Round storage basket (pp. 232–237)

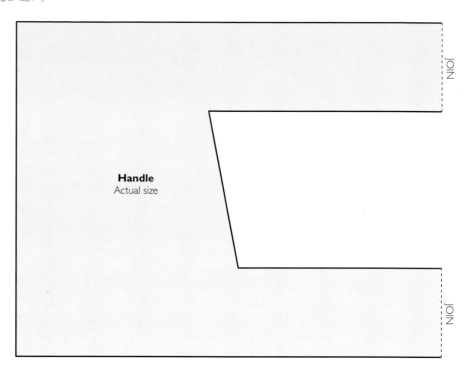

Handle
Actual size

Curtain tieback (pp.198–201)

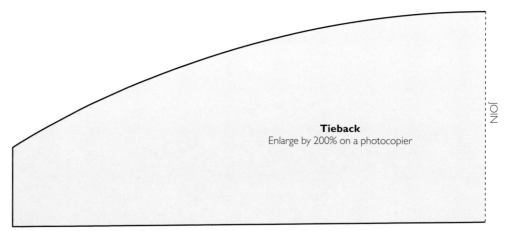

Tieback
Enlarge by 200% on a photocopier

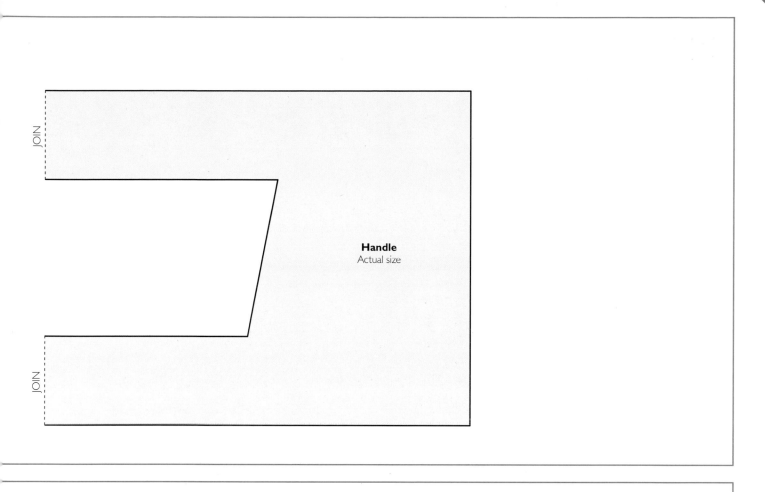

Handle
Actual size

JOIN

JOIN

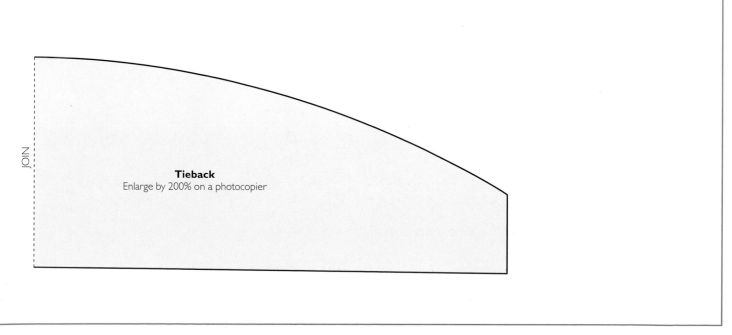

JOIN

Tieback
Enlarge by 200% on a photocopier

Index

Acknowledgments

Contributors

Danielle Budd and Bevelee Jay Regan at Jayworks

Danielle is a graduate of The Royal College of Art, specialising in printed textiles. Her degree show was a collection of unique handcrafted bags and purses, brought to life from her screen printed leather and digital textile designs. Danielle went on to launch a successful accessories label, designed and made in-house and stocked worldwide. She is currently a university lecturer in surface design at the University of the Arts, a freelance designer, and one half of Jayworks.

Bevelee has always been a sewing enthusiast and she has had a varied career in theatre, styling, and merchandising. Bevelee went on to fine-tune her skills in advanced soft furnishing at The Sir John Cass School of Furniture. Currently she is a soft furnishing tutor at Sew Over It, part of the merchandising team at Fabrics Galore, and is the other half of Jayworks.

Danielle and Bevelee have always been friends and are avid makers. Some years ago they decided to bring together their valuable knowledge and plethora of skills and launch Jayworks, a creative soft furnishing company.

Mia Pejcinovic

Mia is a London-based freelance editorial and commercial stylist, as well as design consultant. For the past 15 years she has specialised in styling, set design, art direction, prop sourcing, and production for advertising, editorial, TV, and book publishing, and interior consultancy for residential clients in the UK and abroad.

Mia has worked on numerous exciting projects with some of the industry's most successful photographers. Her many clients include: Debbie Bliss, Designer Yarns, Mothercare, and Retreat Home; the magazines *Beautiful Kitchens, Country Homes & Interiors, Homes & Antiques, House Beautiful, Ideal Home, Image Interiors,* and *Real Homes;* and the Channel 5 TV show *The Hotel Inspector.*

Acknowledgments

Dorling Kindersley would like to thank the following people for their time, input, and expertise:

Photography assistants Emma Ercolani and Amy Barton
Hand models Alice Bowsher and Kate Meeker
Models Miriam Clarke, Ted Daley, Alice Bowsher, and Emma Ercolani
Illustrator Vanessa Hamilton for illustrations on pages 18, 19, 20, 21, 24, 25, 68, 126, 127, 154, 155, 184, 185, 186, and 187
Additional text Clare Steel for ideas and text for the *Putting it all together* section
Indexer Marie Lorimer
Additional cushions Gail Lockwood
Set builder Tim Warren
Locations for photography Light Locations and 1st Option
Prop hire Backgrounds Prop Hire

Additional design and editorial work:
DK India
Project editor Janashree Singha
Project art editor Vikas Sachdeva
Art editor Priyanka Singh
DTP designer Manish Chandra Upreti